1995
4·00

D1296110

Memory, the Holocaust, and French Justice

Contemporary French Culture and Society

edited by

Richard J. Golsan,

Mary Jean Green, and

Lynn A. Higgins

Memory, the Holocaust, and French Justice

THE BOUSQUET AND TOUVIER AFFAIRS

Edited by Richard J. Golsan

Translations by Lucy Golsan and Richard J. Golsan

DARTMOUTH COLLEGE

University Press of New England   •   Hanover and London

Dartmouth College

Published by University Press of New England, Hanover, NH 03755

© 1996 by the Trustees of Dartmouth College

All rights reserved

Printed in the United States of America

5 4 3 2 1

CIP data appear at the end of the book

For my son Jody

and to the memory of

Craig Woods,

scholar, athlete,

gentleman, and

good friend

C O N T E N T S

THE TOUVIER AFFAIR

Reflections on the April 1992 Appeals Court Decision

The Trial of Paul Touvier

ACKNOWLEDGMENTS

I wish to thank a number of colleagues, friends, and relatives without whose advice, help, and support this project would not have been possible. Katie Golsan, Hervé Picton, Jean-Jacques Fleury, and Tom Hilde were most helpful in obtaining newspapers, magazines, and books as they appeared in France that have provided indispensable documentation on the Bousquet and Touvier affairs and the ongoing effects of the "Vichy Syndrome" in France. My colleagues Nathan Bracher and Frank Baumgartner have provided invaluable advice and suggestions along the way. Series editors Mary Jean Green and Lynn Higgins, and David Caffry at UPNE have been most supportive from the outset. Shannon Fogg, Krista May, and Laureen Tedesco provided crucial assistance in preparing the bibliography and editing the manuscript. Nancy, James, Jody, Rocky, and Elvis did their usual superb job of keeping me going throughout the life of this project.

I would also like to thank the College of Liberal Arts, the Department of Modern and Classical Languages, the International Studies Program, the Center for International Business Studies, and especially the Center for Leadership Studies and its director, Arnold Vedlitz, at Texas A&M University for their support.

Finally, special thanks are due to Annette Lévy-Willard, whose help was instrumental in securing the translation rights for these essays from *Libération,* and to Robert Paxton and Bertram Gordon for their generous and helpful advice concerning the manuscript.

June 1995   R.J.G.

CHRONOLOGY

1939

3 September: France, along with Great Britain, Australia, and New Zealand, declares war on Germany.

1940

10 May: Germany launches its western offensive.

14 June: Paris falls to the Germans.

16 June: Premier Paul Reynaud resigns, Marshall Philippe Pétain, who will head the Vichy régime, requests an armistice from the Germans.

22 June: The French government signs the armistice with Nazi Germany at Rethondes.

10 July: The French parliament votes full governing powers to Philippe Pétain and his Etat Français (French State). In so doing, the Third Republic votes itself out of existence.

22 July: The Vichy government creates a commission to review the naturalizations of immigrants, and of foreign Jews in particular, since 1927. According to Serge Klarsfeld, this is the first cornerstone of "Vichy's anti-Jewish edifice."[1] Subsequent measures dated 16 August and

10 September restrict the medical and legal practices to children born of French fathers. Although not explicitly anti-Semitic, the measures further marginalize Jewish immigrants and others fleeing from Nazi Germany and Eastern Europe.

27 August: Vichy repeals the "Marchandeau Law," which outlawed any press attack on "a group of persons who belong by origin to a particular race or religion when [that attack] is intended to arouse hatred among citizens or residents." Henceforth anti-Semitic propaganda becomes a staple of many collaborationist newspapers and magazines.

4 October: The first of Vichy's anti-Jewish statutes is promulgated. It calls for the arbitrary arrest and detainment in French concentration camps of foreign Jews and severely restricts the civil rights of French Jews. Jews are henceforth excluded "from top positions in the public service, from the officer corps and from the ranks of noncommissioned officers, and from professions that influence public opinion: teaching, the press, radio, film, and the theatre." [2]

1941

29 March: Without seeking prior approval from the German military authorities, the Vichy government creates the Commissariat-General for Jewish Affairs under the direction of Xavier Vallat, a well-known anti-Semite and a fierce nationalist who believes Jews are culturally unassimilable. The original idea of a central office for dealing with Jewish affairs and the "Jewish question" initially came from the Germans, who had their own list of potential commissioners in mind. Among them were Louis Darquier de Pellepoix, who would later head the agency, and the notoriously anti-Semitic writer and pamphleteer Louis-Ferdinand Céline. [3]

14 May: The first of Vichy's roundup of foreign Jews is carried out by French police. More than 3,700 Jews are arrested and their civil status reviewed. Most are subsequently interned in French concentration camps at Pithiviers and Beaune-la-Rolande and later deported to Auschwitz.

2 June: The Second Jewish Statute is promulgated. It has been carefully prepared for several months in cabinet meetings at Vichy. According to Marrus and Paxton, it is "a properly French initiative without direct German intervention." The Second Jewish Statute and subsequent ancillary measures limit Jews to comprising two percent of the liberal professions and three percent of students enrolled in institutions of higher education. They also call for a detailed census of all Jews in the Unoccupied Zone, "a grave step which ... was to have fatal consequences later when Jews were being rounded up and deported." On 22 July an "aryanization" law empowers the state "to place all Jewish property in the hands of a non-Jewish trustee who had the authority to liquidate it if it was deemed unnecessary to the French economy, or to sell it to a non-Jewish purchaser."[4]

20 August: A second roundup, occurring over several days, is carried out by the French police. The roundup is undertaken at the behest of the Nazis and in reprisal for communist agitation following the German invasion of the Soviet Union.

12 December: A third roundup of Jews is carried out by the French and German police. This time, numerous Jews are executed in Paris and elsewhere in an effort to discourage the increasing number of anti-German attacks carried out by the Resistance.

1942

20 January: Wannsee Conference decides on the "Final Solution." Reinhard Heidrich, head of the Reich Central Security Office (RSHA) announces to the assembled participants the targeted figures for deportations of Jews from each European country. For France, the figure is "a preposterous 865,000, broken down into 165,000 for the occupied zone and 700,000 for the unoccupied zone."[5] The responsibility for organizing the Final Solution in France falls to SS Captain Theodor Danneker, chief of the Gestapo's Jewish Office in Paris. The age limits on those to be deported are set at between sixteen and forty, because it is the Germans' intention to disguise the deportations as labor convoys.

18 April: Two days after his return to power at Vichy (16 April) Pierre Laval names René Bousquet secretary general for police in the Ministry of the Interior. Bousquet, in turn, designates Jean Leguay as his representative in the Occupied Zone.

6 May: Louis Darquier de Pellepoix is named commissioner-general of Jewish questions. Darquier replaces Xavier Vallat, whom the Germans consider too soft, to carry out the "massive internment and deportation of families, and not just men" that will soon be taking place.[6] During a meeting in Paris with Reinhard Heidrich in early May, René Bousquet learns of the pending deportations of Jews from the Occupied Zone and inquires whether it would be possible to include Jews interned in camps in the Unoccupied Zone in the deportations.

1 June: Jews from the age of six on are required to wear the Yellow Star in the Occupied Zone.

2 July: During a meeting in Paris with German authorities, Bousquet declares that the French are prepared to deport 10,000 foreign Jews from the Unoccupied Zone. At the same meeting, Bousquet initially refuses to accede to German demands that French police participate in the roundup of Jews in Paris and the arrest and deportation of French Jews. After a good deal of German pressure, Bousquet backs down on the first point.

3 July: At a meeting of the cabinet in Vichy, Laval, Pétain, and the Cabinet approve Bousquet's agreements with the Germans the previous day.

4 July: In a meeting with Dannecker, Pierre Laval confirms official French acceptance of the 2 July agreements. Laval also asks that children under the age of sixteen be allowed to accompany their parents during the deportation of foreign Jews from the Unoccupied Zone. Later, on 10 July, Laval presents this as a humanitarian act to the Vichy Council of Ministers, with Pétain himself present.

15 July: Bousquet issues orders to the prefect of the Paris police concerning the roundup to begin the next day.

16–17 July: The so-called "Vel d'Hiv" roundup of foreign Jews by French Police takes place in Paris. Beginning at 4 A.M. on Thursday, 16 July, roughly 4,500 French policemen carrying carefully prepared index cards with the names and addresses of those to be arrested begin their sweeps; 12,884 men, women, and children are arrested and herded into an indoor bicycle racing stadium known as the Vélodrome d'Hiver, kept in abominable conditions for several days, and then deported. The code name for the roundup is "Spring Wind." Bousquet specifically orders that all children over the age of two are to be rounded up with their parents and not "left with neighbors." All those rounded up are foreign Jews, mostly refugees from Eastern Europe, except those children born in France and naturalized as French citizens as a result of their births being declared to the appropriate French authorities.

29 July: First accords between Bousquet and Karl Oberg, head of the SS in France. These accords, which conclude with a letter from Oberg dated 29 July, give greater autonomy to the French police in allowing them to establish reserve units in the Occupied Zone and in guaranteeing that henceforth any orders from the Germans will only be issued through official channels. The French are also exempted from the unpleasant task of designating hostages, and all persons handed over to the occupier by French authorities will not be executed as hostages. The Germans also agree to share information in cases that concern the French. Marrus and Paxton note that in exchange, the French police agree "to act vigorously against 'communists, terrorists, and saboteurs' and to assure 'the repression of all the enemies of the Reich, carrying on this struggle itself, on its own responsibility.'"[7]

18 August: René Bousquet gives instructions to regional prefects concerning the roundup of foreign Jews in the Unoccupied Zone. Dates for the roundups are set, and exemptions for children between the ages of two and sixteen are suspended. Bousquet reminds the prefects of the "absolute necessity of taking the most severe measures to ensure the efficacy of the operation."

26–31 August: Roundups of foreign Jews in the Unoccupied Zone. On orders from Bousquet's office, children between the ages of two and sixteen are deported along with their parents.

19 September: Bousquet issues instructions allowing French Jews to be deported from the Occupied Zone.

11 November: Following the Allied landings in North Africa, the Germans invade the Unoccupied Zone.

31 December: By this date, 41,951 Jews have been deported from France to Auschwitz.

1943

30 January: Creation of the Milice, paramilitary units created by Vichy to fight the Resistance, under the leadership of Joseph Darnand, a decorated veteran of World War I.

5 April: The Vichy Government hands over to the Germans former civil and military leaders of the Third Republic, including Léon Blum, the former Jewish prime minister during the Popular Front, and Georges Mandel. Blum is deported; Mandel will eventually be murdered by the Milice. The Oberg-Bousquet accords of July 1942 are renewed during April as well.

July 1943: Alois Brunner, newly appointed by Eichmann to oversee the Final Solution in France, sets about to seize control of the deportations from the Vichy authorities. With the aid of Parisian collaborators, he launches a violent press campaign against Laval and Bousquet, labeling them protectors of the Jews. On 2 July he seizes control of the Drancy deportation center from French authorities. According to Marrus and Paxton, "Vichy thereby lost control of the key point in the administrative network of the deportation. Thereafter, the French police and bureaucracy were excluded from any influence on the composition of convoys to the east."[8] Arrests of French and foreign Jews are henceforth carried out by German squads and members of the various French fascist movements, including members of the Parti Populaire Français and the Francistes, but not the French police.

31 December: After destroying his records and after ordering the release of several individuals suspected of involvement in the Resistance, René Bousquet resigns his post under pressure.

1944

1 January: Joseph Darnand succeeds Bousquet and assumes the new title of "Secretary General for the Maintenance of Order."

6 January: Philippe Henriot is named state secretary for information and propaganda at Vichy.

10 January: Murder of Victor Basch, former head of the Human Rights League, and his wife by the Milice. As head of the Milice's S-2 unit (intelligence and operations) for the Rhône and Savoy regions, Paul Touvier is known to have been involved in the crimes, although lack of evidence led to their being dropped from the charges against him at his trial.

26 March: Units of the Milice join German troops in attacking Resistance strongholds on the plateau of Glières.

6 June: Allied landings in Normandy begin. Shortly thereafter, German authorities arrest René Bousquet and send him to Germany by private car. He is lodged in a villa, where his wife and his son are allowed to join him.

20 June: Jean Zay, the former minister of education during the Popular Front, imprisoned near Riom, is removed from his cell by three men in Milice uniforms, ostensibly to be transferred to another prison. En route, he is murdered by his captors.

28 June: In the morning, three members of the Resistance, disguised as *miliciens,* gun down Vichy's propaganda minister, Philippe Henriot, at his residence in Paris. The news is announced over Vichy's radio at 12:40 P.M. by Pierre Laval himself. Enraged *miliciens* in Mâcon murder seven citizens in their homes in reprisal. Other reprisals are carried out by the Milice in Toulouse, Clermont-Ferrant, Grenoble, and Voiron. In Lyons, Paul Touvier orders the roundup of seven hostages, and tells his men to arrest Jews. Before dawn on the morning of June 29, seven hostages are taken by the Milice under the orders of Touvier to the cemetery of Rillieux-la-Pape, stood against a wall, and executed at about 5 A.M. It is for these murders, and these murders alone, that Touvier will finally stand trial for crimes against humanity in March and April 1994.

7 July: Georges Mandel, a prewar interior minister, is murdered, apparently by the Milice. As in the case of Jean Zay, the crime is committed while Mandel is supposedly being transferred from one prison to another.

5 August: Pétain disavows the Milice.

25 August: Paris is liberated.

2 September: Liberation of Lyons. Paul Touvier avoids arrest by hiding out in the home of the abbott Vautherin. Touvier begins a long period in hiding, punctuated by robberies, arrests, and escapes. From the beginning, he is frequently sheltered and protected by members of the Catholic clergy.

1945

18 May: After returning voluntarily from exile, René Bousquet is incarcerated at Fresnes Prison.

1946

10 September: Touvier is convicted of treason in absentia by the court of justice in Lyons. He is sentenced to death and *dégradation nationale* (loss of civil rights). His possessions are subject to confiscation. During this period Touvier is on the run with several members of his family, hiding out primarily in Montpellier in the Southwest and then in Paris. On 29 June he is wounded during a holdup attempt.

1947

4 March: The court of justice at Chambéry (Touvier's home town) sentences Touvier to death and *dégradation nationale* in absentia. He is convicted this time for "intelligence with the enemy."

3–9 July: Touvier is arrested in Paris and interrogated by French police for various recent criminal activities. Under suspicious circumstances, he is apparently allowed to escape.

10 December: Xavier Vallat, former commissioner-general for Jewish questions, is condemned by the High Court to ten years in prison. Xavier Vallat's successor as commissioner-general, Darquier de Pellepoix, is condemned to death in absentia.

1949

20 June: A court in Lyons sentences Touvier, who fails to appear, to five years in prison and ten years of *interdiction de séjour* (Touvier will not be permitted to live in the area for ten years) after he is convicted of armed robbery.

23 June: After three and a half years in prison (at the beginning of his prison term, Bousquet prepares the notes for his former boss Laval's defense) and a brief period of release under surveillance, René Bousquet stands trial before the High Court of Justice. He is given a symbolic sentence of five-years' loss of civil rights which is immediately commuted for "acts of resistance." Following his release, Bousquet begins a successful career as a businessman, most notably at the Bank of Indochina, where he will become a director for international affairs in 1952 and associate director general in 1960.

1951

5 January: A general amnesty law is passed for those convicted of *dégradation nationale* and prison terms of less than fifteen years. During the month of October Paul Touvier is allowed to see his criminal file in Lyons.

1953

24 July: A second amnesty law is passed that affects all but the perpetrators of the most serious crimes committed during the Occupation. According to Henry Rousso, the second amnesty law marks the official end of the postwar Purge. Henceforth, sentences meted out to former collaborators returning from exile are extremely mild compared to those handed down in the immediate postwar period.

1954

14 April: A law is passed designating the last Sunday in April as "A National Day of Remembrance for the Victims and Heroes of the Deportation."

1958

November: René Bousquet runs for election to the National Assembly in the Marne district on the Center Republican Party ticket and is soundly beaten by his Gaullist adversary. Bousquet receives only nine percent of the vote. After the death of his friend Jean Baylet, publisher of the Toulousian newspaper, *La Dépêche du Midi* in 1959, Bousquet takes up with Baylet's widow, Evelyne, and runs the newspaper behind the scenes throughout the 1960s. He continues to look for an opening to reenter politics, but a rupture with Evelyne puts an end to these ambitions, because Bousquet no longer has access to the material and other resources of the newspaper.

1959

Paul Touvier meets the singer and songwriter Jacques Brel and becomes his friend. Touvier's allies in the ecclesiastical hierarchy petition the government to amnesty him. In August the request is denied and becomes official on 20 April 1960.

1964

26 December: Crimes against humanity, as defined in the United Nations Resolution of 13 February 1946, are declared imprescriptible in French law.

1965

According to numerous sources, Bousquet, an acquaintance of François Mitterrand through mutual friends, supports the latter's unsuccessful bid for the presidency. Bousquet's contributions include securing the support of the Toulouse newspaper, the *Dépêche du Midi,* as well as financial contributions for Mitterrand's campaign.

1967

The statute of limitations goes into effect on the 1946 and 1947 convictions of Paul Touvier, who has avoided punishment by remaining in hiding. A National Identity Card under the name "Paul Touvier *alias* Berthet" is delivered to him on 7 December at the address of the archdiocese of Lyons. Although the death penalty has lapsed, Touvier is still not allowed to reside in the twelve departments of southern France and cannot lay claim to family property owned there or appear publicly in his home town of Chambéry.

1970

28 January: The prosecutor of the State Security Court asks Jacques Delarue, an historian and specialist on the Occupation, to conduct an investigation into Touvier's past and to assess the fairness of Touvier's earlier convictions. On 10 June Delarue submits his findings, concluding that Touvier's actions were "nefarious, unscrupulous, and inexcusable" and that his past convictions were fully justified.

April–July: In their continuing efforts to have Touvier pardoned, members of the Catholic clergy, Monsignors Duquaire and Gouet, accompanied by Touvier himself, pay visits to officials of the Pompidou government. Those involved in the discussions include Edouard Balladur, prime minister in 1994 at the time of Touvier's trial.

May–December: Monsignors Duquaire and Gouet gather thirty-five letters in support of a pardon for Touvier addressed to the president of the Republic, Georges Pompidou. One of these, dated 17 November 1970, is from the philosopher Gabriel Marcel, who, misinformed, writes that Touvier was in essence a humanitarian influence in the Milice and remained there until the end only to "combat its excesses."

6 August: After conducting an investigation into the circumstances of Touvier's convictions in 1946 and 1947 the minister of the interior recommends against a pardon for Touvier.

1971

January: Monsignor Duquaire begins to write a counter report that refutes the unfavorable report prepared by Delarue. (Extracts of Duquaire's report are included in *Paul Touvier est innocent,* an apology for Touvier written by Jacques Trémolet de Villers, who would eventually defend Touvier in court in Versailles in March-April 1994.)

3 September: Monsignor Duquaire is received by Anne-Marie Dupuy, the principal private secretary of Georges Pompidou. "Reticent" in her reaction to Duquaire's affirmations of Touvier's innocence and his statements concerning the "injustice" of the Delarue report, Dupuy is moved by the fate of Touvier's family. She would later affirm: "Monsignor Duquaire touched the mother in me. His comments on [Touvier's] children moved me."

23 November: Despite the recommendations against the pardon by Delarue and others, Georges Pompidou grants a pardon to Touvier, influenced in part by a sympathy for his family encouraged by Anne-Marie Dupuy. Instructions are that the pardon is to be handled as discreetly as possible.

1972

Public outcry over the Touvier pardon begins, following the publication on 5 June of an article in *L'Express* by Jacques Dérogy exposing the pardon, entitled "Exclusive: *L'Express* has found the Torturer of Lyons."

18 June: 1,500 demonstrators, including former *résistants,* government ministers, and representatives of the Jewish community, gather at the Monument to the Deported in Paris to protest the pardon.

19 June: In *L'Express,* Gabriel Marcel acknowledges he has been duped by Touvier.

21 September: At a press conference Pompidou finally explains his reason for the pardon, stating, "Hasn't the moment come to draw a veil over the past, to forget a time when Frenchmen didn't like one another, attacked one another, and even killed one another?" Few are convinced, and former members of Resistance groups prepare to press charges against Touvier for crimes against humanity.

1973

9 November: Two accusations of crimes against humanity are brought against Touvier before the examining magistrate of Lyons. The accusations are brought by Joë Nordmann and Ugo Iannucci on behalf of Georges Glaeser, the son of one of the victims of Rillieux-la-Pape, and Rosa Vogel, daughter of a deported guardian of the grand synagogue of Lyons, respectively. Over the course of the next several years, the issue will provoke a lengthy legal battle.

1974

12 February: The examining magistrate in Lyons, Henry Ogier, who had received the accusations against Touvier, signs an *ordonnance* declaring himself incompetent to investigate the charges against Touvier. On 30 May the Court of Appeals upholds the *ordonnance.* On 11 July the Court of Appeals of Chambéry upholds a similar declaration of incompetence of the examining magistrate in Chambéry following similar charges of crimes against humanity being brought against Touvier in Chambéry on 27 March.

1975

6 February: The Supreme Court of Appeals in Paris overturns the decisions of the courts in Lyons and Chambéry and assigns the case to the Indictments Division of the Court of Appeals in Paris.

27 October: The Indictments Division declares itself competent . . . but states that the statute of limitations has run out on the crimes in question.

1976

30 June: The Supreme Court of Appeals overturns the Indictments Division's decision and demands that its judges consult with the Ministry of Foreign Affairs concerning international conventions relating to the notion of crimes against humanity.

1978

28 October: L'Express publishes an interview with Louis Darquier de Pellepoix, the former minister of Jewish questions under Vichy now living in exile, who claims René Bousquet was responsible for the deportation of Jews and especially the Vel d'Hiv roundups. Bousquet's role in the Final Solution had been revealed earlier by Joseph Billig in his 1955 book, *Commissariat général aux Questions juives,* but the information was not widely disseminated until the Darquier interview.

15 November: Serge Klarsfeld files a complaint alleging crimes against humanity against Jean Leguay, René Bousquet's representative in the Occupied Zone from May 1942 to the end of 1943, who, as Bousquet's representative, was responsible for the deportation of large numbers of Jews.

1979

12 March: Jean Leguay is indicted by investigative magistrate Martine Anzani for crimes against humanity. This indictment marks the first time that the suspension of the statute of limitations for crimes against humanity is applied to a French citizen.

15 June: The minister of foreign affairs affirms the validity of the principle of imprescriptibility as applied to crimes against humanity.

27 July: The files concerning Touvier's case are ordered transferred to Paris, where Louis Chavanac is named examining magistrate.

Touvier publishes his brochure entitled *Mes Crimes contre l'humanité.*

1981

6 May: The *Canard enchaîné* launches the Papon Affair, accusing Maurice Papon, the former prefect of Paris police and finance minister during the Fifth Republic, of having contributed to the deportation of Jews from Bordeaux during the Occupation.

June: Investigating magistrate Martine Anzani, recently named to handle Touvier's case, decides to indict Touvier for crimes against humanity. Touvier refuses to appear at his hearing. His lawyer, Raymond Geouffre de La Pradelle, resigns, and Judge Anzani issues an international warrant for Touvier's arrest. During the entire period leading up to Judge Anzani's decision, Touvier has been in hiding in friendly monasteries, while clerical allies continue to work behind the scenes on his behalf.

1983

19 January: Maurice Papon is indicted for crimes against humanity.

5 February: Klaus Barbie, the former Gestapo chief in Occupied Lyons known as the "Butcher of Lyons," is indicted for crimes against humanity after being extradited from Bolivia the previous day.

1984

19 September: The "death" of Paul Touvier is announced in the regional newspaper *Dauphiné libéré.*

1985

April: Claude Lanzmann's epic film on the Holocaust, *Shoah,* appears in French movie theatres.

5 October: The magistrate's initial investigation for the trial of Klaus Barbie is completed.

20 December: The Court of Appeals modifies the definition of crimes against humanity, which henceforth can include crimes committed against members of the Resistance.

1986

9 July: A second investigation of Barbie's file is concluded.

1987

11 February: The Court of Appeals cancels the investigation of charges against Maurice Papon. New charges of crimes against humanity will be brought against him in July 1988.

11 May–4 July: The trial of Klaus Barbie takes place before the Assizes Court in Lyons.

13 September: The National Front leader Jean-Marie Le Pen announces to the press that the gas chambers were "a small detail in the history of the Second World War" and that the existence of these chambers is subject to debate among historians.

1989

24 May: Paul "Lacroix" (Touvier) is arrested by the French police at the priory of Saint-François in Nice.

2 July: Jean Leguay dies of natural causes. After ten years, the protracted investigation of his case is complete and is about to be handed over to a Paris court. Breaking with custom, the statement declaring the case closed due to Leguay's death also confirms his guilt on charges of crimes against humanity.

13 September: Represented by Serge Klarsfeld, the Association of the Sons and Daughters of Deported Jews lodges a complaint against René Bousquet, charging him with crimes against humanity. The case is handed over to the Indictments Division of the Court of Appeals in Paris.

1990

10 May: The Jewish Cemetery at Carpentras is desecrated. On 14 May, a massive rally to protest the desecration takes place in Paris and is attended by the president of the republic, François Mitterrand.

16 May: The Indictments Division delivers the materials of the Bousquet case to the prosecutor general, Pierre Truche, who had recently prosecuted the case against Klaus Barbie.

25 September: The prosecutor general orders the Indictments Division to begin its investigation of the charges against Bousquet.

18 October: Doing a complete about-face, Pierre Truche asks the Indictments Division to declare itself incompetent to handle the Bousquet case and proposes that the case be handled instead by the Haute Cour de Justice de la Libération, the Purge court that originally judged Bousquet in 1949 and no longer exists. Truche is apparently acting on the orders of the newly appointed special delegate to the Ministry of Justice, Georges Kiejman, who is himself acting at the behest of the president of the republic, François Mitterrand. The action is clearly a delaying tactic to avoid bringing Bousquet to trial. When asked to justify his action following public outcry, Kiejman claims in a statement made in *Libération* on 22 October to be acting in the name of "civil peace."

19 November: Despite Truche's request, the Indictments Division declares itself competent to proceed with the Bousquet case. Bousquet appeals the decision three days later.

1991

31 January: The Criminal Chamber of the High Court of Appeals rejects Bousquet's appeal. The last obstacle to the indictment of Bousquet for crimes against humanity is removed.

1 March: René Bousquet is indicted on charges of crimes against humanity. The investigating magistrate charged with handling the case, who is responsible for Touvier's case as well as other more routine cases, requests permission to be relieved of these last responsibilities in order to avoid delays in preparing Bousquet's case. The request is denied.

3 April: The court's decision to indict Bousquet is made public.

6 June: The investigating magistrate, Jean-Pierre Getti, delivers his report on Bousquet to the Indictments Division.

July–August: The neofascist magazine *Le Choc du Mois* publishes a dossier entitled *Mitterrand et la Cagoule,* underscoring the president's prewar right-wing activism and his service to Vichy.

8 July: A new penal code is passed which includes a new definition of crimes against humanity, convictions for which are subject to life imprisonment.

11 July: Paul Touvier is ordered released from prison by the Indictments Division of the Court of Appeals in Paris on the grounds that his continued detention "is no longer necessary to the discovery of the truth." The decision causes public consternation and outrage: given Touvier's record, some speculate that the former *milicien* will once again go into hiding. The general prosecutor in Paris announces his intention to appeal the decision.

23 October: Maurice Papon holds a press conference in which he announces that he has written a letter to the president of the republic demanding to be judged or acquitted of the charges against him, eight years having passed since judicial procedures involving charges of crimes against humanity were instituted against him.

1992

6 January: A distinguished panel of historians headed by René Rémond delivers its report on Paul Touvier's links to the Catholic church and its hierarchy to Monsignor Decourtray, the archbishop of Lyon, who had requested the report after Touvier's arrest in June 1989. Although the report does not fault the Church as a whole, it sharply criticizes the activities of many church authorities who helped Touvier evade justice. The report is published in book form as *Paul Touvier et l'Église* by Fayard in March 1992.[9]

13 April: The Court of Appeals in Paris acquits Paul Touvier of charges of crimes against humanity, arguing that the charges do not apply to a servant of Vichy, which was not, according to the judges, a regime that practiced "ideological hegemony." According to the December 1985 definition of crimes against humanity as defined in French law, only actions performed on behalf of such a regime are to be considered crimes against humanity. Public outcry is immediate and intense and is fueled by the fact that the three judges who handed down the decision are known for their right-wing sympathies.

17 May: Ceremonies are held at Pithiviers and at Beaune-la-Garonde, site of former French internment camps, to commemorate the victims of the Vel d'Hiv roundups. Two representatives of the government are present.

17 June: A petition circulated by the "Vel d'Hiv 42 Committee" demands that François Mitterrand recognize officially that "the French State [the Vichy Government] was responsible for the persecution of and crimes committed against French Jews."

6 July: The press reveals new indictments against Maurice Papon and René Bousquet, announced on 19 and 22 June, during the course of the investigation of charges against Papon by the courts in Bordeaux. According to Eric Conan and Henri Rousso, these indictments are "the indirect consequence of the outrage provoked even among the magistrates, by the acquittal of Touvier." [10]

16 July: The fiftieth anniversary of the Vel d'Hiv roundup is commemorated at the site of the former vélodrome. François Mitterrand, who attends the ceremony, is heckled by some members of the crowd (two days earlier, Mitterrand had denied that the French Republic was in any way responsible for the crimes of Vichy).

27 November: The Criminal Chamber of the High Court of Appeals partially overturns the April acquittal of Touvier. The charge retained against Touvier concerns his order to execute seven Jews at the cemetary at Rillieux-la-Pape in June 1944.

1993

3 February: A national day commemorating "racist and anti-Semitic persecutions committed under the authority of the French State (1940–

44) is decreed. The commemoration will occur annually on 16 July, if that date is a Sunday, and if not, the first Sunday following that date.

2 June: The Court of Appeals at Versailles remands the case of Touvier to the Assizes Court at Yvelines.

8 June: Christian Didier, a deranged and unsuccessful writer who had tried to kill Klaus Barbie in 1987, enters René Bousquet's Paris apartment and guns him down. He then flees to a hotel in Lilas near Paris, where he calls a press conference and states, "I had the impression I was crushing a snake."

1994

17 March: The trial of Paul Touvier for crimes against humanity begins in Versailles under tight security. As an added precaution, the synagogue in Versailles is placed under police protection.

20 April: Touvier is convicted of crimes against humanity and sentenced to life in prison. He appeals the verdict immediately. Following the conviction of Touvier, numerous demands are made to put Maurice Papon on trial.

18 May: A plaque commemorating the murder of the seven Jewish hostages at the cemetery of Rillieux-la-Pape is destroyed by persons unknown.

24 May: The Indictments Division of the Court of Appeals of Versailles refuses a request made on 11 May to free Paul Touvier.

14 June: The Correctional Tribunal of Bordeaux agrees to delay the trial of Papon until a ruling is made on Papon's complaint against Gérard Boulanger, author of *Maurice Papon, un technocrate français dans la collaboration,* and the lawyer for several of the plaintiffs in Papon's case. Boulanger is accused of "public defamation of a government functionary."

12 September: As a result of the scandal provoked by the publication of Pierre Péan's *Une Jeunesse française: François Mitterrand, 1934–1947,* the president of the republic appears on French national television to explain his role at Vichy and his postwar friendship with René Bousquet.[11]

Notes

1. Serge Klarsfeld, *Vichy-Auschwitz: Le rôle de Vichy dans la solution finale en France. 1942* (Paris: Fayard, 1983), p. 13.
2. Michael Marrus and Robert Paxton, *Vichy France and the Jews* (New York: Schocken Books, 1983), p. 3.
3. Ibid., pp. 81–84.
4. Ibid., pp. 98, 100, 101.
5. Susan Zuccotti, *The Holocaust, the French, and the Jews* (New York: Basic Books, 1993), pp. 95–96.
6. Serge Klarsfeld, *Vichy-Auschwitz 1942*, p. 50.
7. Marrus and Paxton, *Vichy France and the Jews*, p. 244.
8. Ibid., p. 330.
9. René Rémond et al., *Paul Touvier et l'Eglise: Rapport de la Commission historique instituée par le Cardinal Decourtray* (Paris: Fayard, 1992).
10. Eric Conan and Henri Rousso, *Vichy un passé qui ne passe pas* (Paris: Fayard, 1994), p. 295.
11. Pierre Péan, *Une Jeunesse française: François Mitterrand 1934–1947* (Paris: Fayard, 1994).

Memory, the Holocaust, and French Justice

On Monday night, 12 September 1994, President François Mitterrand went on French national television to discuss his involvement with the Vichy regime during the first few years of the Occupation and his friendship in the postwar years with former high officials of Pétain's Etat Français. Mitterrand chose to address the nation as a result of the scandal provoked by the publication of Pierre Péan's *Une Jeunesse Française: François Mitterrand, 1934–1947*,[1] a detailed account of the president of the republic's right-wing activities and associations as a student in Paris during the 1930s and of his service to the Vichy government, for which he was awarded the regime's highest honor, the Françisque, in 1943. Péan also discussed Mitterrand's involvement since the 1950s with René Bousquet, who served as Vichy's chief of French state police from April 1942 through December 1943. Maintaining offices in Vichy and in Paris, Bousquet was head of French police in both the Occupied and Unoccupied Zones throughout his tenure. After a successful postwar career as a banker and businessman, Bousquet was charged in 1989 with crimes against humanity for his role in the roundup and deportation of Jews during the summer and fall of 1942. Bousquet was murdered in his apartment in Paris's sixteenth *arrondissement* in June 1993 by one Christian Didier, a deranged publicity seeker.

Mitterrand's efforts to explain his lengthy involvement with Vichy did not go over well in all quarters, most notably among his fellow socialists, many of whom felt betrayed by the man who had come to personify the aspirations of the postwar left in France. But what many Frenchmen found most offensive about the recent revelations concerning Mitterrand's past was his association with Bousquet, who in many ways had come to symbolize Vichy's role in the Final Solution as well as the nation's efforts to avoid dealing with this painful subject throughout much of the postwar period. Pierre Moscovici, a former treasurer of the Socialist Party and member of the European Parliament, spoke for disaffected socialists and probably many others in stating: "For me, to be a socialist is to be an anti-fascist and always an anti-fascist! Never to consort with anti-Semitism! What shocks me are Mitterrand's statements about Bousquet, this zealous accomplice of the Final Solution."[2] Indeed, in *Une Jeunesse française*, Mitterrand claims that Bousquet was not "a fanatical Vichyite" and that, in fact, he was a man "of exceptional stature . . . likable, direct, almost brutal" in manner—in short, a man with whom Mitterrand enjoyed spending time (315). In other conversations with Péan, Mitterrand goes on to suggest that the actions for which Bousquet had been charged with crimes against humanity in the late 1980s had already been dealt with during Bousquet's 1949 trial for collaboration (314). This is a misguided and misleading suggestion, and one that Mitterrand was not averse to repeating in his nationally televised interview of September 12: "He [Bousquet] was accused of intolerable acts, but he was acquitted of these crimes by the High Court of Justice, which wasn't lenient. Thereafter he reentered normal society and was welcomed everywhere."[3] In another effort to cast a more favorable light on his erstwhile friend, Mitterrand sought to discredit the man who denounced Bousquet in 1978 for his central role in the July 1942 roundup of foreign Jews in Paris, the former Commissioner of Jewish Affairs during the latter part of the Occupation, Louis Darquier de Pellepoix, as a "very undistinguished personage" and as "someone not to be taken at his word . . . a frightful little man."[4] In press releases from the Elysée Palace at the time of the scandal, Darquier is further characterized as a *personalité horrible*.[5]

It is somewhat surprising that Mitterrand's friendship with Bousquet caused such a stir, if only because the connection between the two men was not news, and neither, in fact, was their strong support for each other in political terms. Indeed, an effort apparently made by the president himself to delay indefinitely the trial of Bousquet for crimes against humanity in October 1990 caused tremendous public outcry. The extreme right-wing press had a field day with what appeared to be presidential intervention on behalf of the accused,[6] gleefully trumpeting the friendship between the two men, including Bousquet's support for Mitterrand's unsuccessful presidential bid in 1965, while taking the opportunity to harp on Mitterrand's right-wing and Vichy past. The neofascist magazine *Le Choc du Mois* went so far as to publish a special issue in the summer of 1991 on *Mitterrand et la Cagoule,* claiming that Mitterrand had once been a member of the infamous prewar reactionary terrorist group. On the cover of the issue was a photo showing the young François Mitterrand, surrounded by the police, participating in a right-wing demonstration in the 1930s.[7] Since the publication of Péan's *Une Jeunesse française,* the photo has been widely disseminated.[8]

In an article published in *Le Monde* on 10 September 1994, Gilles Martinet, a member of the National Council of the Socialist Party, attempted to weigh the implications of Mitterrand's past, especially his connection with Bousquet. Martinet emphasized what he described as Mitterrand's vast, "feudal" system for achieving political success and maintaining power. According to Martinet, this system consisted in essence of a vast array of contacts and supporters covering the entire range of the political spectrum, whose loyalty to Mitterrand derived from the knowledge that their own interests would be protected and served in return. Hence the president's untroubled friendship with the former secretary general of Vichy police, who, as noted, was a powerful figure in banking and industry as well as the press in the postwar period.

Martinet's analysis of Mitterrand's "feudal" system of power explains in general terms the reasons for Mitterrand's friendship with Bousquet. Nevertheless, it ignores the specificity of Bousquet's past and the degree to which the destiny of René Bousquet has become emblematic of the ambiguities and excesses of l'Etat Français and *les années noires,* of a "secret and subterranean Vichy, still so poorly understood." Moreover, the specter of Bousquet, his past, and his violent demise are inseparable from the nation's troubled memory of the period itself, which Henry Rousso has aptly likened to an illness: the "Vichy Syndrome." In short, Bousquet's career and political itinerary can teach us a great deal about recent French history, especially why the Holocaust is more important in France today than it has been at any time since the Liberation.[9]

Born at Montauban in the department of Tarn-et-Garonne in 1909, René Bousquet was the son of a prominent local *notaire,* a lawyer specializing in land transfers, wills, deeds, and so forth, and the only official empowered by the state to give these transactions legal force.[10] Bousquet *père* was also known for his militant radical-socialist politics, which placed him on the moderate left of the political spectrum.

After law studies in Toulouse—which he abandoned after receiving his *licence,* or bachelor's degree, but before completing his doctoral dissertation—Bousquet *fils* quickly established himself as a brilliant young government administrator with a promising political future. By 1929, at the age of twenty, he was already the chief of staff of the prefect of Tarn-et-Garonne.[11]

In 1930 Bousquet achieved national recognition for personally saving several individuals from drowning during the floods that ravaged southwestern France that year.[12] His heroism was made known to the president of the republic, Gaston Doumergue, who congratulated Bousquet personally on a visit to Montauban, as well as the minister of the interior, André Tardieu.[13] In recognition of his efforts, Bousquet was awarded the Médaille d'Or des Belles Actions and made a knight of the légion d'Honneur.

Bousquet's heroism also launched his career at the national level. He served as chief of staff for a number of governmental ministers in the early 1930s and during the course of these activities collaborated closely with Pierre Laval, with whom he became good friends.

Given the extent of his success in the reactionary climate at Vichy, it is of interest to note that Bousquet's own politics, like his father's, were center-left republican and that most of his most significant career advancements in the interwar period occurred after the victory of Léon Blum's leftist Popular Front in the spring of 1936. On 29 May 1936, Bousquet was named assistant bureau chief of the interior ministry and was maintained in this position by Roger Salengro, who in 1937 also placed him in charge of the central records of the Sûreté Nationale.

In 1938, on the recommendation of Albert Sarraut, one of two brothers who were influential radical-socialist politicians and mentors of Bousquet, Bousquet was named subprefect of Vitry-le-François and, one year later, secretary-general of the Marne Department.

The German offensive of May 1940 and the French retreat were followed in June by the evacuation of the Marne department. According to his curriculum vitae presented at the High Court of Justice during his trial for collaboration in 1949, Bousquet was awarded the Croix de Guerre for his "brilliant actions" during the evacuation. The High Court's indictment against Bousquet *(acte d'accusation)* acknowledges his having received the award,[14] but no official record of its conferral exists.[15] In any event, following the Armistice, Bousquet returned to the Marne after a brief visit to Vichy, where he received 30 million francs "to ensure the resumption of the administrative and economic life"[16] of his department. Judged by high officials at Vichy to be "capable of representing the new will" of the regime,[17] Bousquet was named prefect of the Marne by Pétain in September 1940 and then regional prefect of Champagne in August 1941. At the time of his initial appointment in 1940, Bousquet was thirty-one years old and the youngest prefect in France at the time.

From the limited historical accounts available on his tenure as Prefect of the Marne, as well as from testimony he provided at his 1949 trial, Bousquet seems to have remained loyal to radical-socialist colleagues as well as his fellow Freemasons. Indeed, thanks to contacts made directly with the minister of the interior, Bousquet helped the mayor of Vitry-le-François resume his post after he was forced to resign as a result of being denounced as a Freemason in the *Journal officiel,* or official government journal. Bousquet also seems to have been quite successful in restimulating the department's economy, and later claimed that, while serving Vichy during this period, he remained loyal to the republic. He declared after the war that a bust of Marianne, the symbol of the republic, adorned his office at the Marne Prefecture.[18] The High Court's Indictment of Bousquet in 1949, in fact, paints a glowing, if partially inaccurate, picture of his tenure as prefect of the Marne: "He [Bousquet] intervened on behalf of Israelites, Freemasons, syndicalists, and Communists, deflected sanctions against the population, and succeeded in limiting German exactions by providing them with false statistics."

Despite claims made in the passage just cited from the 1949 indictment, not to mention his former association with the Communist Party hierarchy during the Popular Front period, Bousquet proved to be, in fact, an implacable enemy of the communists during his stint as prefect of the Marne. According to the historian Jean-Pierre Husson, Bousquet spent a great deal of energy on the "surveillance of the former Communist Party," keeping lists of important party members prepared commune by commune and conducting investigations into communist presence and influence in private businesses. As a result of one of these investigations, several communists distributing tracts to champagne workers in Reims were arrested and later handed over to the Nazis. Eventually, all were either deported or executed.[19]

His fierce anticommunism notwithstanding, Bousquet kept his distance from overtly pro-Nazi (and anticommunist) collaborationist groups and movements, in part because his Third Republic background made him unwelcome in these milieux. On occasion, however, he did attend events organized in the Marne by groups such as Alphonse de Châteaubriant's Groupe Collaboration, whose primary purpose was to disseminate a refined and intellectually acceptable form of collaborationism to the educated middle and upper classes.[20]

Called to serve in the capacity of "Secretary General for Police in the Ministry of the Interior" by Pierre Laval on 18 April 1942, Bousquet accepted the appointment despite warnings from his friends and confidants concerning the dangers the appointment entailed. According to Yves Cazaux, a friend who joined the Resistance, Bousquet stated at the time: "My duty is there. This is my mission. If I run away from it, I am a deserter and the one who will serve in my place will be terribly dangerous."[21] More explicit after the war concerning which dangerous individual or individuals he was referring to, Bousquet would claim that he had accepted the nomination in part to help keep in check the rising influence in occupied France and at Vichy of the more fanatical pro-Nazi elements. According to Bousquet, this included figures such as Jacques Doriot, the former communist-turned-leader of the fascist Parti Populaire Français, and Joseph Darnand, a decorated World War I hero and head of the Milice, who, as Bousquet's successor at Vichy, was known for his brutality and zeal in fighting the Resistance and in carrying out the Final Solution. In an interview with Jean-Pierre Husson conducted in 1987, Bousquet affirmed: "I went to Vichy to prevent the Germans from arriving too quickly at the Darnand solution."[22] He also asserted that he accepted the nomination to help out his old friend Pierre Laval, who, Bousquet also claimed in the 1987 interview, had remained "a man of the people" possessing a "Leftist and Socialist sensibility."

Few historians would, of course, agree with Bousquet's generous assessment of Laval. Moreover, given Bousquet's role as a principal executor of the Final Solution in France, there is a heavy and ultimately tragic irony in Bousquet's casting himself in a favorable and indeed quasi-heroic light in claiming that he accepted his post at Vichy in order to forestall the "Darnand solution." The implicit self-comparison with Darnand does call, however, for a closer look at Bousquet's tenure at Vichy, a tenure whose apparent ambiguities, as reported in the 1949 indictment, explain in part the High Court's lenient verdict.

According to the 1949 indictment, Bousquet's role in the repression of the Resistance was occasionally damning, but evidence and testimony are also cited to suggest that Bousquet offered valuable assistance to the Resistance on several occasions. The Indictment reports that

> witnesses affirm that Bousquet knew of the activities of many members of the Resistance and never did anything against them. He intervened successfully on behalf of others who had been arrested or condemned by the Germans. He had the commander of the Maquis in the Allier department, Colonel Rossat, warned each time a police operation was to take place. He convinced General Oberg to cancel actions planned against the Maquis of Dordogne, Corrèze and the Plateau de Millevaches.
>
> General Perre, who commanded the Garde Mobile, testified that Bousquet had given him orders forbidding all repressive action against the Resistance.

It was for pro-Resistance activities such as these, the indictment concluded, that Bousquet was constantly under attack from the Milice, Darnand, the collaborationist press, and ultimately, the Germans themselves.

In *Une Jeunesse française*, Pierre Péan offers further possible evidence of Bousquet's pro-Resistance activities. According to Péan, Jean-Paul Martin, a mutual friend of Mitterrand and Bousquet and the man responsible for introducing them to each other following the war,[23] served as administrative assistant in 1943 to Henry Cado, director general of the National Police and one of Bousquet's chief subordinates. In this capacity, Martin funneled "official documents and false identity papers" to "Morland," alias François Mitterrand, now in the Resistance. Was Bousquet aware of this and indeed part of it? Péan's conclusion is that "it is hard to think otherwise."[24]

Bousquet's comportment toward the Resistance was, of course, by no means entirely beyond reproach, according to the 1949 indictment. But in many instances where Bousquet's anti-Resistance activities are discussed, the excuses or justifications he offered for these actions are included without comment or criticism. For example, the indictment makes note of operations by French police carried out against the Resistance in the Corrèze and Savoy regions, but then cites Bousquet's claim that these actions were made to appear "spectacular," whereas they were in reality deliberately ineffectual. The indictment also alleges that Bousquet helped the Germans infiltrate the Resistance and interfere with radio contacts with the Allies by providing German agents with false identity papers. It then records without comment Bousquet's pro-Resistance version of events: the identity cards issued contained deliberate errors that would make them easily recognizable as forgeries.

For other actions recorded in the 1949 indictment, Bousquet apparently had no excuse or justification. None, at least, is recorded, except Bousquet claims to have been just "following orders," a familiar refrain used, of course, by many Nazis and collaborators, especially those involved in the Final Solution. What the indictment describes as the "heaviest charges weighing against the accused" involve efforts in support of German agents and German espionage in the Unoccupied Zone. In October 1942, for example, Bousquet gave specific orders to officers of the Surveillance de Territoire at Vichy not to arrest German agents. According to the indictment, he also allowed German agents to use the official French government telegraph and radio systems to relay information they had gleaned in their infiltration of Resistance-Allied communications. Finally, reports are cited indicating that Bousquet intervened to have sentences lightened or commuted for Frenchmen working for the Nazis.

The 1949 indictment goes on to chronicle a number of other actions, many of which do little, in effect, to clarify the ambiguous presentation of Bousquet's career at Vichy. In a more or less pro-Resistance, or at least anti-Vichy vein, Bousquet, according to his own account, voiced his objections to Laval concerning the creation of the Service de Travail

Obligatoire (STO). The policy required conscripting French citizens to work in Germany to help the Nazi war effort in exchange for the liberation of French prisoners of war. In his efforts to expand the state police force, an objective Bousquet carried out with great zeal, he often provided jobs for those seeking refuge from the STO.

In a less favorable light, the indictment also reports that, following the flight of Generals Giraud and de Lattre de Tassigny to join the Allies, Bousquet, on German orders, assisted in the arrest and deportation of their families to Germany. He also accompanied the German SS officer Knochen, charged with Jewish affairs in the German Embassy in Paris, to Bourrassol, where Third Republic politicians tried at Riom for treason by the Vichy government were imprisoned. There, Bousquet assisted in the "transfer" to Germany of politicians, including Léon Blum, Edouard Daladier, the labor leader Léon Jouhaux, and General Gamelin.

The issue of the "transfer" to Germany of Third Republic leaders raises, of course, the issue of Bousquet's involvement in activities embodying the worst horrors of Nazism, namely, the mass deportations of Jews to death camps in the East. During the spring and summer of 1942 Bousquet negotiated with Karl Oberg, SS chief in France, and later with Reinhard Heidrich, chief of the Central Office of Reich Security, and Reichsführer Heinrich Himmler himself to deport foreign Jews from French soil. The results of these agreements are well known: roundups by French police in Paris and other parts of the Occupied Zone as well as the Unoccupied Zone totaling some seventy-thousand individuals. The most spectacular of these *rafles*, to use the French word, occurred in Paris in July 1942, when over twelve-thousand foreign Jews were rounded up with no help from the Nazis and taken to the Vélodrome d'Hiver, an indoor sports stadium in the fifteenth *arrondissement* used occasionally for political rallies in the interwar years.[25] Those arrested were kept at the Vel d'Hiv for several days under the most inhumane conditions, then sent first to the Drancy depot in Paris and other French concentration camps, and finally deported to Auschwitz.

Given the charges of crimes against humanity pending against Bousquet at the time of his death and François Mitterrand's recent insinuations that *all* of Bousquet's wartime crimes had been dealt with during the 1949 trial, it is instructive to read what the 1949 indictment has to say about Bousquet and the Holocaust. Eight brief and circumspect paragraphs are devoted to the subject. They cover such technical matters as the division of authority in handling Jewish affairs between the national police under Bousquet and the head of the Commissariat for Jewish Affairs at the time, Louis Darquier de Pellepoix.[26] They also deal in very general terms with the Nazi implementation of the Final Solution and the burden supposedly placed on French authorities as a result.

It is hard to avoid the impression in reading the indictment's assessment of Bousquet's role in the Final Solution that the court sought to put as favorable a slant as possible on his activities in this regard. The indictment does acknowledge that Bousquet "consented to serve, in general terms, in his capacity as a high functionary of the regime, the politics of racial persecution with which Vichy associated itself and which the Germans acting alone could only have pursued with greater difficulty." But it also goes to great lengths to underscore Bousquet's supposed efforts to help Jews whenever possible and to dissociate him from some of the more despicable acts of official anti-Semitism of the Vichy regime itself. For example, the indictment notes at the outset of its discussion of the Jewish issue that Bousquet was not involved in the formulation or promulgation of Vichy's own anti-Jewish statutes in 1940 and 1941, because "[the] legislation against the Jews was anterior to Bousquet's arrival at the General Secretariat."[27] It also states that he opposed the extension of the obligatory wearing of the Yellow Star by Jews in the Unoccupied Zone. Finally, in an assertion notable for its historical inaccuracies, the indictment states:

> In 1942, Himmler had ordered the deportation of all foreign and French Jews; Darquier agreed to this, while Laval and Bousquet wanted to oppose it. They could not prevent the deportation of foreign Jews from the Unoccupied Zone, working as they were under a German threat to deport French Jews from the Parisian region, but Bousquet was able to ensure that the deportation was carried out by the French police alone.

The fact that the indictment condemns Bousquet for his role in the Final Solution but then congratulates him for ensuring that the French police alone carried out the 1942 deportations, all in the space of a few paragraphs, is suggestive of a paradoxical attitude toward Vichy that certainly affected the outcome of Bousquet's 1949 trial and continues to color the troubled memory of Vichy today. But what is most striking in the indictment is the implication that Bousquet and Laval generally opposed the deportations of French and foreign Jews alike. This was simply not the case.

That Bousquet did not organize the roundups against his will but instead ordered the operations carried out with the zeal of an efficient bureaucrat is suggested by a number of documents, several of which were indeed included in the dossier of the 1949 trial. These documents, consisting of telegrams sent to the regional prefects on 18, 20, and 22 August 1942, ordered the roundup of foreign Jews in the Unoccupied Zone, including children of less than sixteen years of age, whom the Nazis themselves had originally excluded from the lists of those to be deported. The fact that the High Court essentially ignored these documents is in retrospect surprising to say the least, but it must be remembered that Bousquet was on trial for treason, not crimes against humanity. This is not to excuse the Court, of course, but to underscore, among other considerations, the fallacy, so dear to François Mitterrand, that Bousquet had been judged and exonerated for *all* of his actions at Vichy by the High Court.

The most damaging evidence, however, and the most crucial document later used to justify bringing new charges of crimes against humanity against Bousquet, consisted of a German summary of the 2 July 1942 meeting between Bousquet, the sole French representative present, and Nazi leaders in Paris. The document, which was not contained in the 1949 criminal dossier, outlined what amounted to a blueprint of the Final Solution in France. At the outset of discussions concerning the roundups themselves (the first part of the meeting had been devoted to the respective administrative responsibilities and authority of Bousquet and Darquier de Pellepoix), Bousquet communicated Pétain's and Laval's desire to see roundups in the Occupied Zone handled exclusively by the Germans. The French police would undertake the roundup of Jews in the Unoccupied Zone, as long as the Germans understood that these roundups would not include French Jews. For Oberg, Bousquet's proposal that the Germans carry out the roundups in the Occupied Zone was unacceptable for several reasons. The recently imposed wearing of the Yellow Star in the Occupied Zone had not gone over at all well with the French populace, and the spectacle of massive roundups by German troops could only exacerbate tensions. Moreover, the Germans possessed neither the manpower nor a knowledge of the city of Paris to effectively carry out the roundups there. Finally, a failure by Oberg to secure French acquiescence could damage his own reputation in Berlin. Therefore, Oberg informed Bousquet that Hitler himself would be angry if the French did not handle all the roundups. Faced with this prospect, Bousquet acquiesced. He agreed that the French police would undertake the roundups of foreign Jews "throughout France" in accordance with the figures proposed by the Nazis: 10,000 Jews in the Unoccupied Zone, and twenty thousand in the Occupied Zone. The following day, the Vichy Government ratified these agreements.[28]

Some two weeks later, as a direct consequence of the 2 July agreements, the Vel d'Hiv roundup occurred. On the second day of the *rafles,* July 17, the French authorities went one step further: German minutes of the meeting state that "the representatives of the French police expressed the desire, on several occasions, that the convoys headed for the Reich include children as well as adults."[29]

It is important to stress at this juncture that Bousquet's participation in the Final Solution and his commitment of the police forces at his disposal to that end were not motivated by specifically pro-Nazi sympathies or an overt or pronounced anti-Semitism. According to Robert Paxton, Bousquet was first and foremost a "fonctionnaire, a bureaucrat, who was primarily interested in the continuity and sovereignty of the French State."[30] He was "perhaps the purest example of the phenonenon so characteristic of Vichy called *collaboration d'état'*—i.e., cooperation with the Germans for 'reasons of state,' as distinguished from collaboration for reasons of ideological sympathy."[31] In this and in a number of other ways as well, Bousquet differed from Paul Touvier, a committed pro-Nazi and prewar reactionary and vicious anti-Semite. But Bousquet's lack of sympathy for Nazism did not prevent him from sharing their arrogance and authoritarian outlook. In his recently published *La France à l'heure allemande,* Philippe Burrin offers the following characterization of Bousquet:

> Self-confidence to the point of presumption. Irritated condescension towards the French people who [in his view] understood abso-

lutely nothing. Concern for independence and reciprocity implicit in a politics of collaboration valued for its "realism." A belief in German might which did not include personal sympathy for the occupants. Finally, an unequivocal acceptance of an authoritarian regime.[32]

As Robert Paxton explains in the interview with Annette Lévy-Willard in this volume, Bousquet's "main concern" in organizing the 1942 roundups "was to expand the function of the French police in the Occupied Zone" and indeed throughout France by having the German occupant grant French police greater autonomy to act and by guaranteeing that German intervention in their operations would only be done through the appropriate channels. French police were also relieved of the onerous task of designating hostages. In exchange, French authorities agreed that their police would participate in the struggle against "enemies of the Reich," including "Communists, terrorists, and saboteurs" and, of course, Jews. These accords, known as the Oberg-Bousquet agreements, were formalized at the end of July and the beginning of August 1942 and renewed in April 1943.[33] In a broader context, the increased strength and autonomy of the French police were intended to reinforce the idea that "the Vichy government was not merely a puppet regime," but the agreements also formalized what Philippe Burrin has rightly labeled an "ideological connivance" between Nazi Germany and the French State.[34] Finally, and not coincidentally, the expanded authority of the French police also added to the personal authority of Bousquet himself.

As for the deportation of children, the Vichy authorities claimed that it was to be carried out for "humanitarian" reasons, so as to prevent members of families from being "separated." As Paxton notes, however, the hypocrisy of such a "humanitarian" motive is confirmed by the fact that the children were deported *after* their parents—most of whom had already died at Auschwitz.

Bousquet would later claim that he had nothing to do with these deportations, stating initially that "I systematically refused to deal with Jewish questions. I never agreed to address these issues with the Germans."[35] Later, in the early 1990s, Bousquet would revise these statements in his letter to the president of the Chambre d'Accusation, portions of which are included in this volume, asserting instead that the deportations of foreign Jews were carried out *à contrecœur* in order to protect French Jews. Bousquet also argued that if the deportations of Jews had been left to the Germans, the results would have been much more "cruel."

Both Bousquet's earlier claims and his more recent assertions in his letter to the president of the court seem hollow indeed when placed alongside statements written at the time of the deportations themselves. Bousquet's zeal is evident in a terse and peremptory telegram sent to the regional prefects on 7 August 1942: "I call your attention to the significant gap between the number of foreign Isrealites recorded in the census and the number of those arrested. Pursue and intensify police efforts under way. . . . Have recourse to roundups, identity checks, raids on individual residences, searches in view of further arrests."[36] The same zeal is apparent in the following passage from a speech made to General Oberg in late 1942:

> The vow I take is that the French police, whose task has never been more difficult in technical terms, by the free expression of its independence which is itself the most dazzling proof of the sovereignty of its government, is able to pursue with ferocious energy the struggle against the adversaries of internal French security, against all foreign agents who would wish to have anarchy and disorder reign over our territory, against all those men who, getting their orders from abroad, wish to serve a cause which is not that of France.[37]

Bousquet's enthusiastic courtship of the Nazis and his commitment to carrying out the Final Solution served him well during the early stages of his tenure at Vichy. By their own accounts, the Germans who worked with Bousquet found him an agreeable companion and described their meetings with him as taking place in "an atmosphere of camaraderie." They were convinced as well that Bousquet shared their enthusiasm to create a "new organization of Europe," one in which France would play a leading role.[38] But by late 1943 Bousquet's stock had fallen, and in December the Germans demanded his dismissal.

There were several reasons for Bousquet's removal from office as head of Vichy police. The Germans, detecting a "change in attitude" on Bousquet's part, complained to the French authorities and Laval in particular that Bousquet was allowing the Resistance to develop and that even members of the police under Bousquet were "defecting" to the other side. According to Oberg, Laval concurred with this assessment but had his own reasons for wishing to see Bousquet removed: Bousquet was becoming too powerful in his role as commander of all of Vichy's police and as such represented a threat to Laval himself in his capacity as minister of the interior.[39]

Whatever the validity of claims made concerning Bousquet's "change of heart," it is certainly true that tensions between himself on the one hand and archcollaborationists and Germans on the other were on the rise in late 1943. The assassination of his friend and mentor Maurice Sarrault by French fascist groups and the Gestapo on 2 December, a murder Bousquet vowed to avenge, made his position increasingly untenable. Moreover, Bousquet, like everyone else, had to be aware of German military reversals. Therefore a "double game" of helping the Resistance while working at Vichy was most expedient and could only prove wise in the long run, as the 1949 indictment and trial confirm.

Following his dismissal at Vichy, Bousquet returned to his native Montauban. After the Allied landings in 1944, Bousquet was arrested by the Germans and taken to Germany. The conditions of his "imprisonment" there were hardly trying, however. After being chauffered along with his wife and son in a car made available to him by Oberg, Bousquet was lodged in a villa formerly occupied by Count Ciano, Mussolini's foreign minister. Bousquet's brother, who was working in Germany at the time, was transferred to a neighboring farm to be near the family.

Following the war Bousquet returned to France, was imprisoned and released under surveillance in July 1948, and finally tried in June 1949 before the High Court, a special court created after the Liberation in November 1944 to deal with important cases of official collaboration, or "intelligence with the enemy."[40] Bousquet's trial opened the last session of the court and dealt only marginally with his role in the deportation of the Jews. As noted, Bousquet was charged with treason, not with crimes against humanity.

By all accounts, the proceedings were dominated by Bousquet's skill in presenting his own defense. At times forceful and eloquent, Bousquet described his tenure at Vichy in much the same terms he would use some forty years later in his letter to the president of the Chambre d'Accusation. His role, Laval had assured him, was to act as a "brawny functionary" who would "stand up to the Germans." In heading up the Vichy police, which, Bousquet assured the court, had remained "republican" (!), he had only been doing his duty to France, and "if I had to begin anew in the same conditions, I would act in exactly the same fashion."[41]

When confronted with his role in the deportations of the Jews by the president of the court, Henri Noguères, Bousquet reverted to the all-too-familiar excuse that he was just a small cog in a very large machine. Covering the trial for *Libération*,[42] Madeleine Jacob caustically described Bousquet's self-defense in this instance in the following terms: "At this juncture in the hearings, Bousquet is no longer the near-minister whose ambitions have been crowned with success, but is instead the petty functionary who does everything to diminish his own stature."[43]

Bousquet went on to imply that he was unaware of the ultimate fate of those deported, because the Germans themselves did not refer to "deportations" but, instead, used terms such as "transfer, "regrouping," and 'repatriation."[44] In underscoring his own passivity regarding Vichy's anti-Jewish statutes, Bousquet asserted: "I upheld the racial laws like the rope holds the hanged man"—to which Madeleine Jacob responded bitterly in her column: "Without a rope, Bousquet, there can be no hanged man."[45]

The trial lasted three days. The verdict of the court was as follows:

> No matter how regrettable was Bousquet's comportment [during
> the Occupation], it does not appear that he consciously accom-
> plished deeds whose nature would harm the national defense,
> and, in light of this, he must be acquitted. But in accepting the
> post of Secretary General of Vichy Police, Bousquet has made him-
> self guilty of the crime of National indignity. Conversely, there can
> be no doubt that he rendered important services to the Resistance.

Bousquet was sentenced to five years of loss of civil rights, but the sentence was commuted immediately for acts of resistance.

The verdict did not go over well in all quarters. One newspaper described it as "a conviction to make one laugh," and another characterized it as "one minute . . . of national degradation for Bousquet." Others saw it as "flaunting the memory of the Resistance."[46]

The generosity of the High Court's verdict and the leniency of its sentence were the outcome of the interplay of a number of different factors, some related to how the investigation of Bousquet's activities and the trial itself were conducted, others concerning broader political, legal, and social issues. As recent revelations emerging during the scandal over Mitterrand's past confirm, members of Mitterrand's association of former prisoners of war testified on Bousquet's behalf during the investigation of the case.[47] Their presence was not simply fortuitous. Bousquet's interests were also served by the presence on the jury of one of his powerful prewar mentors, Jean Baylet, editor of the Toulouse newspaper, the *Dépêche du Midi,* as well as other jurors largely indifferent to the proceedings. Madeleine Jacob noted bitterly that, among the jurors, "one . . . worked with great concentration on making paper airplanes, while another dreamed of his Francisque, which he wore proudly in his lapel."

Other factors that affected the outcome of Bousquet's 1949 trial are attributable to the climate of the times themselves. Remarking on the political context of the moment, Edwy Plenel notes that anticommunism predominated in many quarters and the Cold War was fully under way. Moreover, de Gaulle was out of power and was therefore not present on the public stage to serve as a reminder of the glories of resistance to the Nazis and to Vichy. Many French people preferred simply to forget the recent past. Therefore, pardons for collaboration with the Nazis were the order of the day. In fact, during the second day of Bousquet's trial, the Queuille government announced a first large-scale proposal to amnesty those guilty of collaboration. The government spokesperson who made the announcement was the young secretary of state for information—François Mitterrand.

A more thorny, and indeed significant issue, given subsequent judicial proceedings against Bousquet in the 1980s and 1990s, concerns French attitudes toward and legalities concerning the Holocaust in 1949. The indictment itself makes clear the extent to which the court was, at the very least, uncomfortable in dealing with the issue. Moreover, the fact that the indictment describes Bousquet's willingness to aid Nazi agents as "the heaviest of charges weighing against him" is suggestive not only of a disturbing indifference where the deportations are concerned but also of a kind of judicial or legal callousness that at first glance greatly surprises us today. However, one must realize that in 1949, crimes against humanity were not integrated into the French legal apparatus nor were Vichy's own, *autonomous* racist politics acknowledged as such. At the time of Philippe Pétain's trial several years earlier, Vichy's racist legislation of 1940 and 1941 was described as being "a racist legislation copied closely from the German model,"[48] which was, in fact, hardly the case. Nevertheless, this view had not changed in 1949. Moreover, the 1945 drafting and ratification by treaty of the crimes against humanity legislation prior to the opening of the Nuremberg trials of Nazi leaders by the International Military Tribunal was aimed primarily, or at least initially, at the excesses of the Axis powers, the Nazis in particular. According to Geoffrey Best,

"Crimes against humanity" were a canny, cautious half-way house to human rights. They were so to speak invented . . . in order to make possible the prosecution of Axis leaders for the dreadful things they had done distant from battle-fronts and in time of peace as well as war; crimes which the traditional law of war could by no means be stretched to cover.[49]

As defined in the Charter of the International Military Tribunal signed 8 August 1945 in London, crimes against humanity consisted of "murder, extermination, enslavement, deportation, and other inhumane acts committed against any civilian population, before or during the war, or persecutions on political, racial or religious grounds."[50] Those considered liable under law included "[l]eaders, organisers, instigators and accomplices participating in the formulation or execution of a common plan or conspiracy to commit any of the foregoing crimes."[51]

Declared imprescriptible in French law only in 1964, the definition of crimes against humanity would undergo important modifications in France following the 1983 arrest in South America and extradition of Klaus Barbie, the former SS officer and "Butcher of Lyons" who would stand trial for crimes against humanity in 1987. In order to do justice to the memory of martyred members of the Resistance tortured, killed, or deported by Barbie, the court of appeals determined in December 1985 that henceforth crimes against humanity would include "inhuman acts and persecutions committed in the name of a State practicing a politics of ideological hegemony [which] were carried out in a systematic fashion not only against persons by reason of their appurtenance to a racial or religious collectivity but also against adversaries of this politics regardless of the form of this opposition."[52]

Apart from expanding the definition of those to be included as victims of crimes against humanity, the new legislation also offered a more specific codification of the type of regime in whose name crimes against humanity could be carried out—a state "practicing a politics of ideological hegemony." As we shall see, this new specification was to play an important role in the April 1992 acquittal of Paul Touvier.

For René Bousquet, even if the appropriate statutes concerning crimes against humanity like those used later to charge Bousquet and others had been in place in 1949, Frenchmen were simply not targeted for these crimes, because no one cared to look too closely into the nation's role in the deportations. In fact, it would take the conviction of the German Klaus Barbie in Lyons in the mid-1980s to provide the needed impetus to pursue seriously in a legal sense Frenchmen like Bousquet and Touvier for similar crimes.

Historical scholarship in France dealing with the Occupation has recently explored several other important considerations that help contextualize French attitudes toward the Holocaust in the immediate postwar period and at the time of Bousquet's 1949 trial. The majority of these considerations have been summarized in an interview with Henry Rousso and Serge Klarsfeld in the May 1992 issue of *Esprit*. (The interview was part of a special feature on the memory of the Occupation published in the wake of the acquittal of Paul Touvier in April of that year. The issue was entitled, appropriately enough, "Que faire de Vichy?"—"What Is to Be Done about Vichy?") According to Rousso, many of the French, including de Gaulle himself, "never considered Nazism to be anything other than an extreme form of German barbarism. The issue of Nazi biological racism was not at the center of [their] analysis" (p. 22). Moreover, Rousso continues, since the struggle against the Nazis was perceived as a general struggle against anti-Semitism, the specificity of the genocide of the Jews was not adequately addressed. As for the average Frenchperson summing up the horrors of the Occupation as he or she remembered them, the issue of anti-Semitic persecution would finish "far behind" other considerations, including poverty and repression "in the general sense of the term."[53]

From the perspective of the Jews themselves, the issue was even more difficult and complex. Apart from survivors' guilt, which deeply affected many of those who returned from the death camps, Rousso notes that many Jews feared that calling for vengeance and thereby casting themselves in the role of victims would only serve to exclude them from a national community into which they sought at all costs to reintegrate themselves. Therefore, their main concern, as Rousso puts it, was to "forget what had happened."

In his assessment of why the Jews did not seek justice against their French persecutors, Serge Klarsfeld suggests a number of other, more sinister, factors. In many instances, those Jews who had survived the Holocaust found themselves in the postwar era confronted by the same authorities that had persecuted them during the Occupation. Even though the special police of the Ministry of Jewish Affairs had been purged, the national police, previously under the direction of René Bousquet, had not. The same held true for many government administrators and functionaries, who had been completely rehabilitated in the postwar era. Klarsfeld cites as an example Maurice Papon, currently under indictment for crimes against humanity, who, in October 1944, gave a speech in Bordeaux in homage to the deportees, many of whom he had helped to deport a short while before, by organizing the railway cars that would take them to the East. (For a discussion of Papon's role in the deportations, see the afterword to this volume.) Bousquet, in effect, then, benefited from political, legal, and social circumstances that, although not necessarily apparent at the time, virtually guaranteed him a favorable outcome at his trial, not to mention very little significant protest following the announcement of the verdict.

Thus acquitted and free to pursue a new career, Bousquet quickly established himself as a brilliant and powerful banker and businessman. In his recent biography of Bousquet Cyril Aouizerate enumerates the former chief of Vichy Police's list of corporate and banking titles, a list that is astonishing in its length. Apart from his important positions in the Bank of Indochina, where he began his postwar career, and later the Indo-Suez Bank, Bousquet sat on the board of the Indochina Rubber Company, the Indochina Cinema Films Company, the Indochinese

Water and Electricity Company, the French Asian Bank, the French Distillery Company of Indochina, The Indochinese Cigarette Manufacturer's Company, the French Commercial Company, the General Mining Company, the Baccarat Crystal Company, and the UTA Airline Company. Given Bousquet's obvious experience and expertise in the Far East, as the list of corporate titles suggests, it is not surprising that François Mitterrand turned to him for assistance in preparing a trip to China in 1961.[54]

The list of postwar professional titles continues and includes among other positions the direction of the Toulouse newspaper, the *Dépêche du Midi*, which Bousquet ran during the 1960s following the untimely death of Jean Baylet, its director. It was this newspaper that, at Bousquet's behest, backed François Mitterrand's unsuccessful presidential bid in 1965, contributing 500,000 francs to his campaign, printing campaign posters for him free of charge, and devoting a number of favorable editorials to his cause.[55]

It is perhaps safe to say that Bousquet would have finished his days as a powerful and successful businessman if Louis Darquier de Pellepoix, the rabid anti-Semite and former director of Jewish affairs under Vichy, had not denounced him as the organizer of the Vel d'Hiv roundup. In an interview published in *L'Express* on 28 October 1978 whose title was "At Auschwitz, They Only Gassed the Fleas," Darquier laid the blame for the entire operation squarely on Bousquet's shoulders and noted that the former principal French organizer of the Final Solution in France was living comfortably as a banker in Paris.

Darquier's accusations sent shock waves through the nation, and Bousquet's career began to unravel.[56] Antoine Weil, the chairman of the UTA aviation group and the husband of Simone Weil, a government minister and former deportee, pressured Bousquet to resign his position in the company, and other resignations followed in short order.[57] In September 1989 Serge Klarsfeld, on behalf of the Association of Sons and Daughters of Jewish Deportees of France, brought charges against Bousquet for crimes not examined during his 1949 trial. According to Klarsfeld, the *fait nouveau* not covered in the earlier trial consisted of "the responsibility taken by Bousquet to elaborate in concert with the SS an agreement entailing the cooperation of the French Police in the arrests of thousands of Jewish families." The primary documentary source of this information, the aforementioned German summary of the 2 July 1942 meeting between Bousquet and the German authorities, had been located in the Centre de Documentation Juive Contemporaine following the war and discussed in a three-volume account by Joseph Billig published in 1955, and later reproduced by Serge Klarsfeld.[58] According to French law, the crime was imprescriptible, because it constituted a crime against humanity.

It is at this juncture, following the charges brought against Bousquet by Klarsfeld, that the role of the Mitterrand government and the French justice system itself becomes particularly troubling. To many, if not most, of the French, juridical and administrative decisions taken after this point suggest a deliberate effort to delay the trial and indeed to allow the aging Bousquet to die comfortably in his bed. Following the charges brought by Klarsfeld, it took six months for the Cour de Cassation (the Supreme Court) to assign the case to the Paris Court of Appeals. Six more months elapsed before the prosecutor general, Pierre Truche, ordered the investigation to begin.[59] Then, according to Cyril Aouizerate, when the examining magistrate charged with investigating both the Bousquet and Touvier cases requested permission to be relieved of other investigations under way in order to concentrate his energy on the two crimes against humanity cases, the request was denied. Moreover, the courts assigned only one translator to translate the thousand pages in German that were crucial evidence in Bousquet's case.[60]

The case only made front-page headlines, however, when in October 1990, Pierre Truche, who had previously prosecuted the case against Klaus Barbie, reversed an earlier decision and asked the Chambre d'Accusation, the court that would hear the case, to declare itself incompetent to judge Bousquet. Truche went on to argue that the case should be heard by the High Court constituted during the Purge, which had originally passed judgment on Bousquet. The proposal gave every appearance of being completely ludicrous, since the High Court had been dissolved for many years and many of its original members were long since dead. Given legal and other difficulties, the reconstitution of the High Court, if possible at all, would take years, and the accused would in all likelihood have died of old age in the interim. The entire proposal was apparently a subterfuge intended to delay Bousquet's trial indefinitely. The man behind the proposal was Georges Kiejman, the newly appointed *ministre délégué à la Justice*, a post that itself had just been created. According to recent accounts, Kiejman, who has also been Mitterrand's friend and personal lawyer since 1981, intervened at the behest of the president himself.[61]

Public outcry following Truche's decision was immediate and intense. As noted, the right crowed over Bousquet's friendship with Mitterrand, remarked on the president's Vichy past, and also took advantage of the occasion to note the involvement of the left with Vichy and in Bousquet's case in collaborating with the Nazis. For the left, and the communists in particular, the protection accorded Bousquet in the highest reaches of government testified to the worst excesses of class privilege still rampant in contemporary France.

Despite pressure from the highest levels of government and the judicial system itself, the Chambre d'Accusation eventually declared itself competent to hear the case, arguing that a decision to disqualify itself could be considered by the civil parties involved as a denial of justice and a violation of Article Six of the European Convention for Safeguarding the Rights of Man and Fundamental Liberties, which states that every person has the right to have his or her complaint heard equitably and publicly and within a reasonable period of time by an independent and impartial tribunal.[62]

On 1 March 1991, Bousquet was charged with crimes against humanity. The indictment stated in part that Bousquet was accused of

> having knowingly made himself the accomplice to arbitrary arrests and sequestrations committed by the representatives and agents of the German government against expatriates [living in France] and foreigners of Jewish origin; with having knowingly been the accomplice of the violent removal of minors from the Occupied and Free Zones; with having addressed telegrams on the 18, 20, and 22 August 1942 extending to groups, notably children, in the Unoccupied Zone not previously designated, measures including arrests, internments, and deliveries [to the enemy].[63]

The charge was made public on 3 April. On 6 June the examining magistrate, Jean-Pierre Getti, presented his final report on Bousquet to President Moatty of the Chambre d'Accusation. On 6 July 1992, the press revealed that further charges of crimes against humanity had been brought against Bousquet by the courts in Bordeaux as a result of the investigation into similar charges against the aforementioned Maurice Papon, administrative officer in the prefecture of Bordeaux during the Occupation and later prefect of the Paris Police and a minister in the government of Valéry Giscard-d'Estaing. On 16 July 1992, in conjunction with commemorations of the Vel d'Hiv roundups, antiracist militants and former members of the Resistance gathered in front of Bousquet's apartment building in Paris and spread barbed wire in symbolic protest of Bousquet's role during the Occupation. Bousquet himself was not present, having left town the day before to avoid the hate phone calls he had been receiving. In failing health—he was nearly blind and had recently undergone two lung operations—Bousquet had begun to crack under the pressure.[64]

Bousquet's trial was finally scheduled to get under way in the fall of 1993, when on the morning of 8 June Christian Didier, a deranged and unsuccessful writer, claiming to be a messenger of the court, gained entrance into Bousquet's apartment and gunned him down.[65] After fleeing Bousquet's residence, Didier fled to a modest hotel in the suburbs, telephoned members of the press, and invited them to come and hear his confession. Didier described the crime in detail and expressed his feeling of "having killed a serpent" to the assembled members of the media before the police arrived and arrested him. To date, Didier has not been tried.

Lest one be tempted to see in Christian Didier a deranged but well-intentioned avenger of Bousquet's many victims, frustrated, in effect, by the numerous and lengthy delays in efforts to bring Bousquet to justice, it is sobering to look at his background. As Ian Buruma describes him, Didier was a man "obsessed with spectacle and publicity" who "desperately wanted to be famous."[66] Born in the village of Saint-Die-des-Vosges near the end of World War II, Didier aspired at an early age to be a renowned writer. Known to his schoolmates as "Rimbaud"—more for "his weirdness than his literary talent," as Buruma asserts—Didier spent much of his life attempting to convince others, by increasingly demented means, of his literary genius. A stint as a "literary beatnik" traveling in Australia and the United States was followed by a career in France driving stretch limos for the likes of Salvador Dali, Catherine Deneuve, and Alain Delon. Efforts to find a publisher for a first novel, *The Ballad of Early Bird*, were unsuccessful.

As Buruma notes, Didier's attempts to gain fame and notoriety became increasingly bizarre as time passed. He disrupted live television and award shows and jumped at Jacques Chirac, the mayor of Paris, during the Tour de France, waving a sign encouraging Chirac to read *The Ballad of Early Bird*. He wrote letters to the Ayatollah Khomeini and broke into the Elysée Palace, proclaiming himself a "literary Zorro." In further efforts to promote his career, Didier chained himself to a traffic light on the Champs Elysées and walked from Paris to Strasbourg to get attention for his novel.

Not all of Didier's antics were so innocuous, however. By pretending to be a doctor, he gained access to the prison where Klaus Barbie was held prisoner during the 1980s. His intention was to kill the murderer of Jean Moulin. His plan failed, needless to say, and he was imprisoned for a year. His efforts to gain notoriety through murder proved more successful in the case of René Bousquet. Indeed, Didier's success and the apparent ease with which he carried out his plan have prompted speculation in some quarters that the murder of Bousquet was not merely a publicity stunt but perhaps attributable to more suspicious and unknown factors.[67]

If René Bousquet's career and spectacular demise sound like a dark parable of the evils of the modern era, that perhaps explains in part why the French are today having so much difficulty forgiving their president his lengthy friendship with the man. Moreover, the fact that in his television interview, Mitterrand had subtly attempted to whitewash Bousquet by claiming that Bousquet had been exonerated in his 1949 trial "almost with congratulations," while failing to mention more recent and serious charges against Bousquet, must have struck even the most charitable of French aware of the facts of the case against Bousquet as disingenuous if not outright evidence of bad faith on the part of Mitterrand.

But, as noted, the career of René Bousquet is not merely of momentary interest stemming from the scandal surrounding Mitterrand's dubious past. Bousquet's role at Vichy has become emblematic of the worst excesses of the regime's collaboration with the Nazis, specifically its willingness, and indeed eagerness, to do its part in forwarding the aims of the Final Solution in exchange for an illusory autonomy and position of privilege in Hitler's "new European order." Moreover, the fact that Bousquet's 1949 trial downplayed his role in the deportations underscores the degree to which Vichy's anti-Semitic character was swept under the rug in the postwar years, when the Gaullist myth of Resistance held sway and the French preferred to think of themselves as a people who had opposed Nazi ideology and hegemony and disdained pro-German right-wing collaborationist sycophants in Paris and the Pétainist regime at Vichy.[68] It was during this period, in fact, that collaboration was dismissed as the policy or attitude of a few marginal fanatics[69] and opportunists and Vichy was defended by those who would defend it for having provided a protective "shield" for France while de Gaulle furnished the sword. Bousquet's career prior to the war and his actions on behalf of the Pétain government put the lie, of course, to all that. Moreover, Bousquet's light sentence in 1949, his postwar success as a banker and a businessman, and his protection at the hands of high government officials confirmed what Eric Conan and Henri Rousso have argued recently, which is that the *guerre franco-française* that typified the Occupation was *also* about class struggle and privilege and that that aspect of the conflict is far from being resolved.[70] François Mitterrand's comments to Olivier Wieviorka in a recent interview to the effect that Bousquet was a "high functionary" caught up in the machinery of the Final Solution and that he did not attribute to Bousquet the "base character" he associated with political "rabble" like the *milicien* Paul Touvier, could only exacerbate these animosities, at least in certain quarters.[71]

So when Bousquet was shot, many French people saw the nation as having lost the opportunity to sort out the tangled history of Vichy and its legacy in postwar France and to mete out a more thorough and comprehensive form of justice than the Purge courts had managed to do. In short, the trial of Bousquet was to have been the trial of Vichy as it was now understood, as well a corrective to the flawed justice of the Purge. Moreover, the stakes were not simply "respect for history and the memory of the victims," as Gaston Plissonier, the militant communist and former Resistance leader put it,[72] but something more urgent as well. According to Plissonier, "we are in the presence of a dangerous reactivation of neo-Nazi movements, of those of a fascistic extreme right, as well as repeated efforts to revise and falsify history."[73] Under such circumstances, a trial that would supposedly inform the general public of the realities of Vichy and the brutalities of fascism would prove all the more timely and important.

For several years, historians such as Henry Rousso have been warning of the dangers inherent in putting the Vichy past on trial. The most significant consideration is that judges and magistrates, not better qualified specialists, would inevitably be making judgments concerning the historical realities of the Vichy regime. Moreover, as Paul Thibaut argued in a 1991 essay entitled "French Guilt," by the very nature of its judgments, a court decides guilt or innocence, right or wrong, by a process of "cutting and excluding" and therefore necessarily oversimplifies the complexities of the issues involved. These complexities, Thibaut continued, are better understood and digested within the framework of "political" or "moral" debates, which, by definition, "compare experiences . . . and distinguish among them only by also showing their continuities."[74] Finally, according to Thibaut, in dealing in absolutes of right and wrong, the court would allow the nation as a whole to avoid the troubling ambiguities of its past by dumping the entire burden of its guilt on a few "extreme cases."

In conversations with Olivier Wieviorka recorded in 1990 and 1991 concerning efforts to try Bousquet as well as Touvier and Papon, Jacques Chaban-Delmas, another former Resistance leader who served as prime minister under Georges Pompidou and ran for president in 1974, voiced other concerns of a more broadly philosophical bent. Chaban-Delmas wondered if some fifty years after the fact the accused in each case was indeed the same man who had committed the crimes in the first place. As for the notion that the trials would get at "the truth" concerning Vichy, Chaban-Delmas responded: "Where is the truth? How does one untangle it after all this time? I think it's better to let the dead bury the dead."[75]

In Bousquet's case, finally, any new trial would almost inevitably have left the impression that the Purge had done its job very poorly or not at all, a view that many historians contest. Although it is true that certain groups and professions were purged more thoroughly than others, largely for reasons of postwar continuity and renewal, the general consensus is that these inequalities were not as extreme as they are often presented in the context of current debates. Besides, as Henry Rousso warns in his interview in *Esprit*, renewing the national debate concerning the efficacy of the Purge in the context of a trial of Bousquet would likely have resulted "in the trial of French society in the postwar years,"[76] a process that would have opened a whole different can of worms. Another danger implicit in the condemnation of the justice of the Purge, and one that Rousso does not mention, is that it plays directly into the hands of unrepentant collaborators and pro-Nazis, who have always claimed that the Purge was merely the vengeance of the victors.

Nevertheless, despite dangers such as these, after the murder of Bousquet, a sense a incompletion or unfulfillment still prevailed. For many, France still needed to expiate its sins, especially where the Jews were concerned. Some argued that even in comparison with the Germans, France had failed miserably in this regard. According to Christian Pineau, a former Resistance fighter and politician in the postwar period: "Not only did we not excuse ourselves but we hid what we did."[77]

Therefore, when the trial of Paul Touvier for crimes against humanity committed during the Occupation opened in Versailles in March 1994, a feeling of anticipation that Vichy and its crimes would finally be tried was quite palpable, certainly in the media. The "Trial for Remembrance," as the Parisian daily *Libération* put it in their front page headlines on 17 March, was about to begin.

Unlike the case of René Bousquet, which has only been discussed intermittently in this country and, for the most part, in the context of the scandal surrounding Mitterrand's past, the facts of the Touvier case, especially his trial, have been more widely reported. A trial for crimes against humanity is of course always newsworthy in itself, and newspapers across the country provided regular updates. In the *New York Times*, reports on the trial appeared almost daily. At the conclusion of the trial, numerous magazines and periodicals ran synopses of the court's deliberations as well as commentary on their implications. On 22 May 1994, the *New York Times Magazine* devoted its cover story, entitled "The Last War Criminal," to Touvier's past and his trial. The essay was a follow-up to an earlier piece, published in 1989, following Touvier's arrests by the *gendarmes* at the right-wing *intégriste* Saint-François priory in Nice on 24 May of that year.

In France, at least, interest in the case of Paul Touvier was not simply a function of the fact that he was charged and convicted of crimes against humanity. His long *cavale*, or flight from justice, lasted more than forty years and would have been impossible without the help of Catholic clerics and powerful groups within the Church, who, among other forms of assistance, provided him with shelter, money and in 1971 secured him a presidential pardon from Georges Pompidou. Thus Touvier, like Bousquet, was, in several important ways, symbolically linked to a larger institution, the Catholic church, whose role during the Occupation, like the Vichy government itself, was fraught with ambiguities.[78] Moreover, his condemnation would also constitute, as Serge Klarsfeld suggested in the 1992 interview in *Esprit*, a judgment against the dreaded and openly fascist Milice, a pillar of Vichy's authority and power in the closing year of the war.[79]

But even Touvier's links with the Catholic Church, as well as his status as a sort of living reminder of the Milice and its abuses, could not fully explain the interest in (and, in some quarters, fanatical devotion to) the man. For Touvier was (and is), for many, a *personnage de roman*, a character out of a novel, a con artist and mythomaniac who succeeded in duping not only members of the clergy, who came to see him as a victim of persecution and indeed a modern-day Christian martyr, but also others, including media stars such as the singer Jacques Brel and intellectuals such as the philosopher Gabriel Marcel. Indeed, a look at Touvier's own account of his past published in 1979 entitled, appropriately enough, *Mes Crimes contre l'humanité*,[80] confirms that as a writer at least, he is not lacking in certain perverse and histrionic persuasiveness, and is all too ready to assume the role of the victimized martyr and misunderstood man of virtue. Along with comparing himself to Saint Paul, Touvier offers in germ the infamous "Schindler defense" later used during his trial: in the face of heavy exactions from German and French superiors, he claims to have been able to reduce greatly the number of Jewish victims at Rillieux-la-Pape in 1944, an event to which we return later.

Touvier's self-apology is also filled with apocalyptic forebodings and characterized by a Manichaean vision of the world in which the "free" Christian forces of good struggle incessantly against the dark forces of communism. The Occupation itself is described as a civil war instigated by the communists, whose attacks on German officers interrupted the peaceful harmony of Pétainist France ("Under the protection of the Armistice, France lived in peace . . .). According to Touvier, as a result of these attacks, the "infernal cycle, 'terrorism-repression,' had commenced."[81] The presence of the Germans, apparently, had nothing to do with it.

That this extreme right-wing Catholic, not to mention pro-Nazi, vision of the world and history, coupled with Touvier's self-portrait as a martyr to the forces of evil, found a receptive audience among neofascists and right-wing Catholic traditionalists outside the clergy is not particularly surprising. In June 1992, for example, *Le Choc du Mois* published a dossier entitled "The Truth about the Milice" that laid out the "exemplary itinerary" of Paul Touvier and characterized the Milice itself as France's righteous self-defense in the face of communist insurgency. Two years earlier, Jacques Trémolet de Villers, Touvier's lawyer, published a book entitled, bluntly enough, *Paul Touvier est innocent* and presented his subject as the modest, humble, and virtuous victim of all the evils of modernity.[82]

Any number of factual accounts of Touvier's past, whether published in the press or in book form or gathered in testimony for the courts, of course, contradict these blatantly hagiographic accounts of the man *L'Express* more aptly labeled in 1978 the "executioner of Lyons." A closer look at Touvier, whom Charles de Gaulle once described as fully deserving of the firing squad, is therefore in order.

It is worth noting from the outset that the backgrounds, careers, and crimes of Touvier and Bousquet could hardly be more different. Unlike Bousquet, Touvier was the son of right-wing Catholic lower-class provincials. Touvier's father, François, was a small-town tax collector, who was by all accounts fanatically reactionary and nationalistic both politically and religiously. A member of Action Française and the Croix de Feu, both fascist movements active in France before World War II, Touvier senior opposed his sons' joining the Boy Scouts because of the Scouts' British origins and later refused to attend Paul's wedding to his first wife in 1937 because her father was a Freemason. Besides, François had wished to see Paul become a priest. Authoritarian in his politics, François was a tyrant at home as well, harshly indoctrinating his children in his own beliefs. His children called him "the Pope."[83]

Touvier's mother, to whom he was devoted, was apparently quite different from his father. Mild-mannered and unassertive, she appeared to accept her role as the bearer of numerous children conceived, in her husband's view at least, as part of an obligation to the Church and God. Her acquiescence eventually cost her her life. She died in 1931 bearing her eleventh child, conceived against the advice of her doctor. At the time, her son Paul was sixteen years old.

Like his father, Paul Touvier was not well educated, nor was he particularly ambitious or successful. He went to work as a clerk for the national railroads (SNCF) in 1936, where he did not distinguish himself. When the war broke out, he was conscripted into the army, and following the French defeat, returned to his native Chambéry, where he resumed work for the railroads. According to a pamphlet prepared by LICRA (Ligue Internationale contre le Racisme et l'Antisémitisme) and published shortly before Touvier's trial, Touvier was accused of desertion, but nothing came of it.[84]

In October 1940 Touvier joined Vichy's veterans' organization, the Légion des Combattants, a strongly Pétainist group whose activities were comprised chiefly of parades and other shows of support for the Vichy régime. Under pressure from extreme right-wing elements at Vichy, a more muscular and politicized subsidiary, the Service d'Ordre Légionnaire (SOL) was created in December 1941. On the urging of his father, Touvier quickly signed up, and by January 1942 he was the unpaid secretary of the Chambéry section.[85]

Touvier's zeal in the SOL earned him the recognition of his superiors, and when the SOL became the Milice in January 1943, Touvier climbed expeditiously through the ranks. After apparently attending a training period for the élite of the Milice at the officers training school at Uriage during March 1943,[86] Touvier was quickly promoted, becoming head of the Second Service for the Savoy Department in April of that year. His success in that post earned him another promotion in August to the position of head of the Second Service of the entire Rhône region. In that capacity, Touvier "was responsible for a large area covering ten departments with a population of four million. He reported directly to Vichy rather than to the Milice chief for the Lyons region."[87] Moreover, as a head of the Second Service, which could be described in general terms as the intelligence branch of the organization, Touvier enjoyed a privileged position within the Milice itself, because his job entailed "filtering and accumulating all sorts of information that could be exploited to act both within the Milice and against its adversaries."[88] Politically powerful and by all accounts arrogant to boot, Touvier inspired both jealousy and animosity within the organization.

Despite claims made by Touvier and his supporters in the postwar years, the young *milicien* hardly lived a life characterized by Christian virtue. His first wife having died in 1939, Touvier had taken up with a prostitute, Marie-Louise Charroin, and pimped for her in order to help support his own expensive, not to say lavish, tastes. In Jacques Dérogy's 1972 article revealing the Pompidou pardon, Dérogy claims that Touvier put Charroin up in the confiscated apartment in Chambéry of a Jew named Zavelick and installed himself in a confiscated apartment in Lyons belonging to a Jewish textile industrialist from the Lorraine named Lehman. Dérogy also reports that Touvier sold Lehman's furniture for profit and used his car. The plundering of the Milice's victims by Touvier and his fellow *miliciens* occasionally became so extreme that members of rival groups got into fights over the division of booty and wound up wounding and killing each other in pitched battles. Dérogy's account of Touvier the *milicien* coincides, moreover, with testimony given by a former colleague in 1946: "the fruits of searches, money, jewels, and furniture brought back by the Milice were confiscated by Touvier and sold or exchanged by him . . . he was an authoritarian man, without scruples, a veritable gangster."[89] Needless to say, the actions of Touvier and his fellows as just described are hardly in keeping with the Milice's self-image as the noble and virtuous protector of Christian civilization.

Touvier's crimes in the Milice were not limited to dispossessing Jews of apartments, cars, and other valuables or to warring, gangsterlike, with rival factions in the Milice. The LICRA pamphlet lists ten other charges against Touvier, not counting the massacre at Rillieux-la-Pape, the sole charge for which Touvier finally stood trial in the Spring of 1994. For the most part, these crimes consisted of attacks against Jews. For example, witnesses claimed that Touvier was one of two men who attacked with hand grenades the Jewish synagogue on the Quai de Tilsitt in Lyons on 10 December 1943. Two people were wounded in the blast. On 13 June 1944 Touvier was reported by witnesses as being in charge of the roundup (and eventual deportation) of all Jews present at the same synagogue. In another, particularly well-known episode Touvier was implicated in the arrest and murder of Victor Basch, a Hungarian Jewish immigrant who became a professor at the Sorbonne and president of the League of the Rights of Man, along with his wife. According to several accounts, German officers who accompanied the Milice considered Basch and his wife too old to be bothered with and left them with their French colleagues, who executed them. On the morning of 11 January 1944, the bodies of Basch and his wife, both eighty-one years old, were discovered in a ditch, with bullets in their heads.

The list of Touvier's crimes cited in the LICRA Bulletin continues. All were denied by Touvier, and all were eventually disallowed by the April 1992 Paris Court of Appeals decision.

After the war Touvier's career also differed markedly from René Bousquet's. Convicted of treason and sentenced to death in absentia for treason and "intelligence with the enemy," first in Lyons in 1946 and then in his native Chambéry in 1947, Touvier spent the postwar period largely in hiding and on the run. Sneaking out of Lyons following the liberation of the city in September 1944 (but not before liberating some forty political prisoners as an "insurance policy" for later on),[90] Touvier fled to Montpellier where he purchased a dilapidated rooming house with the 300,000 francs he had extorted from his victims while in the Milice. Within a year, Touvier had restored the building, which he sold for a million francs.

Moving to Paris, Touvier took up a life of petty crime, involving himself in counterfeiting schemes and robbery. During an attempted car theft, he was shot in the arm and nursed back to health by the sister of a friend, Monique Berthet, whom Touvier married in August 1947. Arrested for robbery earlier that year, Touvier had been told by the police that he would be returned to Lyons, where his death sentence would be carried out. Following a number of visits from Monique, who provided Touvier with proper clothes in which to make his escape, he was left deliberately unattended by the police, and escaped with no difficulty whatsoever. Following his escape, Touvier lived, apparently miserably, in the suburbs of Paris, doing odd jobs to survive. According to Trémolet de Villers in *Paul Touvier est innocent*, these included wall painting, tutoring, and scrubbing floors.[91]

In November 1949 Touvier returned to Chambéry to live in hiding in his father's house with his wife, their daughter, Chantal, born in 1948, and Touvier's son by his first marriage, twelve-year-old François. In 1950 a second son, Pierre, was born. In order to pay the bills while remaining in hiding, Touvier typed lengthy manuscripts of beatification trials brought by friendly priests.

From the outset, Touvier's postwar odyssey and his survival itself had been assured by the assistance of friendly priests. Just before his escape from Lyons in 1944, Touvier had hidden beneath a trap door of a priest, Stéphane Vautherin, who had served as a Milice chaplain. During his subsequent journeys, Touvier made a habit of contacting the local priest, ingratiating himself by relaying greetings from other priests he had contacted, and recounting his tale of woe. Over the years, Touvier became friends with powerful figures and groups within the Church, the most important being Monsignor Charles Duquaire, secretary to the powerful Cardinal Gerlier of Lyons. It was Duquaire who finally secured a presidential pardon for Touvier in 1971, but the campaign itself was initiated by other clerics as early as the 1950s.

Although Georges Pompidou's pardon of Touvier hardly turned out to be a blessing in the long run, the tenacity with which it was pursued by powerful figures in the Church and at the highest level of the French government is testimony to Touvier's extraordinary capacity to arouse sympathy and to secure champions among what can only be described as misguided, but apparently charitably inclined, priests. Over the years other motives have been attributed to Catholic clerics who sought to assist Touvier, some honorable and some not. One theory was that, through Stéphane Vautherin, Cardinal Gerlier had offered Touvier protection after the war in exchange for freeing the Milice's prisoners. Another theory offered a more unsavory version of events: in his capacity as an intelligence officer for the Milice, Touvier had gathered compromising information on the Church and its representatives during the Occupation, and the Church's protection was offered in exchange for Touvier's silence. Finally, some speculated that Touvier had shared Milice booty with the Church and that his generosity was being returned. While all these theories ultimately proved groundless, the remarkable extent of the Church's support for Touvier fueled them continually. It was largely in an effort to put an end to such rumors and allegations that, following Touvier's arrest in 1989, Cardinal Decourtray of Lyons opened the Church's archives and named a distinguished panel of historians and political scientist headed by René Rémond to investigate the full extent of the Church's lengthy and complicated dealings with Touvier. The report, entitled *Paul Touvier et l'Eglise*, was published in book form in 1992.[92]

According to Rémond and his colleagues, there really was no "Touvier Affair" until Pompidou's 1971 presidential pardon and its subsequent revelation by Dérogy in *L'Express* in June 1972. But the circumstances leading up to the pardon itself are disturbing enough and deserve closer scrutiny here.[93]

In his essay on Touvier's trial in the *New York Times Magazine*, Ted Morgan states that the episode began when Duquaire approached Pierre Arpaillange, the director of pardons at the Ministry of Justice in 1969, asking for a pardon for Touvier. Following Duquaire's visit, Arpaillange, as he testified at Touvier's trial, began to receive all sorts of letters in support of Touvier. Finding this to be quite unusual, Arpaillange initiated an investigation into the matter, assigning the case to Commisioner Jacques Delarue in February 1970. Delarue testified at the trial that on beginning his investigation, he was astonished to discover that Duquaire had already contacted all the witnesses in advance.[94] While Delarue conducted his investigation, moreover, Duquaire was busy pleading his cause to other government officials, including Edouard Balladur, at the time adjunct secretary general of the presidency of the republic, responsible for religious affairs.[95]

Delarue's report, turned in on 10 June 1970, was highly unfavorable, and at this point, according to his testimony at the trial, Arpaillange notified Duquaire that he should discontinue his campaign on behalf of Touvier.[96] But Duquaire and Touvier's other supporters in the Church hierarchy did not desist. In the fall of 1970 a letter campaign from famous individuals on behalf of Touvier was launched but soon abandoned when the philosopher Gabriel Marcel, originally favorably disposed toward Touvier, retracted his letter and asked a number of embarrassing questions concerning Touvier's past of his ecclesiastical supporters.

A final, and ultimately successful, phase of the campaign was inaugurated in the Fall of 1971, when Duquaire, who had written his own report refuting Delarue's findings,[97] approached Anne-Marie Dupuy, chief of staff to the president of the republic. According to Dupuy's testimony at the trial, Duquaire appealed to the mother in her, arguing that Touvier's family and children were being made to suffer unjustly as a result of their father's illegal status. At first skeptical, Dupuy was finally swayed and supported Duquaire's petition in her conversations with Georges Pompidou. On 23 November 1971, Pompidou signed the pardon. Notification of the pardon was sent to Touvier at 1 Place de Fourvières, Lyons, the address of the Archbishopric.

Touvier enjoyed his pardon for only a short time. The publication of Dérogy's article in *L'Express* precipitated a veritable avalanche in the press against Touvier. According to Trémolet, this "campaign of hatred" generated more than 2,000 articles in six months.[98] Whatever the exact figures, media attention, as well as public protest, were so intense that Touvier and his family felt obliged to go into hiding once again. A belated effort by Pompidou at a news conference on 21 September 1972 to justify the pardon by stating it was time "to draw a veil over the past" convinced only a very few.[99] The *grâce*, or pardon, according to Rémond, had become *la pire des disgrâces*, the "worst of disgraces."[100]

The irony underlying the whole "imbroglio of the pardon" is that it was accorded only for *peines accessoires*, restrictions accompanying the 1946 and 1947 convictions that prevented Touvier from residing in Chambéry, where his crimes had been committed, and from inheriting his father's property. The statute of limitations had run out on the convictions themselves in 1966 and 1967, respectively, but not on the *peines accessoires*.

Touvier's second *cavale*, or period in hiding, was characterized by continuing support from Catholic clerics and organizations, albeit of an increasingly reactionary stripe, and new criminal charges against him. For the first time, however, these charges involved crimes against humanity, brought against Touvier in November 1973, imprescriptible in French law since 1964, as noted earlier. There followed an intense and complicated legal battle, the details of which are discussed in the Chronology, which resulted, finally, in the arrest of Touvier in May 1989. When the gendarmes arrested him, Touvier was using the alias "Paul Lacroix."

For those who assumed, following the fugitive's arrest in Nice, that the "Touvier Affair" was finally over and that the former *milicien* was about to face justice, the next several years would bring a number of harsh disappointments. The wheels of justice, as in the case of Bousquet, were to turn notoriously slowly, and indeed were to encounter a number of distractions and interruptions that shocked and even outraged the French public. On 11 July 1991, the Chambre d'Accusation of the Paris Court of Appeals decided to release Touvier on his own recognizance, after paying 60,000 francs in bail. He was required by the court to report in once a week.

In justifying its decision, the Chambre d'Accusation claimed that Touvier's "detention was no longer necessary to the discovery of truth." The reason for the court's clemency, moreover, was supposedly humanitarian in nature. As was well known, Touvier suffered from prostate cancer, although the seriousness of the disease in his case was subject to debate. Touvier's lawyer, Trémolet de Villers, argued that Touvier was "gravely ill" *("un grand malade")* and that to detain him further would be "inhuman." A court-appointed doctor found his condition to be much less severe. In any case, for the examining magistrate, Jean-Pierre Getti, who had almost completed his investigation, the decision was a source of "extreme surprise." More disturbing, in his view, it fit a pattern of delays by the court consistent with efforts to avoid bringing Frenchmen charged with crimes against humanity to trial. Getti's consternation was shared by the prosecutor general of Paris, who sought immediately to have the decision overturned.[101]

Public outrage, while short-lived, was intense. The court's show of humaneness toward Touvier seemed out of place, especially in light of Touvier's own brutality towards his victims, his long flight from justice, and the dubious nature of his lawyer's claims concerning the severity of his malady. In retrospect, it is clear that Trémolet exaggerated the seriousness of Touvier's condition. In the long run, the court's misplaced generosity could only add to the growing conviction in many quarters that the French justice system simply did not want to try Frenchmen for crimes against humanity. In releasing Touvier, after all, the court was releasing a man whose entire postwar raison d'être had been to avoid justice at all costs.

If Touvier's 1991 release by the Chambre d'Accusation provoked a strong public reaction, that reaction was nothing compared to the veritable storm of protest that followed the Paris Court of Appeal's decision to acquit Touvier of all charges on 13 April 1992. The basis of the decision, as several of the essays included in this collection make clear, was that Touvier was acting on behalf of the Vichy regime in committing his crimes. Moreover, since the regime did not practice a "politics of ideological hegemony," any actions committed on behalf of the regime could not be construed as crimes against humanity, by definition imprescriptible. Therefore, Touvier's actions had to be qualified as "war crimes," in which case the statute of limitations had long since gone into effect. Moreover, the court's lengthy report on its decision also made it clear that it was disinclined to believe the testimony of many of the witnesses against Touvier.

Public consternation and outrage were immediate and intense. When informed of the decision, François Mitterrand announced his "surprise" and affirmed that the word itself was an understatement. Simone Weil, herself a former deportee, described the acquittal as "a terrible decision." The National Assembly, in session at the time the acquittal was announced, went into recess upon receiving the news in order to allow deputies to attend a vigil at the Memorial of the Deportation on the Ile de la Cité. Within days, a group of more than forty lawyers signed a petition and presented it to the court stating that they had lost confidence in the three judges who had handed down Touvier's acquittal. The two lawyers who inaugurated the petition, Françoise Cotta and Aube Catala, refused to plead cases before the judges in question. The president of the Paris Court of Appeals, Myriam Ezratty, spoke out vehemently against the petition, arguing that actions such as these "seriously damage the normal functioning of the judicial institution." At Ezratty's request, the head of the Paris Bar disavowed the two lawyers, but the damage was done: the Touvier acquittal had provoked what one newspaper described as a *fronde* in the halls of justice themselves.[102]

On 28 April protest came from another quarter. Some twenty of the most distinguished historians of modern France signed a petition calling for public protest to the acquittal. The petition stated:

> We have learned with consternation of the decision of the *chambre d'accusation* concerning the Touvier affair.
> Aware of our responsibility to seek truth in all its forms, we are indignant that a sad and somber period of our history symbolized by the Vichy regime is travestied by specious reasoning, linguistic artifice, and solid ignorance. Far from reestablishing "civil peace," this decision by the justice system can only trouble the younger generations, shock the older ones and breed confusion.
> We protest a decision that surpasses the juridical framework.
> We object to the abuse of history for false ends.[103]

Although the historians' petition did not mention the personalities involved, their outrage was compounded by the fact that of the three judges responsible for the decision, one had spent his entire career in the colonies, removed from the complex affairs of the metropole, whereas another belonged to a strongly right-wing magistrates association. The *Canard enchaîné* cast further doubt on the impartiality of the court by pointing out that a president of the Paris Court of Appeals, Henri Gleize, along with an examining magistrate, Claude Linais, had earlier founded an organization in support of the "persecuted former *milicien.*"[104]

Given the massive public outcry over the April 1992 acquittal, not to mention the "specious reasoning" and "solid [historical] ignorance" that characterized the verdict itself, it is not surprising that the decision was partially overturned by the Criminal Chamber of the Supreme Court on 27 November 1992. Unlike the lower court, and in all likelihood because of the lengthy and misguided opinion it handed down, the Supreme Court carefully avoided entering the historical debate over the nature of the Vichy regime itself. Moreover, the Supreme Court chose not to comment on the Milice itself, other than to stress its subordination to and complicity with the Gestapo. The Supreme Court did, however, reject the lower court's de facto decision concerning the massacres at Rilleux-la-Pape. According to the lower court, Touvier was not an "agent of the German State." The murder of the seven Jews on the morning of 29 June 1944, ordered by Touvier in reprisal for the Resistance's murder the previous day of Philippe Henriot, Vichy's minister of information, was therefore by definition a French affair. But, as the Supreme Court noted, on numerous occasions, Touvier himself had stated that the murders were carried out on the orders of the Germans. Indeed, in *Mes Crimes contre l'humanité,* Touvier had claimed that the German commander Knab had ordered Touvier's superior, de Bourmont, to execute one hundred Jews in reprisal. On the evening of 28 June, de Bourmont met with Touvier and ordered him to round up thirty Jews. "Totally distraught" by his own account, Touvier succeeded in reducing the number to seven (hence, the "Schindler defense").[105] Therefore, Touvier had acted on German orders, on behalf of a regime all agreed had practiced "a politics of ideological hegemony" and could therefore stand trial for crimes against humanity on that count.

Although the Supreme Court decision of November 1992 did pave the way, finally, for the trial of Paul Touvier on charges of crimes against humanity, the nature of its decision not only let stand some highly dubious legal decisions concerning the history of the Vichy regime but also hamstrung the proceedings themselves. In order to convict Touvier, it was necessary to *prove* that he had acted at the behest of the Germans in ordering the Rilleux-la-Pape executions. In historical terms, this was a highly dubious proposition, in spite of Touvier's earlier pronouncements. The Milice were known to have wanted to avenge the murder of Henriot themselves, and, in fact, several other acts of reprisal had been carried out the same day in other towns.[106] Although both Knab and de Bourmont were dead and could not contradict Touvier's account, other evidence, often circumstantial in nature, suggested that Rillieux was an exclusively French crime. In his plea before the court during Touvier's trial in April 1994, Arno Klarsfeld, Serge's son and the lawyer for several of the plaintiffs, noted that after the Liberation, several of Touvier's subordinates had testified that Touvier alone had ordered the reprisals.[107] Klarsfeld also argued that at a dinner party on the evening of Henriot's assassination, Knab did not once mention his name. For Klarsfeld at least, for Knab not to utter Henriot's name on the same day he ordered one hundred victims executed in reprisal for his death stretched credulity to the breaking point. Moreover, as Klarsfeld also argued, all evidence suggested that the Germans were indifferent to Henriot and that Knab disliked him personally.[108]

Other factors also made Touvier's story seem doubtful. As noted, Touvier took his orders directly from Vichy, and his subordination to de Bourmont in this particular instance seemed unlikely. Finally, as Ted Morgan noted in his essay on the trial, the Germans had plenty of Jews in captivity in Lyons and hardly needed Touvier to round up more.[109]

For many, it was one of the bitter ironies of the trial that in order to secure a conviction, it would be necessary not only to distort the historical record where the Rillieux-la-Pape massacre was concerned, but also, indirectly, to let Vichy off the hook in the process. The stakes were so high, however, that some were willing to contradict their own previous testimony in order to see Touvier convicted. Jacques Delarue, whose report on Touvier had failed ultimately to prevent Pompidou's 1971 presidential pardon, had earlier claimed that Touvier had acted solely on French orders. During his testimony before the court on 1 April, however, Delarue changed his tune completely, testifying this time that orders had come from the Germans.[110] Others were also willing to make the same about-face, especially among the lawyers for the civil plaintiffs and the prosecution, who desired a conviction at all costs. Among the lawyers for the civil parties, only Arno Klarsfeld refused to accept this line, arguing that one should not distort history to secure a conviction. In his final plea before the court, which was later published under the appropriate title of *Touvier, un crime français*, Klarsfeld insisted that the murders at Rillieux were a French crime, but that in the larger context of the Milice's subordination to the Gestapo, it could be traced back to a Nazi "politics of ideological hegemony."

Regardless of who was ultimately responsible for ordering the murders at Rillieux-la-Pape, the trial of Paul Touvier could hardly be considered the trial of Vichy itself, considering that Vichy's culpability in the Final Solution was bracketed from the outset. Moreover, any successful attempt to link Touvier directly and exclusively to Vichy would have guaranteed his acquittal. The "Trial for Memory" turned into the trial of a sickly and voluble old man, prone to convenient lapses of memory and occasionally, careless and self-condemnatory slips of the tongue. At one point, Touvier blurted out that "it was horrible for us [the Milice] that it was the Germans who avenged Henriot." He labeled valuables extorted from Jews "gifts to the Milice." Touvier also denied being an anti-Semite, an assertion later belied by the contents of his *cahier vert*, a secret notebook Touvier kept during the 1980s filled with rancourous and often obscene anti-Semitic statements. The reading of this notebook before the court shocked the jury as well as the public and, according to several accounts, contributed greatly to Touvier's conviction.

Given the constraints placed upon Touvier's trial from the outset as well as the historical burden so many wished it to assume, it is not surprising that reactions to its outcome proved to be mixed. In an article entitled "La Leçon Touvier" published in *Le Monde* on 21 April, Laurent Greilsamer struck an optimistic note, arguing that at the very least the French had had the courage to assume responsibility for their past in judging one of their own for crimes against humanity. Ted Morgan offered a similarly positive assessment, arguing that the trial "presented the French past as it really was, so that the nation could face up to it and pass it on to future generations."[111]

But the fact remained that Touvier was just a "mediocrity," a rancourous and vicious cog in the machine of the Holocaust, whose full dimensions in Vichy France would have come more clearly and fully to light in the trial of a René Bousquet, or even a Maurice Papon, still untried. Moreover, as Eric Conan and Henry Rousso have pointed out recently in *Vichy, un passé qui ne passe pas*, the trial raised as many troubling issues as it resolved, the most obvious being that some fifty years after the crimes, it is very hard to get to the truth. The difficulty in this case was compounded, moreover, by the perverse constraints placed on the witnesses' testimony as a result of the November 1992 Supreme Court decision.

In one very real sense, however, the court's verdict was profoundly satisfying, and, ironically, in a manner in which Touvier himself might well have been aware. The last of the "Twenty-one Points" to which Touvier and other members of the SOL swore allegiance during the Occupation reads: "Against the Forgetting of Crimes. For the Punishment of Those Responsible." Whatever its failings, the trial of Paul Touvier at the Yvelines Court of Assizes had certainly accomplished that.

Notes

1. Pierre Péan, *Une Jeunesse française: François Mitterrand, 1934–1947* (Paris: Fayard, 1994).

2. Quoted in Richard Wolin's unpublished essay, "The Ghosts of Vichy and French Politics of Memory." It is important to note at this juncture that Bousquet had no history of anti-Semitism or of pro-Nazi sympathies, and his most recent biographer, Pascale Froment, confirms this view. We shall return to the motivations behind his participation in the Final Solution later.

3. Quoted in *Le Monde*, 14 September 1994.

4. Ibid. At the time of the interview in *L'Express*, Darquier was living in exile under the name "Estève" in Madrid, where he taught French at a language school. He had fled France at the end of the war and was sentenced to death in absentia in 1947 for his activities as commissioner of Jewish Affairs during the war (see Chronology for further details). According to Serge Klarsfeld, the postwar government did not seek Darquier's extradition because they did not want a trial that would inevitably publicize Vichy's role in the Final Solution. See *Vichy-Auschwitz, 1942* (Paris: Fayard, 1983), 540. Bousquet's role in the Final Solution had first been revealed by Joseph Billig in his 1955 book, *Le Commissariat général aux questions juives*. The information did not provoke a scandal until the 1978 interview with Darquier. See the comments of Robert Paxton in the "Symposium on Mitterrand's Past," *French Politics and Society* 13:1 (Winter 1995), 20.

5. See the "Symposium on Mitterrand's Past," *French Politics and Society* 13:1 (Winter 1995), 34.

6. The specifics of Mitterrand's intervention on behalf of Bousquet are discussed later.

7. Mitterrand's connections with various members of the Cagoule are discussed in detail in Péan, *Une Jeunesse française.*

8. Following the publication of *Une Jeunesse Française* many on the extreme right pointed out that Mitterrand's past and his connection with Bousquet were old news for readers of their reviews, including *Crapouillot* and the official weekly of Le Pen's National Front, *National-Hebdo.* As *National-Hebdo* pointed out, "This is not a scoop." Some on the extreme right expressed sympathy for Mitterrand and praised his attitudes and assertions. One National Front leader, Hubert Massol, denounced what he described as a "politico-media plot which exploits Franco-French hatred with political ends in view on the eve of the presidential elections." He went on to praise the president for "his sense of history" and to congratulate him for "his courage and his loyalty to friends and youthful commitments on the eve of his life."

9. Pierre Miquel, "Le Président qui aime l'histoire," *Le Monde,* 16 September 1994. See also Henry Rousso, *The Vichy Syndrome: History and Memory in France since 1944* (Cambridge: Harvard University Press, 1991).

10. I am endebted to Robert Paxton for this information.

11. The best sources of information on Bousquet's career before and during the Occupation are Jean-Pierre Husson, "L'Itinéraire d'un haut fonctionnaire: René Bousquet," in *Vichy et les Français* ed. Jean-Pierre Azéma et al. (Paris: Fayard, 1992), pp. 287–302; Cyril Aouizerate, *Bousquet: Biographie d'un collabo* (Paris: Editions du forum, 1994), and Pascale Froment, *René Bousquet* (Paris: Stock, 1994). Husson's essay is the most authoritative and precise treatment of Bousquet's early career and has been used extensively here.

12. In Emmanuel Faux, Thomas Legrand, and Gilles Perez's *La main droite de Dieu: Enquête sur François Mitterrand et l'extrême droite* (Paris: Seuil, 1994), a conversation occurring in 1978 is reported in which Mitterrand describes the episode to Jacques Attali in the following terms: "When he [Bousquet] was a young subprefect in Toulouse, he didn't hesitate to throw himself into a swollen river to save a little girl. He owes the beginning of his career to this act of courage" (p. 92).

13. See Froment, *René Bousquet,* p. 66.

14. This information is taken from the *Acte d'Accusation.* All translations are my own. I am indebted to Annette Lévy-Willard for providing me access to this document.

15. See Husson, "René Bousquet," p. 289.

16. Ibid.

17. Ibid.

18. Ibid., p. 290.

19. Ibid., p. 291. Although the Nazis and the Soviet Union were officially allies during Bousquet's stint as prefect of the Marne, the Vichy regime was

implacably anticommunist from the outset. Bousquet's anticommunism could therefore be attributable in some measure to his bureaucratic zeal in serving Vichy.

20. For a discussion of Châteaubriant and the Groupe Collaboration, see Bertram Gordon, *Collaboration in France during the Second World War* (Ithaca: Cornell University Press, 1980), pp. 230–43.

21. Quoted in Sorj Chalandon, "L'Ami Bousquet: Une histoire française," *Le Magazine de Libératin*, 3–9 December 1994.

22. Ibid., p. 294. Bousquet apparently made the same claim during the war to a mutual friend of his and François Mitterrand's, Yves Cazaux. See Péan, *Une Jeunesse française*, p. 317.

23. Faux, Legrand, and Perez conclude that Mitterrand and Bousquet actually met during the Occupation through their mutual friendship with Martin (*La Main droite de Dieu*, p. 93). It is perhaps worth noting at this juncture that these authors take a more skeptical and indeed hostile attitude toward Mitterrand and the version of events he presents than does Péan in *Une Jeunesse française*.

24. Péan, *Une Jeunesse française*, p. 313.

25. In *Vichy France and the Jews* (New York: Schocken Books, 1983), Michael R. Marrus and Robert O. Paxton note that the Vel d'Hiv hosted a rally of prominent anti-Semites and other supporters of Action Française in July 1937 following the release from prison of Action Française's leader, Charles Maurras. Maurras had been imprisoned for incitement to murder for his verbal assaults on premier Léon Blum (p. 250).

26. For a brief discussion of the Commissariat for Jewish Affairs and its two commissioners, Xavier Vallat and Darquier de Pellepoix, see the chronology at the beginning of this volume.

27. For a description of Vichy's Anti-Jewish Statutes, see the chronology.

28. For a detailed discussion of the 2 July meeting and the events leading up to it, see Serge Klarsfeld, *Vichy-Auschwitz, 1942*, pp. 89–95. Extracts of the text of the German summary of the meeting are included in *Libération*'s Bousquet Dossier.

29. Quoted in *Le Monde*, 14 September 1994.

30. Letter from Robert Paxton to the author, 31 January 1995.

31. Ibid.

32. Philippe Burrin, *La France à l'heure allemande* (Paris: Seuil, 1995), p. 159. Although Burrin seems to share Paxton's view that Bousquet was not sympathetic to Nazism, he does note that in 1941 Bousquet expressed sympathy for a single-party system and the Italian Fascist Party in particular, noting at one point to Italian interlocutors: "It is you who have taught us that without a single party system there can be no authoritarian regime" (p. 158). On the issue of anti-Semitism, Burrin also notes that in a conversation with the Protestant Pasteur Boegner, Bousquet affirmed that "whatever the outcome of the war, the Jewish problem will need to be resolved" and expressed his view that even the French Jews that Vichy claimed to protect would be subject to "strict obligations" and "limited rights" (p. 162). In his recent article on Bousquet in

Le Magazine de Libération, Sorj Chalandon cites the case of a prewar Jewish friend who came to request Bousquet's assistance in Vichy. Bousquet refused to see him, but did not turn him in either. While these anecdotes do not confirm a visceral anti-Semitism on Bousquet's part, they do reveal a ready compliance with prevailing attitudes and policies at Vichy and a willingness to forsake former friends in the name of ambition.

33. For more detailed discussions of the Oberg-Bousquet agreements, see Marrus and Paxton, *Vichy France and the Jews,* pp. 241–45, and Burrin, *La France à l'heure allemande,* pp. 160–61.

34. Burrin, *Le France à l'heure allemande,* p. 160.

35. Quoted in Annette Lévy-Willard, "Why Bousquet Risks the Assizes Court," *Libération,* 8 February 1993.

36. Quoted in *Le Monde,* 14 September 1994.

37. Quoted in Aouizerate, *Bousquet,* p. 65.

38. For the initial German reactions to Bousquet, see ibid., p. 70.

39. Oberg's comments on Bousquet's removal are taken from his deposition of 20 February 1946, quoted in ibid., p. 72. Aouizerate also speculates that Laval wished to be rid of Bousquet for more personal reasons. Bousquet, rumor had it, was paying frequent visits to Laval's daughter (p. 72).

40. The High Court's charter specified that it was competent to deal with cases involving "the head of State, the head of Government, ministers, secretaries of State, under secretaries of State, commissioners general, secretaries general of the chief of State, of the government, and of the ministers, residents general, governors general, and high commissioners." See "Les Affaires Bousquet-Papon-Touvier: État des lieux établi par la Fédération internationale des droit de l'Homme," *Actes* 71 (April 1991), 33.

41. Quoted in Edwy Plenel, "L'Affaire Bousquet," *Le Monde,* 14 September 1994.

42. This is not the same newspaper that the essays in the present volume are taken from, but an earlier, now defunct, post-Liberation newspaper.

43. Quoted in Plenel, "L'Affaire Bousquet."

44. In his biography of Bousquet, Cyril Aouizerate argues that Bousquet was fully aware of the ultimate fate of the Jews and that, rather than slow down the deportations, he only accelerated them as a result. Aouizerate also states that "in September 1942, Bousquet received a message from the Central Jewish Consistory explaining that 'it has been established from detailed and corroborative sources that several hundreds of thousands of Jews have been exterminated in eastern Europe. It is not the German government's intention to use the deportees for labor but rather to arrest and exterminate them'" (p. 61).

45. Quoted in Plenel, "L'Affaire Bousquet."

46. All the preceding newspaper commentaries on the 1949 verdict are quoted in ibid.

47. Edwy Plenel, "Une Longue amitié avec René Bousquet," *Le Monde,* 9 September 1994.

48. Quoted in Pierre Truche, "La Notion de crime contre l'humanité," *Esprit* 181 (May 1992), 74.

49. Geoffrey Best, *War and Law since 1945* (Oxford: Oxford University Press, 1994), p. 67.

50. Quoted in Michael Reisman and Chris T. Antoniou, eds., *The Laws of War: A Comprehensive Collection of Primary Documents on International Laws Governing Armed Conflict* (New York: Vintage, 1994), p. 319.

51. Ibid., p. 320.

52. Quoted in Henry Rousso, "Les Rivalités de l'histoire et de la justice," *Libération,* 17 March 1994.

53. Serge Klarsfeld and Henry Rousso, "Histoire et Justice," *Esprit* 181 (May 1992), p. 22.

54. Faux, Legrand, and Perez, *La Main droite de Dieu,* p. 97.

55. Ibid., pp. 95–96. The authors also note that the paper has continued to support Mitterrand and that in recent presidential campaigns Mitterrand has chosen to hold his final meeting of the campaign in Toulouse.

56. It is of interest to note that in the interview Darquier provides no hard evidence or indeed new information concerning Bousquet's role in the Vel d'Hiv roundups. As a matter of fact, *L'Express*'s interviewer, Philippe Ganier-Raymond, discredits many of Darquier's more outlandish and patently false assertions during the course of the interview itself, making him appear a much less than credible witness. What is clear is that Darquier remained an unrepentant anti-Semite to the end, as repeated assertions concerning Jewish "plots" and the Jews' responsibility for French "decadence" confirm.

57. Aouizerate, *Bousquet,* p. 86.

58. Joseph Billig, *Le Commissariat général aux Questions juives (1941–1944),* 3 vols. (Paris: Editions du Centre, 1955). See Klarsfeld's 13 September 1989 letter to the examining magistrate, quoted in its entirety in Aouizerate, *Bousquet,* pp. 92–93.

59. Faux, Legrand, and Perez, *La Main droite de Dieu,* p. 90.

60. Aouizerate, *Bousquet,* p. 93.

61. Ibid., p. 90. In *La Main droite de Dieu,* Robert Badinter is quoted as saying that Georges Keijman now regrets his role in delaying the trial of René Bousquet, a role he played at Mitterrand's request. Badinter goes on to affirm: "I'm sure Mitterrand did not want a 'Bousquet Affair'" (p. 91). In a recent letter to *Le Monde* (12 September 1994), at the height of the controversy swirling around Mitterrand's past, Keijman asserted: "at no time did I receive instructions from the President of the Republic to interfere in any way with the procedure involving René Bousquet. Nor did I attempt to do so on my own initiative."

62. Quoted in "Les Affaires Bousquet-Papon-Touvier," p. 32.

63. Quoted in Péan, p. 315.

64. For details of Bousquet's physical and mental condition and public reaction to him in the months before his assassination, see Froment, 575–80.

65. According to Pascale Froment, at the time of Bousquet's death, another charge against Bousquet for crimes against humanity was under investigation

by the court. A former *résistant*, Gérard Hisard, located a German document in Coblenz that implicated Bousquet for denouncing to the Germans a Resistance group that tapped into a telephone cable connecting Berlin to Paris and passed along secret information gleaned from the tap to the Allies. As a result, the Germans arrested and deported a French postal engineer, Robert Keller. Following confirmation of the authenticity of the document, the new charges were filed. The crime would constitute a crime against humanity in France, even though it did not involve racial persecution, because, following decisions made during the Barbie Affair, the arrest and deportation of *résistants* could be included in the definition as well.

66. Ian Buruma, "The Vichy Syndrome," *Tikkun* 10:1 (Jan-Feb. 1995), p. 92. The details of Didier's past are taken from this essay.

67. In his recent *The Death of Politics: France under Mitterrand* (London: Michael Joseph, 1994), John Laughland writes: "the extraordinary circumstances of Bousquet's death were met with hardly any comment or investigation by the French media. It was extraordinary that, Bousquet's case having taken years to come to court, he should have been killed immediately before he was due to stand trial. . . . Nor was there any questioning of the claim that Didier just rang the doorbell and walked into the apartment with a gun in his bag. Professional photographers testified that a contemporary photograph of Bousquet was worth 100,000 francs, yet if it was so difficult to shoot him with a telephoto lens, it is strange that he could so easily be shot with a Remington 38" (p. 219).

68. For a discussion of French attitudes toward the Occupation in the postwar period, see Henry Rousso, *The Vichy Syndrome* (Cambridge: Harvard University Press, 1991), chap. 1 and 2.

69. Along these lines, see Jean-Paul Sartre's classic essay, "Qu'est-ce qu'un collaborateur?" in *Situations III* (Paris: Gallimard: 1949).

70. Eric Conan and Henry Rousso, *Vichy, un passé qui ne passe pas* (Paris: Fayard, 1994), p. 11.

71. Olivier Wieviorka, *Nous entrerons dans la carrière: De la Résistance à l'exercice de pouvoir* (Paris: Seuil, 1994), p. 350.

72. Quoted in ibid., p. 194.

73. Ibid.

74. Paul Thibault, "La Culpabilité française," *Esprit* (January 1991), 24.

75. Quoted in Wieviorka, *Nous entrerons*, p. 318.

76. *Esprit* 181 (May 1992), 36.

77. Pineau's comments are in Wieviorka, *Nous entrerons*, p. 272.

78. In this regard, it is of interest to note that in a special issue of *Esprit*, "Que faire de Vichy?," published following Touvier's acquittal in April 1992, one of the articles, by François and Renée Bédarida, was devoted to "L'Eglise sous l'Occupation."

79. For Klarsfeld's comments along these lines, see the interview with Klarsfeld and Rousso in *Esprit* (May 1992), 19–20.

80. Paul Touvier, *Mes Crimes contre l'humanité* (n.p.: 1979).

81. Ibid., p. 9. All of this discussion occurs under the heading "Provocation of Civil War."

82. Jacques Trémolet de Villers, *Paul Touvier est innocent* (Bouère: Editions Dominique Martin Morin, 1990).

83. The best account in English of Touvier's family and background is contained in Ted Morgan, "The Last War Criminal: The Trial of Paul Touvier," *New York Times Magazine*, 22 May 1994, p. 36.

84. P. Quentin and P. Bataille, "Paul Touvier devant ses juges" (1994), p. 2.

85. For a brief description of the origins of the SOL, the Milice and the beginnings of Touvier's career in these organizations, see René Rémond et al., *Paul Touvier et l'Eglise* (Paris: Fayard, 1992), pp. 63–75. According to the LICRA document, Touvier actually doubled his salary once he quit the SNCF and went to work for the SOL full-time.

86. Touvier's training session at Uriage is reported in *Le Choc du Mois* 53 (juin 1992), p. 27, not the most reliable of sources. For a discussion of the Milice and Uriage, see John Helman, *The Knight-Monks of Vichy France: Uriage, 1940–1945* (Montreal: McGill-Queens University Press, 1993), pp. 182–94.

87. Morgan, "Last War Criminal," p. 32.

88. Rémond et al., *Paul Touvier et l'Eglise*, p. 72.

89. Quoted in Quentin and Bataille, "Paul Touvier devant ses juges," p. 2.

90. Morgan, "Last War Criminal," p. 37.

91. Trémolet de Villers, *Paul Touvier est innocent*, p. 24.

92. For an account of speculation concerning the motives for the Church's assistance to Touvier and the constitution of the Decourtray panel, see the *Présentation* to Rémond et al., *Paul Touvier et l'Eglise*, pp. 10–15.

93. Indeed, the chapter in *Paul Touvier est innocent* dealing with the presidential pardon is entitled "L'Imbroglio de la grâce."

94. Morgan, "Last War Criminal," pp. 45, 56.

95. Rémond et al., *Paul Touvier et l'Eglise*, p. 218.

96. Morgan, "Last War Criminal," p. 56. Rémond provides a more detailed and complex account of the Delarue report, both as to its origins and impact. See *Paul Touvier et l'Eglise*, pp. 211–75.

97. Portions of Duquaire's counter report are included as an appendix to Trémolet de Villers, *Paul Touvier est innocent*, pp. 120–21.

98. Ibid., p. 25.

99. Pompidou's statement is quoted at length in Henry Rousso, *The Vichy Syndrome* (Cambridge: Harvard University Press, 1991), p. 123.

100. Rémond et al., *Paul Touvier et l'Eglise*, p. 221.

101. For an account of Touvier's 1991 release and its repercussions, see "Paul Touvier remis en liberté," *Libération*, 12 July 1991.

102. See "Touvier: La Fronde," *Le Figaro*, 24 April 1992.

103. Quoted in *Libération*, 28 April 1992.

104. See "La Justice 'révise' l'histoire de Pétain et de Vichy," *Le Canard enchaîné*, 15 April 1992.

105. During his trial, Touvier would alter his account as to who ordered the

Rillieux massacre as well how many victims were designated and by whom. See Chalandon's report of the proceedings of the trial on 29 March included in this volume.

106. For the murder of Henriot and the reprisals that followed, see Jacques Delperrié de Bayac, *Histoire de la Milice, 1918–1945* (Paris: Fayard, 1969), pp. 500–505.

107. Arno Klarsfeld, *Paul Touvier, un Crime français* (Paris: Fayard, 1994), pp. 49–53.

108. Ibid., pp. 71–72.

109. Morgan, "Last War Criminal," p. 35.

110. See Klarsfeld, *Paul Touvier*, pp. 66–67.

111. Morgan, "Last War Criminal," p. 78.

THE BOUSQUET AFFAIR

The essays and documents assembled here, all of which originally appeared in the Parisian newspaper *Libération*, underscore the wide range of issues raised by the accusation and indictment of René Bousquet on charges of crimes against humanity. Indeed, had the trial of Bousquet actually taken place, many still believe it would have been the trial of Vichy itself, and especially of its complicity in the Final Solution.

In his interview with Annette Lévy-Willard published at the moment of commemorations surrounding the fiftieth anniversary of the Vel d'Hiv round-ups, Robert Paxton situates the 1942 deportations of Jews ordered by Bousquet in the broader context of the policies and ambitions of the Vichy regime and of the implementation of the Final Solution throughout Europe. Paxton provides further specifics on these other related issues in his subsequent essay, "Did Vichy France Protect French Jews?"

Paxton's essay, along with the remaining documents and essays in this section, originally appeared as a supplement in the 13 July 1993 issue of *Libération*. Published five days after Bousquet's murder, the supplement was entitled "The Bousquet Dossier: Essential Evidence in a Trial That Will Never Occur." The materials translated here include a brief summary of the Bousquet Affair by Annette Lévy-Willard, excerpts of a lengthy letter from Bousquet to the court written in the Summer 1992 in which Bousquet offers essentially the same defense he presented in 1949, and brief essays addressing "Six Questions for History." These essays, written by distinguished historians Robert Paxton, Henry Rousso, Pierre Laborie, and Denis Peschanski, were intended to address issues raised by Bousquet's letter in his own defense. The six questions include the aforementioned "Did Vichy France Protect French Jews?" as well as "Did Bousquet Falsify History in His Defense Plea?"; "Was There Massive Collaboration of Top Administrative Officials?"; "Was the France of 1940–42 Anti-Semitic?"; "Why did the High Court Acquit Bousquet?"; and "Did the Purge Achieve Its Goals?" These essays can be read independently of Bousquet's letter.

ANNETTE LÉVY·WILLARD

Vichy Did the Work of the Nazis:

An Interview with Robert Paxton

Lévy-Willard: In July 1942 René Bousquet, secretary general of the Vichy police, ordered the French police in Paris to arrest foreign Jews—including their children born in France—thereby condemning them to death, without, one might add, the least crisis of conscience on Bousquet's part, as his declarations before the High Court in 1949 indicate. Could Bousquet have done otherwise than to order the arrests?

Paxton: It is important to understand that in the summer of 1942, Bousquet's main concern was to expand the functions of the French police in the Occupied Zone. The logic of power was to show the world that the Vichy government was not merely a puppet regime. In order to prove this, it was necessary that the French police control internal affairs and not leave it up to the Germans alone to designate hostages and arrest French people. The result was that the French police did the work of the Germans. This was the logical consequence of Vichy's decision to create a "new State" rather than limit itself to a caretaker's role in keeping within the framework of the [1940] armistice. As the war dragged on, German demands became increasingly difficult to bear, but Vichy continued [to accommodate them].

When the Germans extended the Final Solution into France, the Vichy government did something completely unprecedented, exceptional in World War II Europe: it turned over to the Germans Jews who were completely under its own authority in the Unoccupied Zone. This initiative on the part of Vichy is stupefying. The French state had other options that would have permitted it to refuse to hand over these Jews, including referring to the terms of the Armistice agreement itself, which recognized an unoccupied zone. Vichy could have affirmed: "This operation exceeds the legal limits set by the armistice; we do not have the means to prevent you from deporting people but we will not participate in the deportations." And, finally, Vichy could have chosen a more daring option, which would simply have been to oppose the arrests, as did Admiral Horthy in Hungary, for example, between 1942 and March 1944. But the Vichy regime, in wishing to create a desirable situation for itself in Nazi Europe, put itself from the outset in the position of going beyond the terms of the Armistice [in its efforts to please the Germans].

The Germans had less than 3,000 police for all of France. If Vichy had refused to participate, the Germans would not have had sufficient manpower to carry out all these arrests.

Lévy-Willard: You show in your book, *Vichy France: Old Guard and New Order,* that Vichy was not an accident in the history of France, that Vichy's "National Revolution" constituted a continuation of a xenophobic and antirepublican tradition. Besides, one of Vichy's first decisions was to review the naturalization of thousands of refugees residing in France.

Paxton: The question of citizenship was already at the heart of political debates in France in the 1930s. The opposition claimed that the republic accepted too many immigrants and naturalized too many refugees. When this antirepublican opposition arrived in power in June 1940, it began reviewing naturalizations and, as of 22 July, forbade those not born of a French father to practice law or medicine. The reasons given to justify these measures was that "cosmopolitanism" had been one of the major causes of the French defeat, and so foreigners became Vichy's targets in summer 1940.

Contrary to what is often assumed, Vichy's policies toward the Jews were from the beginning in conflict with those of the Germans. As of the fall of 1940, the Nazis expelled German Jews, who then sought refuge in the French Unoccupied Zone. Vichy did not want these refugees. It is therefore completely false to claim that the first anti-Jewish measures of the French State were the work of the Germans. In fact Vichy "resisted" Germany . . . by attempting to block the arrival in France of trains full of German Jews chased out of Germany by the Nazis. When this effort proved unsuccessful, the Vichy government decided to intern these German Jews in camps at Gurs and elsewhere.

To understand the behavior of Vichy's leaders, one must understand that they were delighted to learn in May 1942 that the Germans were going to round up German Jewish refugees in the Occupied Zone and put them in trains headed "toward the East." On 7 May, René Bousquet asked Reinhard Heidrich, Himmler's subordinate: "Couldn't you also deport the refugees in our zone, the Unoccupied Zone?"

This request was consonant with the politics of Vichy and an outgrowth of the refugee crisis of the 1930s. "At last someone is going to rid us of these refugees," the Vichy leaders told themselves. The Nazis had something else in mind.

Lévy-Willard: During the summer of 1942 Vichy's political leaders, and Pétain and Laval in particular, received reports of massacres of Jews in Poland. Didn't they ask any questions? Didn't Bousquet, who organized the roundups, ask what was going to happen to these families he was handing over to the Germans?

Paxton: He knew and he didn't know. The Germans followed a policy of systematic disinformation and secrecy. The key word in France was "deportation." When one mentioned "deportation" in 1942–43, one thought of the Service du Travail Obligatoire, the conscripted labor force, and deported resistance partisans, and some Frenchmen were even indignant that Jews were not subject to obligatory labor, and thus to deportation. The available information [about the deportation of Jews] was contradictory. Even the Jewish Agency in Palestine was not sure enough of the information it had to publish a report denouncing the massacre of Jews until November 1942, even though the Final Solution had been under way at Auschwitz and Birkenau for nine months.

Besides, Laval had already asked how to present the deportations to the public. What term should be used? The German answer was "agricultural labor." And that became the official version. The organizations of the departures themselves did not correspond to this explanation. It was enough to look at the conditions of travel, but people did not want to know.

Lévy-Willard: Vichy's functionaries took away the citizenship of recently naturalized refugees, but how could they justify legally the deportation of children born in France?

Paxton: It was against the law, but the authorities argued that families should remain together, which is not abnormal. What was aberrant, and demented, was when they sent the children along *after* the parents had already been deported. Weeks after the departure of their parents, and alone.

Lévy-Willard: It is noteworthy that in the postwar trials, Vichy was more often judged for treason than for anti-Semitism.

Paxton: Absolutely. Two Commissioners for Jewish Questions, Xavier Vallat and Darquier de Pellepoix, were convicted, the latter to death in absentia. But it is true that the question of the Jews played only a minor role in other trials such as the trial of Bousquet, who, however, did more harm than authentic anti-Semites. After the war a kind of repression of this issue took place. Even the survivors of the Holocaust did not wish to speak about it, because they felt guilty for having survived it, because it disturbed others, because the survivors wished to begin a new life. In order to understand the postwar trials of collaborators, it is necessary to understand that the magistrates handling the cases had all previously pledged an oath to Pétain. The purge of the magistrates was limited to judges who had participated in the Special Jurisdictions (Special Sections). The others continued their careers in an entirely normal fashion. And besides, these judges, like the majority of Frenchmen, believed in the shield thesis and saw the deportation of Jews as an exclusively German project. Their experience as magistrates under Vichy had very much clouded the issue.

In studying these trials, I have been struck by the lacunae in the procedures themselves. Vichy functionaries were charged in accordance with Article 75 which punished conspiring with the enemy ["intelligence with the enemy"]. The juridical point of departure for these trials was thus very narrow. The issue of official Vichy anti-Semitism was never raised because the subject was not covered under Article 75.

Lévy-Willard: The idea that Vichy acted as a "protective shield" against the Germans, which was for quite some time the official version of its role, relies on statistical evidence: fewer Jews were deported from France than from other European countries.

Paxton: This thesis seems convincing because of the exactness of the figures, but the thesis itself is entirely false. For example, comparisons are made between the deportation figures for France and those for Holland, but the comparison does not hold up. In Holland, Jews were concentrated in the ghetto in Amsterdam. Holland was also a small country completely occupied by the Germans. France was a large country with a varied geography as well as an Unoccupied Zone. If you wish to be scientific, you must compare everything, not just the figures: governmental policies, the extent of occupation, the resources the geography offered refugees, and public opinion as well. Considering the dispersion of the Jews in France and shelter offered them by French people, the number of those deported would have been lower if the French administration had not been under the orders of the Vichy regime. If you insist on comparing raw statistics alone, you must also take into consideration the number of Jews turned over to the Nazis from areas not occupied by the German army. In this category, Vichy France gets the highest award for all of Europe.

Lévy-Willard: In 1973 the publication of your book *Vichy France* in French translation provoked a shockwave here. For the first time, another version of the history of Occupation was proposed and the thesis of a French state totally subjugated by the Nazis was destroyed. Why was it necessary for twenty years to pass before the truth could emerge concerning Vichy?

Paxton: My book caused a sensation because the work of other historians, including the German Eberhard Jaeckel (author of *France in Hitler's*

Europe) and the Frenchman Yves Durand, had been ignored. The preferred, "official" version of history was that of Robert Aron: France under the German heel, Vichy as protective shield. I had the good fortune to be translated into French as public opinion was changing. As Henry Rousso has demonstrated in *The Vichy Syndrome,* it took May 1968, *The Sorrow and the Pity,* and a change of outlook brought about by a change of generations. My book, which showed that the armistice and the National Revolution were political choices, that internal political initiatives did not originate in Berlin, situated Vichy within the continuity of French history. To my complete surprise, the book stirred tremendous controversy. Some university historians were very critical. For instance the *Revue française de sciences politiques* published a review underscoring a dozen minor errors in the book and concluded that I knew nothing about France and that my book was not "scientific." Since then there has been a reversal. It is not unusual that people prefer gentler versions of history: this was certainly the case for the Indians in American history. The more painful history is, the more innocuous one seeks to make it.

Lévy-Willard: After *Vichy France,* you went on to publish *Vichy France and the Jews* ten years later. Why did you choose to add another component to your history of Vichy?

Paxton: The thesis of *Vichy France and the Jews* was already in the first book, but not sufficiently documented. I must add that the study of Vichy's relations with the Jews is a very painful subject, and I was disheartened to undertake it. To carry out this research alone would be too depressing, and I wanted to abandon it. And so I asked one of my former students, Michael Marrus, now a professor in Canada, to help me with it. Marrus and I worked in the archives for five years. For this project, I had access to the French archives thanks to Roger Errera (director of the Diaspora collection owned by the Calmann-Lévy publishing house). I regret that in our book we did not adequately emphasize the actions of French citizens who helped the Jews. As one refugee told me: "All the Jews who perished perished because of the Vichy regime, but all those who survived survived due to the efforts of French citizens." Our research focused deliberately on the actions of the Vichy government, and thus the darkest part of this story. The work was depressing from beginning to end.

Lévy-Willard: As an American, why have you spent all of these years studying the history of Vichy?

Paxton: As an adolescent in 1945 I was fascinated by the history of the war. The subject of Vichy was particularly interesting because of the uniqueness of the French situation during World War II. Several questions emerged: What type of sovereignty prevailed in France? Where was the true government? In Vichy? in London? France was more divided than other European nations.

A second point of interest was the conflict between two conceptions of citizenship where one witnessed in 1940 the revenge of the xenophobic camp that had been in opposition since 1789.

A third point unique to the French situation was that Vichy enjoyed more autonomy than the other occupied countries.

Last, the Final Solution was applied in France at the very beginning, in 1942, which explains why the vast majority of the deportees were exterminated. The Final Solution was launched in Poland, and then in Slovakia, in the Spring of 1942, and in Western Europe in the Summer of 1942. Why in France before other countries such as Hungary and Denmark, for example? Perhaps because of the accommodativeness of the French government.

Lévy-Willard: Not a single Frenchman has been tried for crimes against humanity. Are such trials necessary? [It should be noted that Bousquet was still alive and Touvier had yet to be tried at the time this interview took place.]

Paxton: The trials of Bousquet and Papon would be salutary. It would be healthy to be finished with this, to address the questions directly and then close the book. But if the trials do not take place, research and education will accomplish the task of the courts, especially since so many French historians are now working on the Vichy period. Thus progress will be made and new questions will be asked. History is never finished.

Lévy-Willard: Were you surprised by the [April 1992] decision not to try Paul Touvier?

Paxton: Completely. I thought judges based their opinions on juridical and not historical arguments. Here, however, their historical analysis was completely false. The Touvier decision provoked a great deal of indignation, of course. Although as a foreigner I prefer not to give my opinion concerning the petition sent to the president of the republic to recognize publicly the role of the Vichy regime in the deportation of the Jews, I must admit that, if I were a French citizen, I would sign.

But I must say that I do not wish to point the finger at one country alone, because no country has reason to be proud of its actions in this regard during this period. David Wyman's book shows that the United States kept the door half closed to refugees at the end of the 1930s. The Allies failed to react to information they received concerning the Final Solution. The British historian Martin Gilbert shows that the Allied Command refused to bomb Auschwitz because they wished to concentrate all their efforts on a military defeat. All this suggests that in a certain sense, every country made the Final Solution possible. No one reacted strongly enough.

16 July 1992

A N N E T T E   L É V Y - W I L L A R D

Fifteen Years of an Interminable Affair

René Bousquet, 69, knight of the Legion of Honor and honored with a Military Croix de Guerre 1935–45 (?), was living peacefully on the Avenue Raphaël, overlooking the Ranelagh Gardens, in the wealthy 16th Arrondissement of Paris. At the time it seems that his name stirred no memories among the respectable financiers who sat beside him in numerous executive meetings. But a journalist from *L'Express* located Louis Darquier de Pellepoix in Spain, a man who had been the commissioner for Jewish affairs in the Vichy government and who, between long, anti-Semitic diatribes, named Bousquet as the man responsible for the Vel d'Hiv roundups. "It was Bousquet who organized the big roundup of Jews, from A to Z. Bousquet was the chief of police. He is the one who did everything."

The following week, during a protest meeting against the xenophobic and anti-Semitic declarations of Darquier, the lawyer Serge Klarsfeld, president of the Association of Sons and Daughters of the Jewish Deportees of France, described the involvement of the former chief of French police in the roundup of Jews from 1942 to 1943. He immediately brought charges against Bousquet's associate Jean Leguay, who, unlike his boss, who was judged by the High Court in 1949, had never been brought to trial. Klarsfeld made no attempt to reopen the Bousquet case because it had already been ruled on. "I attacked Bousquet," explained Klarsfeld, "then I brought suit against Leguay."

The publication of the interview with Darquier de Pellepoix had enormous repercussions, and Alain Peyrefitte, the minister of justice at the time, announced that he planned to ask finally for the extradition of the former commissioner for Jewish affairs. He never did.

The political uneasiness surrounding the Bousquet affair was already palpable and Agence France Presse reporters, censored by editors who were blocking any stories about the Bousquet–Leguay affair, threatened to call a strike on 17 December to protest against this unofficial censorship. René Bousquet, the cold and brilliant retired banker, had become one of the last living symbols of French collaboration in the extermination of European Jews.

The personnel representatives on the administrative board of the airline UTA, of which Bousquet was a member, then issued a statement refusing to "tolerate such dishonorable fraternizing," and on 14 December 1978 Bousquet offered his resignation.

At the beginning of 1979 Bousquet was still a member of the governing board of the Bank of Indo-Suez (formerly the Bank of Indochina), where he had built a career for himself following the war. But demonstrations took place demanding his resignation, and an Anti-Fascist Committee of the Suez Banks distributed tracts denouncing this "unworthy person who sits on boards beside a host of important people." Bousquet resigned from his post.

Meanwhile, the suit brought against Leguay was accepted by the Public Prosecutor's Office of the Paris Tribunal. For the first time in France the committing magistrate, Martine Anzani, pronounced an accusation of "crimes against humanity." But the government allowed the case to drag on, and the foreign affairs minister, who was responsible for deciding if the agreement of 8 August 1945 between the Allies on the imprescriptibility of crimes against humanity applied to France, remained silent. It took the appearance in June 1979 of a full-page ad paid for by Serge Klarsfeld's association denouncing this silence to force a decision by the minister, who then affirmed that these were indeed imprescriptible crimes. The gathering of evidence lasted ten years, and Jean Leguay died on 2 July 1989, without ever going to trial.

1989

Klarsfeld once more took up the fight against Bousquet and brought the charge, "Leguay is Bousquet." Supporting this charge were declarations Bousquet himself had made in 1985 during the Leguay hearing: "As for the functions of Leguay, he had no power to make decisions, but was in charge of transmitting all the information and orders from the SS authorities to me or to the Minister of the Interior."

Since Bousquet had already been tried by the High Court, the lawyers set to work unearthing new documents, such as the minutes from the meeting of 2 July 1942 in which the SS and Bousquet planned the roundups of the Vel d'Hiv and telegrams signed by him ordering the deportation of parents of small children and minors younger than eighteen who had been protected up until that time.

The telegrams were part of the file of the proceedings of the 1949 trial but had never been examined by the High Court as possibly constituting crimes against humanity.

The left replaced the right in power and turned out to be no more anxious to try Bousquet than their predecessors had been to try Leguay. This was the political left that had not hesitated to kidnap the German Klaus Barbie in Bolivia so that he could be tried in Lyon.

In April 1990 *L'Express* reminded the public of the crimes of Bousquet and of the Vichy government—the martyrdom of 3,500 Jewish children interned at Pithiviers and at Beaune-la-Rolande, separated from their parents, abandoned to their fate, transferred to Drancy, and finally killed at Auschwitz. These children had been arrested in the Vel' d'Hiv roundup organized by René Bousquet. The children had not been included before, but now the French authorities insisted that they, too, be handed over to the Germans. The mothers were deported first, followed by the children.

There were demonstrations under Bousquet's windows, but the court remained unruffled. It was six more months before the criminal court of the Paris Court of Appeals was asked to investigate the affair. The case would later be passed back and forth between the Court of Appeals and the Paris prosecuting attorney.

The Public Prosecutor's Office finally handed down the absurd decision that only the High Court of Justice, created at the time of the Liberation (in 1944) could try the former Vichy official. Surely this was some kind of hoax: according to the law, this high court must be composed of jurors chosen from a list of senators and deputies serving their terms on 1 September 1939. It was clearly an attempt to prevent a trial of Bousquet.

The political initiative, coming from the Elysée Palace itself, was clearly meant to block the procedure. In October 1990 Serge Klarsfeld asked for the resignation of Georges Kiejman, who had just been assigned to the Ministry of Justice (and who was responsible for the decision calling for the High Court to handle Bousquet's case). "This about face in the Public Prosecutor's office, which takes its instructions from the Chancellery, was evident in the change that took place on 2 October at the head of the Ministry of Justice. A son of a deported Jew [Robert Badinter] was Minister of Justice when the Gestapo chief of Lyon was brought back to France to be tried. The son of a deported Jew [George Kiejman] was named Minister assigned to the Judiciary to ensure the impunity of the Vichy Chief of Police."

Georges Kiejman responded in *Libération*: "It might seem desirable today that this high court, or its equivalent, try Bousquet. But if one thinks beyond the technical problem, it is equally important to take into consideration that, beyond the necessary struggle to recall what has been forgotten, it is also important to preserve peace among the citizens. There are other ways besides a trial to punish the cowardice of the Vichy government." This argument is hardly surprising coming from a lawyer who made his opposition to a Bousquet trial even clearer in an interview with Reuters: "Is this man the same as he was in 1942? I don't see why the gentlemen of the left would embrace daily the idea of change and would refuse this idea of change a half century later." Thus he confirmed that the chancellery—and therefore the political authorities—did not want Bousquet to be tried for his crimes.

The surprise came from the Judiciary on 19 November 1990, when the magistrates of the criminal court, presided over by Albert Moatty, decided that they were competent to judge the former Vichy police chief. On 1 March 1991 René Bousquet, almost a half-century after the events, joined the likes of Paul Touvier, the former member of the Lyons Milice, and Maurice Papon, former police chief and minister, accused of having organized the deportation of 1,690 Jews in Bordeaux, in being indicted on charges of crimes against humanity.

The trial date drew nearer but the Bousquet case continued to be handled with kid gloves. The news of his indictment was kept secret for several weeks as was the other charge against him (in June 1992) by the Criminal Court of Bordeaux in the context of the Papon case. To avoid speeding up the investigation, the public prosecutor's office refused to free Judge Getti from other duties in order to examine the facts of the case.

1993

In spite of all obstacles, it seemed as if Bousquet would eventually come to trial. In June 1993, after a highly controversial decision [in April 1992] to dismiss the case against him, the *milicien* Paul Touvier was nevertheless brought before the appellate court, the case against Bousquet was completed, and Judge Anzani refused the last request for a delay by his lawyers. The criminal court would be able to deal with the case in the autumn of 1993.

One person still did not believe it. René Bousquet, himself. At eighty-four, alert and without remorse, he had lost none of his aggressiveness: "If they give me a hard time, well, we'll just start all over, like the 1949 trial. I'll defend myself! And I have the means to do it! But I will be greatly surprised if there is a trial."

Where did this certainty come from? We will never know.

Libération
13 July 1993

Six Questions for History

Bousquet's Letter (Defense Plea) to the Court,

19 August 1992

Editor's Note: In August 1992 René Bousquet wrote a letter to the Paris Court of Appeals detailing his actions during the Occupation and offering reasons why he should not be tried for crimes against humanity. The original text of the letter is over sixty manuscript pages long and was reproduced in its entirety in the *Dossier Bousquet* published by *Libération* shortly after Bousquet's murder. Since the letter is often quite technical and confusing, not to mention repetitive, I have attempted to reproduce here only the essential points Bousquet makes. I have followed the original text in using capital letters where Bousquet uses them to emphasize what he considers a crucial argument or comment.

From: René Bousquet
34 Avenue Raphaël
75016 Paris

To: Monsieur le Président MOATTY
Chambre d'Accusation
PARIS COURT OF APPEALS
DOSSIER: René BOUSQUET
Paris, 19 August 1992

Monsieur le Président:

I have reflected sufficiently during the years 1940 and 1943 and since on the tragic situation of FRANCE, resulting from the Armistice Convention and the German Occupation, and all that the latter have brought with them, to understand that this period of our History must remain a painful subject, inscribed in our collective memory.

My thoughts will always be directed toward the victims of this war,

—which, by its very nature, was a harbinger of dramas and sufferings, because it generated, beyond the level of individuals, collective phenomena that surpassed them and that they could not master.

—a war whose consequences, in this instance, were aggravated by a destructive ideology that was the cornerstone of the "Hitlerien enterprise."

Against such an enterprise, everyone, according to his circumstances, was obliged to struggle when he could and to the extent of his means.

This is what I did, facing the difficulties, obstacles, and risks of all sorts which such a struggle entailed. . . .

This is why I am deeply wounded by the charges brought against me.

These charges have as their object

—without taking into account the fact that I have already been judged more than forty years ago,

—to call into question the verdict handed down by the High Court of Justice which stated on 23 June 1949:

—that there was reason to "pronounce my acquittal"

—"that there existed, as a consequence of [the Court's] investigations and debates, proof that in numerous circumstances, I had, through my actions, participated in an active and sustained fashion in resistance efforts against the occupant," and that as a result, the sentence handed down—five years' loss of civil rights—was commuted.

THE ACTIONS OF THE CIVIL PARTIES HAVE AS THEIR OBJECT TO RETRY ME ON CHARGES FOR WHICH I HAVE ALREADY BEEN JUDGED AND TO CALL THE EARLIER VERDICT INTO QUESTION. . . .

I believe, nevertheless, that in carrying out my functions, I tried with all my might to limit the fearful effects of the Occupation, even though my accusers wish to charge me . . . with the consequences of the German racial policy, and with the situation that policy created. . . .

To make of me the accomplice of the genocide of the Jews is perhaps a thesis that the tragic circumstances of the time can give the appearance of sustaining, especially since this thesis has been elaborated several decades after the events, when the war is long since over and the occupant has been removed from France's national territories. This thesis, however, suffers from the fundamental flaw of being developed without taking into account precisely the tragic reality in which I found myself at the time when I was Secretary General [for Police] in the Ministry of the Interior. And this tragic reality was brought about by the fact that the Germans:

—who had infiltrated French services, and notably the Paris Prefecture of Police, and this with the active assistance of the Commissariat for Jewish Questions, who were dependent upon the Germans,

—had decided to arrest, on orders from their government, French and foreign Jews, without distinction, in order, in their own words, to transfer them to provinces in the East. The sinister reality [of the genocide] only became clear much later when, at the end of the war, the existence of the concentration camps was discovered,

—and this [German] decision formed part of a group of measures (reprisals, the execution of hostages, deportations [of individuals] to perform forced labor) which in each case created *immediate* problems of exceptional gravity,

—and this while, given the developments of the war itself, no one knew how much time the Germans had to carry out their plans.

Having been obliged to carry out my functions in these circumstances, the moments of decision have marked, indeed wounded me profoundly, and the question of what it was possible to do in the situation will forever remain unanswered:

—*On the one hand*, to resign would in no way have provided a solution to the problems France faced. On the contrary, [my resignation] would only have aggravated the situation (e.g., the appointment of Darnand in 1944, and its consequences). . . .

—*On the other hand*, it seems difficult, given the circumstances of the moment, to maintain that duty required one to let the occupant act on his own, while making no effort to save those who could be saved among those subject to deportation.

Certainly, room to maneuver was extremely limited, but in light of the painful reality of the moment—a reality fundamentally different from the manner in which it is perceived and presented fifty years later—it was essential to try to limit the extent of the disaster. . . .

Given what happened in BELGIUM, HOLLAND and elsewhere, it is reasonable to believe that, if nothing had been done, racial persecution in FRANCE would have been more extensive, rapid, and cruel, and that French Jews would have found themselves in exactly the same boat as the foreign Jews. . . .

I note that it strikes me as untruthful to claim today that the Germans did not possess the means at the time to carry out the decisions [concerning the Final Solution] taken at the highest levels.

And the events that occurred after my departure [as head of police], notably in 1944, a year during which German divisions intervened against the Maquis, provide proof that the Germans had the means to carry out their plans. . . .

French policy—in the face of the German threat to arrest all Jews without distinction, a threat, moreover, accompanied by a German imperative to carry out these operations immediately—was, at the very least, to protect French Jews because it was impossible to do more, given the situation in which France found herself. . . .

[If] one decided to do what could be done in order to help French

Jews escape the measures imposed by the occupant—and this was the policy of the French government and its administration ... —one found oneself necessarily implicated in and constrained by an action against foreign Jews and—as the result of an astonishing change of policy on the part of the German occupant—German Jews and others of German origin, many of whom had earlier been deported by the Germans into FRANCE after 18 June 1940. ...

It is easy today to reproach me either for having negotiated with the Germans to limit the powers of their police, or for having obtained only those concessions they were ready to agree to. ... But it is clear that if I had not negotiated with them, the consequences for the Jews, especially for the French Jews, would have been much more cruel. ...

THE PURPOSE [of the current proceedings against me] HAS BEEN CLEARLY INDICATED (SEE SERGE KLARSFELD, *VICHY-AUSCHWITZ 1942*— PAGES 7 ON): IT IS TO PUT ON TRIAL THE GOVERNMENT, THE ADMINISTRA- TION, AND THE POLICE [of Vichy] BY FOCUSING ON THE JEWISH PROBLEM DURING THE GERMAN OCCUPATION [and] BY USING ME [as a scapegoat] IN MY CAPACITY AS A SURVIVOR OF THIS PERIOD. ...

[In Reference to] THE NEW CHARGES [of crimes against humanity]:

The Civil Party plaintiffs ... have stressed that the crimes against humanity charges brought against me apply to infractions of individ- ual rights committed against persons by virtue of their appurtenance to a specific race or religion—[these crimes consist of] illegal arrests and the removal of children—which were not at issue during the delib- erations of the High Court [in 1949].

It is important to recall at this juncture that Articles 6 and 368 of the Penal Code, taken in concert, do not permit new and different charges to be filed in relation to actions previously adjudicated. ...

It should also be recalled that, as the stenotypy of the discussions before the High Court confirms, all of my activities beginning from 18 June 1940 and including most notably my functions as Secretary Gen- eral for Police in the Ministry of the Interior fell under the exclusive jurisdiction of that Court. ...

Hence the inclusive nature of the indictment against me (. . .), which resulted finally in the decision to acquit me, handed down by the High Court of Justice. My conviction and sentence [of five years'] loss of civil rights was commuted by reason of my active and continuous par- ticipation in the Resistance against the occupant.

In conclusion, my dossier closed, I would like to say a few simple things. As a young functionary, I sacrificed a great deal to carry out my responsibilities, motivated by a desire to serve.

As fate would have it, I was called to serve in the Ministry of the Interior at precisely the moment when the German police apparatus was extending its reach throughout France and when German decisions harmful to French and foreign Jews were being carried out.

Faced with this aggression by the occupant, who was already being aided in this by the Commissariat for Jewish Questions, I did what was in my power to limit the damage.

Then the High Court of Justice pronounced its verdict.

More than forty years later, certain individuals wish to try me again.

I will confront [these charges], as I have always done in the past, first on behalf of my country, which one wishes to hold accountable for things for which she was not responsible.

Please accept, *Monsieur le Président*, the expression of my respectful regards.

RENÉ BOUSQUET

1. Did Bousquet Falsify History in His Defense Plea?

Denis Peschanski and Henry Rousso

Bousquet's plea in his own defense, like the summing-up of the prosecution, is a judicial document. The first is a plea presenting the version of the accused, the second tries to prove the guilt of one man, even if the trial for crimes against humanity goes far beyond individual cases. For the historian, these documents can reflect only a partial truth because they were created in the framework of a judicial procedure and not of a historical study. Only a part of the archives is there, isolated pieces of evidence lifted from the rest when needed by the prosecution or the defense. Furthermore, thanks to the imprescriptibility of the charge, the entire procedure against Bousquet is focused on his participation in the Final Solution, leaving aside a crucial aspect of his activities—the struggle against the Resistance in general and the communists in particular.

It is not a question here of returning a verdict or of judging the affair but, rather, of analyzing Bousquet's defense in light of current historical knowledge, which, judging from his defense, he himself possessed at the time.

An Important Absentee: The Ideology of Vichy

The defense statement speaks from the beginning about "the destructive ideology of Hitler's project" as the source of the extermination of the Jews, and it was the Nazis, and they alone, who set in motion the "Final Solution," later profiting from the complicity, passive or active, of the countries they occupied. But the Vichy regime had also championed a racist ideology that went along with the German aims even if Vichy did not have the extermination of the Jews as an objective.

In this way Bousquet managed to exclude both the context in which he rose to the position of General Secretary of the Police and any question about the policies of Vichy that had been put into practice two years earlier. Reminding us that he was named to this post in April 1942, he failed to point out that he had long been close to Laval and that he was well known in government circles before the war. He therefore did not remain in a job he had had before but accepted, with full knowledge of what was taking place, new and highly visible functions that Laval could offer only to a man he could trust completely.

By April 1942, the government had already signed into law most of its anti-Semitic legislation in statutes regarding Jews dated October 1940 and June 1941. Measures of enforcement in the white-collar professions and at the university, a census, "aryanization" of Jewish businesses, and so on were measures taken without pressure from the Germans, and they had been in force for two years in the context of a governmental anti-Semitism that had been an integral part of the Vichy policy of exclusion. In 1946 the former director of Pétain's civilian cabinet, Moulin de Labarthète, stated during an interrogation, while speaking of the Statute on Jews of 3 October 1940, that "Germany was not the author of the anti-Jewish legislation of Pétain. This legislation was spontaneous and homegrown."

The Objectives of Laval and Bousquet

According to the defense case, for Vichy it was a matter of limiting the damage by saving those it could among French Jews. "In doing this, the French government showed it had no desire to attack this group of Jews."

As for foreign Jews, it is noteworthy that whereas Bousquet borrowed several quotes from the historian Raymond Tournoux on the minutes of the Council of Ministers of 26 June 1942, he did not quote this same historian when he spoke of the meeting of the Council of Ministers of 3 July 1942, which swallowed the Franco-German accord on police collaboration and heard Laval pronounce himself ready to deliver what he himself called "the trash."

Even before totally rejecting the "Shield" theory (cf. article by Robert Paxton, this volume, pp. 81ff), two nuances of some importance need to be considered when examining the claim that Vichy tried to "save" French Jews. First, among the victims of these laws were children of non-native parents born on French soil, and therefore French. Second, Laval had already signed the denaturalization decree for Jews who had entered France after 1927, which could affect more than ten thousand French Jews, but he was forced to cancel it in the spring of 1943 under very strong pressure form the Catholic hierarchy. This being true, it is undeniable that throughout the negotiations on the deportation contingencies, Laval and Bousquet argued for a sort of "national preference."

However, and this is crucial, by its policy of exclusion and its own anti-Semitic laws, Vichy had already weakened the whole Jewish community, French as well as non-French. A good part of the census reports that helped to make the roundups possible was made with the backing of French law. From the moment in the summer of 1942 when Vichy agreed to codirect the implementation of the Final Solution in France according to its policy of government collaboration in order to reaffirm its sovereignty vis-à-vis the occupier, it embraced another policy, that of massive deportations that called for agreements within the framework of a policy that was not its own.

Then what was Laval after? Although undeniably immersed in the anti-Semitic atmosphere of the 1930s, he was without doubt less obsessed by it than Pétain and a good part of his entourage. Laval thought more on a European scale. Gambling on a German victory, he thought he would be able to play Hitler's great game and that in so doing he would have trump cards he could play as needed, thinking that he could thereby check Hitler when, in actuality, he found himself more and more enmeshed in a one-way collaboration. He felt no remorse about abandoning foreign Jews because he was totally indifferent to their fate. One will also recall that Bousquet never explained the roundups in the Unoccupied Zone, which, in principle, did not suffer from the German threat before November 1942. For instance, even if he does allude to the expulsion to the Unoccupied Zone by the Nazis in October 1940 of German Jews from the Baden, the Palatinat, and Sarre regions (7,700 total), he does not mention that they were sent to French camps in the Unoccupied Zone, notably the one at Gurs, where 1,200 died of cold and hunger. He seemed to forget, too, that the Vichy government had protested in vain to Berlin about this massive influx of foreign Jews.

Also omitted in the defense's story is the fact that more than 10,000 Jews in the Unoccupied Zone were deported between August and November 1942, before it was invaded by the Germans. In this case, the argument that the French police were preferable to German police certainly does not hold.

Forgetting the Children

There was an important omission in the defense's case—the tragic question of the children. Here, the indifference of those responsible in the Vichy government is demonstrated in a striking manner. In the spring of 1942 the Germans demanded that the French authorities deport Jews ages sixteen to sixty (fifty-five for the women). The agreement was made, and Laval proposed that from 4 July on children under sixteen should also be arrested and deported. Even before receiving a response from Berlin, he ordered children included in the Vel d'Hiv roundup that was set for the 16 and 17 of July 1942. For some weeks after the roundup, they were interned in the Beaune-la-Rolande and Pithiviers camps, separated from their parents who had already been deported.

Did Laval and Bousquet want to exterminate them? Taking into account the date when the request was made, the answer is no. Did they act out of compassion or humanity, hoping thus to reunite separated families? Nothing points to this. On the other hand, three hypotheses can be put forward that could explain Vichy's decision. First, they included the children in the convoy in order to rid themselves of the bureaucratic problem of what to do with thousands of orphans. Second, Laval could have feared the reaction of public opinion when they learned of the separation of these families, a reaction that did, indeed, take place. Third, it is likely that including the children in the convoys allowed the government to fulfill the quotas demanded by the Germans, even if they were not demanding the roundup of Jewish children at that time.

What Did Vichy Know?

Bousquet, like the other French responsible for the deportation, claimed that he did not know about the "sinister reality" of the extermination until the spring of 1945.

But, just as it is necessary to avoid the anachronisms so frequent today and the assumption that everyone knew everything about the operation even before its execution, it is also necessary to dispute claims of ignorance by the secretary general of the police, right arm to the head of government. Vichy had access to extensive networks of information. From 1 July 1942 in a broadcast of Free France on the BBC giving reports sent to London by the Polish government, Jean Marin spoke of the massacre of 700,000 Polish Jews and mentioned gas chambers. Even in France, several underground newspapers, carefully monitored by the police, tried to alert the public. Certainly the sources of these reports could be seen as unreliable by those who wanted to see it that way, but the reports at least are there to prove that these articles were known to Vichy.

There were also the accounts of ambassadors, from Romania on 17 August and from the United States on 16 September, which reported the same information. In Vichy's eyes these were not propaganda documents because the government was in official contact with an extensive and widely dispersed diplomatic corps.

There were also the religious authorities. On 25 August 1942 the Assembly of Cardinals wrote to Pétain that they had "no doubt about the fate which awaited the deportees after they had endured a terrible martyrdom. . . . The program of extermination had been applied methodically in Germany and in the countries occupied by it." Thus alerted, the pastor Boegner met Laval on 9 September 1942 for an interview that he related after the war in this way: "What could I get out of a man whom the Germans had led to believe—or who pretended to believe—that the Jews taken out of France were going to the south of Poland to cultivate the lands of a Jewish state? I told him of massacres, he answered me with gardening."

Pressure from the Catholic hierarchy was still very unobtrusive in June and the beginning of July 1942 at the time of the first agreements, but it was nevertheless being applied in private meetings.

In addition to these various sources, reports were being issued by international aid agencies who since 1940 had been organizing aid to the internees of the French camps in the south of France and had access to the most precise information.

All in all, Vichy had access to the same sources of information as other countries. Even taking into account the credibility they might have accorded to some and not to others, the chronology is worth examining. In July of 1942 information was still sketchy and limited. By the end of the summer, however, the convergence of all these sources made the situation clearer if not easier to understand. By the beginning of 1943 doubt was no longer possible. The supervision of the prisoner roundups was not turned over to the Germans until the end of spring 1943. Whatever the conditions, this is a long way from the spring of 1945.

It seems apparent, therefore, that Laval and Bousquet did not want to know. Proof of this can be found in the minutes from a conversation between Laval and Oberg on 2 September 1942, signed by Hagen and entitled "Agreement on Language":

> During the discussion . . . President Laval indicated that foreign diplomats had several times asked him where the Jews given over to occupation authorities were being sent. He had answered that they were supposed to be sent to the south of Poland. He then asked to be told how he should respond to these queries so as to avoid contradicting our own statements. It was agreed that the Jews transferred from the unoccupied zone to the occupation authorities are being transported to be employed by the government (i.e., in Poland).

Were the French Police Preferable to the Germans?

To support his argument that the French police were the "lesser evil," Bousquet cited the first three roundups of Jews in Paris in 1941. In his eyes this was proof that the Germans did not need French police to carry out arrests against the Jews and that they could arrest foreigners as well as the French.

In actuality, the first roundup on 14 May 1941 led to the internment of 3,710 Poles, Czechs, and Austrians in the camps of Beaune-la-Rolande and Pithiviers. This was carried out by the Paris police at the request of the Germans but with Vichy's backing. The second roundup, from 20 to 23 August, was called a response to communist agitation. A total of 4,230 foreign Jews and a number of French Jews were interned at Drancy. Once again, it was the Paris police who carried out the operation, but did not advise the Interior Minister until afterward. Going over the heads of the authorities in this fashion was something Bousquet did not want to see happen again. Only the third roundup, on 12 December 1941 was essentially carried out by the Germans, who arrested 743 Jews in response to individual attacks on the German military in the name of the struggle against "Jewish Bolshevism." These three roundups included only men and nine out of ten of those arrested were arrested by French police. The roundups of the summer of 1942 included women as well as men, old people, and then children. This was the beginning of the road that led to the Final Solution in France. Bousquet could not have been ignorant of the difference in nature of the persecutions of 1941 and those of 1942.

A final objection of simple logic—if the Germans had no need of the French police, why did they push so hard to obtain their services?

The Real Influence of the High Commissioner for Jewish Affairs in Questions Concerning the Jews

Bousquet wildly overestimated the role of the High Commissioner for Jewish Affairs. It is undeniable that Darquier de Pellepoix, named to this post by Laval in May 1942, was a died-in-the-wool anti-Semite and a fanatical supporter of National Socialism, but it is just as obvious that, from the time of his appointment, he had only limited power to intervene and, unlike his predecessor, Xavier Vallat, he was marginalized even while remaining at the center of the government team. As for the police for Jewish affairs, it was not eliminated as Bousquet claimed but, instead, was integrated into his services.

2. Did Vichy France Protect French Jews?

Robert O. Paxton

René Bousquet claimed that the Vichy government saved some French Jews by sacrificing foreign ones. Leaving aside the infamous character of this selection, let us try to determine to what extent this claim is believable. A central element of Bousquet's argument is a comparison between the 78 percent of the Jewish population in Holland deported between 1942 and 1944 and the 24 to 26 percent of the Jewish population of France deported during these same years.

This comparison is attractive in its simplicity. René Bousquet was able to cite certain recent authors such as Annie Kriegel and François-Georges Dreyfus in support of his claim. This argument is not new, however. It was Xavier Vallat, the High Commissioner for Jewish Affairs in Vichy, who used it first, during his trial by the High Court in 1948.

With the same kind of argument, certain Americans try to make us believe that, since the Indian population in North America is bigger than it was in 1600, the policy of European colonizers in North America toward the Indians cannot have done too much harm. Thus, one sees how history can be distorted in referring exclusively to raw statistics. Such statistics have to be analyzed less abstractly and in a more historical context.

In order to make a legitimate comparison between Holland and France concerning the fate of Jews, it is especially important to examine the choices made at every turn and in the light of available options, for it becomes immediately clear that the Jews of Holland were much more vulnerable than those in France. Concentrated near the diamond markets in a few large Dutch cities, often traditionally dressed, this population was not difficult to spot or to arrest, in spite of the opposition of the people of Amsterdam to German racism. They were the only citizens in occupied Europe to march in the streets in protest of the anti-Jewish actions of the Germans, and they did this in February 1941. In contrast, the Jewish population in France had certain advantages: they were widely dispersed over a large territory, they had assimilated to a high degree, they were invisible in their civil status, and they could flee to the Unoccupied Zone. Limited to their own resources, the German police in France, who numbered roughly 1,000 in 1942, would not have been able to find and arrest 76,000 Jews. Far from profiting from these advantages, however, the Vichy government, by its own authority and for its own reasons, made the Jewish population more visible and more vulnerable, and they did it in three ways.

It is true that René Bousquet was only prefect of the Marne when the first anti-Jewish measures were adopted by the Vichy government. He claimed, moreover, to have opposed others in his departmental administration by retaining a Jew as counselor general. The manner in which the prefect of the Marne presided over the application of the first and second statutes on Jews in his department remains to be examined in the archives in Reims.

First, the Vichy regime decided to identify and list all the Jews in France and reduce their role in the economic and cultural life of the nation, and this included French Jews as well as foreigners and stateless individuals.[1] As secretary general of the police René Bousquet continued to enforce these measures, which made all future efforts to differentiate between the fate of the French and all other Jews very difficult. In December 1942 Bousquet contributed another potentially disastrous identification requirement to the file, adding to the stripping away of their rights already inflicted on French Jews by his predecessors. This was the stamp JUIF added in red ink to identity and rations cards. For some Jews, French and non-French alike, this turned out to be their passport to death.

Second, the Vichy regime insisted from the beginning on keeping all administrative and police actions in the two zones concerning the Jews in its own hands. The first commissioner for Jewish affairs, Xavier

Vallat, had already allowed himself to be caught in the collaboration trap. When René Bousquet arrived in April 1942, Vichy had long since gone far beyond the terms of the Armistice in order to keep the administration of the two zones in its own hands. René Bousquet was even more zealous in showing the Germans that the French authorities were capable of doing everything themselves, even if his "everything" went beyond the armistice stipulations or what was permitted by simple humanity.

Third, the anti-Jewish policy of Vichy was conceived partly to prevent the arrival of German Jews in the Midi, the Unoccupied Zone, expelled from their native land by the Nazis in the autumn of 1940 and the winter of 1940–41, culminating in the expulsion of 6,504 Jews from Baden and Sarre-Palatinat on 25 October 1940, at the very moment of the Montoire meeting. This massive influx of foreign Jews provoked strong protests from the Vichy authorities. As long as Hitler's policy was to expel Jews to foreign countries, the Vichy government would request that the refugees be returned to their homeland. In the spring of 1942 the Nazi policy toward the Jews changed. This was the beginning of the Final Solution; expulsion was replaced by extermination. René Bousquet himself, the new secretary general of the police, continued to apply the policy followed by Vichy since the autumn of 1940, trying to convince the German authorities to take back their Jewish refugees.

On 6 May 1942, in his first conversation with the top German police authorities (notably Heidrich, Himmler's associate, and the SS chief Karl Oberg, the new chief of German police in France), René Bousquet answered the German declarations with a French counterproposition. The Germans had announced that they would soon have trains at their disposal to deport stateless Jews in the Occupied Zone to the East. According to a telegram from the German Embassy in Paris, "Bousquet asked Heidrich if the Jews interned for more than a year and a half in the Unoccupied Zone could be evacuated with the first ones. The question was left open at the time because of transportation difficulties."[2]

This document naturally does not appear in the Bousquet defense, although it is full of other documents and lofty references. The informed reader would not be fooled by the authentic appearance of the document prepared by Bousquet and his legal counselors. It is a plea for the defense, full of large gaps as well as cleverly distorted historical interpretations.

For example, as the Final Solution got under way in France, it was René Bousquet who pushed for the extension of the operation into the Unoccupied Zone. The Germans, for their part, were reticent at first. It is false to pretend, as Bousquet does, that all the initiatives came from the Germans, whereas on the Vichy side there was only opposition.

It is true that, according to the terms of the agreement of 2–3 July 1942, the Vichy authorities preferred to see foreign or stateless Jews depart rather than French ones. The roundups of French Jews, done at the request of the Germans but carried out by the French police in August 1941 in Paris, had made a very bad impression. Public opinion was an important element in the very complicated negotiations between the French and German authorities and between the different German services from the end of June 1942 to the Vichy accord of 3 July 1942. The occupying authority was also sensitive to public opinion, with the exception of the anti-Jewish services. In Belgium, where no local government existed to soften German policies, the Nazis deported stateless and foreign Jews first, so as not to upset Belgian public opinion.[3] Thus Vichy obtained nothing more than what had been freely accorded to the Belgians.

Above all Bousquet wanted to convince the German police of the usefulness of the French police because he was simultaneously engaged in negotiations which would lead to the Oberg-Bousquet agreements of 29 July. According to these agreements, the German chief of police in France accepted a certain "liberty of action" of the French police on the condition that it prove its usefulness in the struggle against "terrorists" and other enemies of the Third Reich.

The legal independence of the French police was more important in the eyes of Bousquet than refusing to take part in the Final Solution.

And what if the Vichy government had simply refused the help of its police in the Nazi deportation project for Jews? Here is an example of a refusal mustered by the Pétain government: the yellow star would not be required in the Unoccupied Zone in the summer of 1942.

Contrary to this, the "defense plea" of Bousquet creates the image of an all-powerful Nazi Germany, capable of doing everything alone all over Europe, even beyond the zones of direct occupation. If one looks closely at the map and follows the chronology of the Final Solution, it is evident that Hitler would not have been able to enforce the Final Solution simultaneously in all the occupied countries. Without local collaboration he did not have enough troops. So, the Hungary of Admiral Horthy refused to deport a single Jew between 1942 and the summer of 1944. After this date it is true that the Nazis ultimately carried out in Hungary the most brutal operation anywhere in the Final Solution.

No doubt the German police would have continued to arrest French Jews itself, as had been done in December 1941 (without any real opposition from Vichy). At the rate of the roundup of 12 December 1941 (460 German police arrested 743 Jews of French nationality), it would have taken a long time to finish the work in the Occupied Zone alone.

According to the most generous interpretation permitted by historical documents available, Vichy might have obtained, at best, the delay of the deportation of Jews of French nationality. On 4 July 1942 Bousquet informed the German authorities that Pétain and Laval "had expressed their consent to the evacuation, with the first wave, of all the stateless Jews staying in both the Occupied and Unoccupied Zones."[4] With the first wave? Could anyone in Vichy believe that the turn of French Jews would not follow? Even if they did, Dannecker must have removed any doubt when he reminded Leguay, Bousquet's representative in Paris, on 13 August 1942 that the German authorities had "let President Laval know very clearly that this was a permanent action whose final phase included French Jews as well."[5]

Thus it was not the cynical offer of foreign Jews, which Bousquet bragged about, that saved the largest part of the Jewish population. It was instead the end of German occupation and the actions of a large number of people and French organizations, sometimes even a lack of action by men such as the mayors who threw the orders to register all Jews, including those of French nationality, into the wastebasket instead of sending these lists to the prefecture.

The Vichy government had not envisaged the arrest and deportation to death camps of the Jews of French nationality, but it had certainly carried out their registration, their being discredited with their fellow citizens, their exclusion from public office and the white-collar professions, and the confiscation of their property. In this way it had made them more visible and vulnerable to the operation of extermination put into action by the Nazis and their accomplices in the spring of 1942. If one-third of the Jews of France who were murdered in the course of the genocide were of French nationality, Vichy was an accomplice in their fate. If a great number of Jews of French nationality escaped this fate, it was in spite of what their government did.

There remains one last point, the almost unique character of the action of the Vichy government in turning over to the Nazis Jews who were in a territory that was free of any German presence. Only three other cases have been found of the deportation of Jews of unoccupied countries in all of Europe during World War II: Hungary in the regions of Galicia after their conquest of the Russians in the summer of 1941, the Slovaks, who turned over the Jews of their own nonoccupied territory, and the Bulgarians in February 1943 in territories recently acquired in Macedonia.

Finally, it must not be forgotten that, along with the foreign Jews who were refugees in France's Unoccupied Zone and turned over to the Nazis through Bousquet's initiative, children born in France, and therefore French citizens, were also deported.

Notes

1. The Jews of French nationality enjoyed some preferential treatment in comparison with foreign or stateless Jews. There were exemptions for former service men in certain jobs. However, French Jews were required to be registered along with the other Jews.

2. Telegram from the counselor of the German Embassy in Paris, Schleier, to the German minister of foreign affairs, 11 September 1942. Nuremberg Document MG-5209. Michael R. Marrus and Robert O. Paxton, *Vichy France and the Jews* (New York: Schocken Books, 1983), p. 232; Serge Klarsfeld, *Vichy-Auschwitz 1942* (Paris: Fayard, 1983), p. 55.

3. Maxine Steinberg, "Le Paradoxe Français Dans la Solution Finale à l'Ouest," *ANNALES: ECONOMIES, SOCIETIES, CIVILISATIONS,* 48:3 (May-June 1993), 588–89.

4. Report of Dannecker, 6 July 1942. Document of the International Tribunal of Nuremberg, RF-1234. Marrus and Paxton, *Vichy France and the Jews,* p. 218; Klarsfeld *Vichy–Auschwitz,* p. 104.

5. International Military Tribunal of Nuremberg, document RF-1234. Marrus and Paxton, *Vichy France and the Jews,* p. 234.

3. Was There Massive Collaboration of Top Administrative Officials?

Denis Peschanski

It is impossible to understand the Vichy government and the attitude of its state institutions if, as confusion and disagreement now seem to demand, we attribute to them an intent to exterminate the Jews and a plan to carry it out. It is enough to say that the French government put a policy of exclusion at the very heart of its political and ideological plans and that from the summer of 1942 on it agreed to codirect the implementation of the German Final Solution in France.

Since the armistice of 1940 the new administration sought to explain the defeat by denouncing the decadence of the Third Republic and attributing the defeat to a plot hatched by the forces of the "Anti-France," composed of Jews, Freemasons, Communists, and foreigners. It did no good, argued the new administration, to struggle against the German occupation, which was only a symptom of this decadence. The first objective was the reconstruction of the national and social fabric.

The necessary internal "cleansing" was achieved through a rallying of "pure" elements around the traditional values of work, family, country, order, and piety and the exclusion of "impure" and corrupting elements of society. Pétain wrote in August 1940: "Neutrality is not possible between the true and the false, between good and evil, between health and sickness, between order and disorder, between France and 'Anti-France.'"

Thus, from the summer of 1940 and with no pressure from the Germans, a series of measures was written into law that extended from the creation of a review board on naturalizations to the dissolving of Masonic lodges, from an increased repression of communists to the first statute concerning Jews, and to the law that permitted the internment of foreign Jews for the simple reason that they were Jews and foreigners. These actions and exclusions constituted an integral part of the politics of the new regime.

Sanctified by the Hitler-Pétain meeting at Montoire in October 1940, the dual choice of "National Revolution" and collaboration was written into the armistice, and French and German records agree that collaboration was a French initiative. Pétain believed in a German victory, and he hoped in the short run to make daily life easier and in the long run to secure a special place for France in the new Europe. He also wanted to consolidate his power over all of the national territory, even to the point of taking charge of the darkest duties of repression and persecution. At the same time, he wanted a free hand in putting into operation his National Revolution.

As for German objectives, they could not have been clearer. Foremost among these was to place French production at the service of the German war economy, to ensure the safety of occupying troops, and, beginning in the summer of 1942, to put into operation the deportation and the extermination of French Jews. In order to do this, the existence of a very conservative power with influence over its citizens was highly desirable, for it was better for the occupation authorities to achieve their objectives by dividing and conquering, playing the Parisian "collaborationists," such as Déat or Doriot, against Vichy and even certain individuals in Vichy against Vichy itself. Elmar Michel, chief of the economic section attached to the military command in France, wrote frankly in his assessment of the economic collaboration in July 1942:

> The whole of the French economy, including the unoccupied territories, has been put to work satisfying in large measure the needs of the German war economy. . . . Even today, the idea is that the French economy be directed by the French government. . . . Germany edits the regulations or decisions which must be carried out, or limits itself to directives. . . . This system offers not only the advantage of using a minimum of German experts, but also of having the French services intervene so that the French people will see their government as responsible.

The attitude of the important agencies of the French government was largely conditioned by these restraints. The armistice agreement, carefully observed, specified in Article 3 that

> In the occupied regions of France, the German Reich exercises all the rights of an occupying power. The French government agrees

to facilitate by all possible means the regulations relating to the exercise of these rights and their execution with the help of the French administration. [It] encourages all administrative authorities and services in the occupied territory to conform to the regulations of German authorities and to collaborate with these authorities in a dutiful manner.

Beyond this, the major responsibility of Vichy was to furnish authority for legal supervision to the French administrators. To counteract an order, administrators would have had both to commit an act of resistance and to disobey their own authority of supervision. Most of the time the duty to disobey was forgotten.

On 9 June 1941 Admiral Darlan, vice-president of the Counsel, wrote to the prefects: "Marshal Pétain, chief of the state and of the government, who received a mandate from the National Assembly to lay the foundation for the new order, understands that you are the pioneers as well as the representatives of the new regime to be built on the ruins of the old one, which was responsible for the defeat." The prefects were the first step in implementing the program of the new regime, particularly since their power was no longer moderated by elected officials. But they did have to reckon with former soldiers who in the southern zone had reorganized in the Legion, "The eyes and ears of the Marshal." Later the prefects were forced to reckon with the Milice. They also bowed to the very direct pressures of the German administration in the Occupied Zone. In drawing up a tally sheet of the prefectural corps, one should not overlook the few Resistance fighters among the department prefects. Among these were Jean Moulin and Edouard Bonnefoy, the regional prefect in Lyon, denounced by the Milice, arrested by the Gestapo, and deported to Neuengamme. Altogether, there were 36 prefects and assistant prefects who died because of deportation or their participation in the Resistance. Thirty-five others who were deported returned. For most of these the turning point when they joined the Resistance was in the first half of 1944 when Darnand, the chief of the Milice, took over the reins of the Maintenance of Order.

The chronology is important, and the profiles of these men are different. More than four-fifths of the prefects had begun their careers under the Third Republic. In general they made very good pipelines for the new regime. The most important part of their time was given over to solving the problems of daily life, with food supplies as the most significant concern. They often showed themselves to be zealous in repressing communists, as the obsession with order and the endless anticommunism of the Vichy government from 1940 to 1944 was largely shared by the top departmental administrators. They usually carried out the orders when anti-Semitic persecutions were the order of the day. On 13 August René Bousquet sent regional prefects a note from Oberg, the top officer of the SS and of German police that laid out the new procedure of police collaboration. He accompanied the note with this comment: "It won't escape you . . . that, if this note from General Oberg gives the French police ways of acting it hasn't had before, both on a moral and material level, it is important that, by the results of their increased activity, the police services show proof of their usefulness. It is up to you to give a new impetus to these services since you must realize, as I do, the necessity of doing this in the present circumstances."

A limited, but in no way exceptional, example of police collaboration is that of the Special Brigades (BS) of the RG (Information Center) of Paris. In 1943 the political and military structures of the communist Resistance, located in Paris, were dismantled by the Special Brigades in three dragnet operations over an entire year. Nearly three hundred militants were arrested. These men and women were singled out, followed, arrested, and tortured by the French police before being handed over to the Germans. In close collaboration with the German occupiers, the French did indeed track down foreigners who were taking part in the Resistance fight to liberate national territory. It is important, however, not to overgeneralize. The relative failure of the Vel d'Hiv roundup was attributable to the fact that certain members of the police leaked information to prospective victims and German mistrust of French police only grew with time. In spite of this, the French police were a useful instrument in the hands of those in power and useful for their policies. The period was marked by a growing centralization. "We were interested in having the French police united under one direction," Oberg said at his trial—and by a clever management of the services. An example of this was the transfer of suspect members of the Parisian Information Section to the Third Section, held by resisters, while hardened reliable police were concentrated in the Special Brigades.

The judiciary furnishes us with a final example of government support. Because they interpreted the laws and even the history of Vichy, judges are now beginning to examine their own history. It is clear that, between 1940 and 1944, and because of tradition, it was unthinkable for a group of men who cultivated deference and discipline toward political power to doubt the authority of the state. Murmurs of revolt were even more muted because these men essentially shared Vichy's values. Only one magistrate, Didier, refused to swear allegiance to Marshal Pétain in 1941.

There was little reaction to the purge of the magistrates themselves, which aimed at the Jews within the group from the autumn of 1940 and the Freemasons beginning the following summer. In addition, there was a less well-known law of 17 July 1940 that suspended the life term of seated judges. It was used as often as the other two measures combined and was an even more constant threat to judges.

In the face of this purge, it is striking that there was no collective protest by the magistrates. There were a few individual efforts, sometimes an attempt to create solidarity, attributable largely to honorary magistrates. Rarer still were those who joined the Resistance.

In judicial practice, with more or less zeal, the laws were applied, old or new, including the anti-Semitic laws. Without resistance, the magistrature, whose function it is to interpret the law, consented to everything. Examining the details one finds that the criminal judges interpreted the laws more liberally than the state counselors. But, the important thing is that they accepted, along with a number of doctrinaire jurists, the anti-Semitic legislation as a branch of the law. In this way they made it commonplace. They also legitimized it, enhancing the legitimacy of the political power of those who had written it into law.

By these few examples one understands the unusual merging of the policy of exclusion with the propaganda of unification around traditional values and the weight carried by administrative policies. The verdict is not favorable for the top French administration.

4. Was the France of 1940–42 Anti-Semitic?

Pierre Laborie

"When someone asks me today how the French treated refugees at that time, Jewish and political, how the French behaved toward us, I don't know how to answer.

France, What France?

The French. . . . What do you mean by that?"[1]

The doubts of Lisa Fittko illustrate the uncertainties a study of collective attitudes under Vichy encounters. The questions of a woman who was there are the same as those of historians. They remind us of the difficulty of getting a grip on such elusive material and make clear the impossibility of reducing to clichés or approximations or summarizing generalities a whole scale of reactions in an ever-changing evolution—numerous and contradictory, spread out over time and scattered among all the nuances that separate a fervent acquiescence from active disapproval.

To inquire into the anti-Semitism of the French in general terms is perhaps not the best approach to understanding the relations between public opinion and the Jews during the Occupation. Because of the attitude such an inquiry encourages and the elastic definitions and emotional charge that inevitably result, it can too easily use the past to excuse or condemn.

The problem of anti-Semitism must be examined, but with a realization of the limits of such an examination. Anti-Jewish behavior is too often nourished by oversimplified stereotypes, and we must not deceive ourselves by this same sort of oversimplification in assessing its effects.

The crisis of the 1930s accelerated the spread of a latent anti-Semitism that transcended the political division of left and right. On the eve of the war it could be found alongside a certain kind of republican outlook of which René Bousquet was a product. Following the defeat, the language of hate that was directed at the "guilty" ones and expressed itself openly in a sympathetic press—often an eyewitness to bursts of violence that made good copy—easily became part of the atmosphere of the period. During 1940 and 1941 the anti-Semitic policy of Vichy caused only a general indifference and, sporadically, a feeling of satisfaction. The administration, the police, the gendarmerie, the courts, all were participants, claiming to serve the state through this process of exclusion and persecution. The Catholic Church was slow to break its silence. In the beginning the Resistance seemed divided on the "Jewish Question." The 65,000 copies of Les Décombres, the anti-Semitic firebrand publication by the fascist Lucien Rebatet, were bought up and more than 130,000 orders went unfilled for lack of paper.

The cowardly acts, the practice of informing, the cupidity of the plundering, all formed the setting for ordinary life. Finally, faced with genocide, a new and heavy silence was noted at the time of the Liberation.

The list could be longer. A trial of Vichy or the trial of a pilloried France? Those who vigorously track down the evidence of an anti-Semitism linked to national identity and who have concluded this was a reality clearly believe that the majority of the French recognize themselves in the image reflected in the mirrors of 1940 Vichy. The opinion expressed by Xavier Vallat on 19 October 1946, legitimizing his own actions during his trial is echoed here. Xavier Vallat stated that the anti-Semitism of Vichy was nothing more than the exact reflection of French wishes. This kind of thinking could lead, as is sometimes believed, to the radicalizing of discourse and the denunciation of the conscious complicity of the population in carrying out genocide.

The bulk of the evidence, however, points to less categorical judgments. There was an awakening of conscience at the singling out of Jews in the Occupied Zone; the roundups of the summer of 1942 provoked outrage; and the solemn protestations of spiritual authorities were supported by many. There was a turnabout of opinion, and groups formed that were determined to save the children, and finally, in spite of the tragedy, there were the facts evident in the final balance sheet—76,000 deported and 80,000 victims, of which 11,000 were children. Of the 330,000 Jews living in France in 1940, three-fourths managed to survive and 85 percent of the children were able to escape extermination. From this, inevitably the question arises, which does not in any way erase the shadowy areas: Could it have been thus in a France where the majority were deeply anti-Semitic?

Everything did not begin with the collapse of 1940 and with Vichy. By the end of the 1930s, with the perception the country had of its own decadence, the "Jewish problem" became a sort of accepted idea in every group. The Jewish community in France, confronted with an immigration of foreign Jews that it began to see as a burden, was itself not free from sliding. The anti-Semitic rhetoric, until then clearly identified with the extreme right, spread far beyond these limits. The year 1938 constitutes an important date in the process of a widespread new growth of anti-Semitic sentiment. In a France bled white, sick with fear, and paralyzed by the specter of a new and murderous conflict, the image of the Jew thus became one of the key elements in a whole system of closely linked representations that produced its own kind of thinking. It was in looking through this prism that the nation saw, in a confused way, a serious identity crisis. The denunciation of the intruder, of the *undesirable* foreigner, of the exploiter, the corrupter, the traitorous competitor, the international plotter, the Bolshevik, the enemy within, the instigator of the war, all of this originated with the Jew and was attributable to him. Expressed or not in polite hints, explicit or insinuated, everyday talk, religiously inspired or out of deep conviction, anti-Semitism and its prejudices, in close relationship with xenophobia, made up some of the patterns that before Vichy molded collective everyday thinking. To judge by this, it is easy to appreciate the delicate tone in which, in July 1939,[2] the subtle spirit of Jean Giraudoux evoked the "hundreds of thousands of Askenasis escaped from Polish or Roumanian ghettos" and the "horde" of foreigners "swarming" around who "deface our country by their presence and their action and rarely beautify it by their personal appearance." The same ones, according to Giraudoux, multiply "in a spontaneous generation which reminds one of fleas on a newborn puppy." Other examples could be given. Over this field of fantasy produced by the twin evils of anti-Semitism and xenophobia, Vichy could advance into familiar country.

In 1940 and 1941, if we exclude a few isolated and muted objections, no widespread protests were heard over the laws of exclusion and spoliation. It was with indifference, with an immense and heavy silence, that an apathetic public opinion, anesthetized by the cult of the Marshal and obsessed with everyday cares, accepted without objection the enforcement of Vichy's anti-Semitic measures. It seems an oversimplified explanation to see in this surrender by the public only the prolongation of a visceral anti-Semitism. Even if it is viewed now at some distance, this idea is shocking. It is clear that for most French people, at least until 1941, the fate of Jews was not a main preoccupation. It was perceived as a more or less insignificant problem, depending on individual sensibility, but just one problem among many and not of the first priority for most of those "neither enchanted nor revolted," according to a familiar expression. In the same way, the Jews were considered just one category of reprobates among others. In 1941, however, those who resisted—communist or not, as well as both Protestant and Catholic authorities—began to coalesce to show their indignation.

In 1942 the forced wearing of the yellow star in the Occupied Zone and the massive roundups that summer in both zones brought about a reawakening of conscience. These events provoked a decisive change in public opinion. Two important facts should be stressed. First, for most French citizens, came the "physical" discovery of the realities of a persecution that up until that time had been carried out with relative discretion. The population was shocked. The sight of convoys, the separations, and especially the fate of the children provoked considerable emotion. Popular reaction was intensified by the public protestations of several bishops, the first and most celebrated coming from the Archbishop of Toulouse, Monsignor Saliège, and from the National Committee of the Reformed Church. This changed significantly the image of the Jew in its dominant representations: from a guilty and responsible abstraction, the Jew was transformed into a real human being, persecuted and victimized—a victim, among others, of a collaboration hated a little more for this as well.

Second, the turning point in 1942 accelerated the development of bonds of solidarity. The silent complicities made organizing the rescue of the victims more efficient and reinforced the Jews in their determination to become active in their own survival.

Still, not all the ambiguities have disappeared. We must remind ourselves of the discrepancy between the development of a way of thinking and of conscience. The fate of Jews counted for very little in the ruptures that distanced public opinion from the Vichy regime in the second half of 1941. The events of 1942 modified the French outlook toward the Jews, but it is difficult to assess to what extent. The persistence of confusion as to the nature of the deportations and the troubled silence surrounding these events following the Liberation show that a good deal of murkiness still existed. Traces can be found in the results of an Institut Français d'Opinion Public poll of February 1946. Out of all those questioned at that time, fewer than four out of ten believed that the Jews were French like everybody else.

Notes

1. Lisa Fittko, *Le Chemin des Pyrénées* (Paris: Maren Sell, 1987).
2. Jean Giraudoux, *Pleins Pouvoirs* (Paris: Gallimard, 1939).

5. Why Did the High Court Acquit Bousquet?

Henry Rousso

"These proceedings were lively at times and even picturesque." Thus began Prosecutor Frette-Damicourt's closing argument at the trial of René Bousquet on 23 June 1949. Although recorded during the last session of the High Court, they passed almost unnoticed at the time. A half-century later however, they raise burning questions: How can René Bousquet's acquittal and the Court's decision to commute the charge of "national indignity" (shameful behavior toward the nation) because of "acts of resistance" be explained? Was it the result of an inability at the time to understand fully the responsibility of the French government in the deportation of Jews? Was it due to the timing, considering his trial took place relatively late? Or was it because of special treatment or protection, or both, accorded Bousquet?

Despite the passage of time, the answers remain uncertain, but several points need to be underscored. Regarding the general context of the trial, it must be remembered that from 1948 on the High Court no longer handed down severe sentences. As a consequence of political ruptures in 1947, communists no longer sat on juries, which were appointed by parliamentary members, and the chambers were engaged in a long debate on the necessity of amnesty laws. A first law had been voted in 1947, a second followed in 1951, and the last was passed in 1953. Therefore, the same judges presiding over the cases of the last two or three accused men out of the hundred handed over to the High Court since 1945 (cf. Henry Rousso's discussion of the Purge following this essay) were simultaneously engaged in trying to decide whether or not to close the book on Vichy and collaboration. Undoubtedly, the context of the trial worked in favor of Bousquet, as it had for several other dignitaries of the regime, but this does not explain everything.

Another decisive element was Bousquet's own defense, which was almost identical to the defense he presented in 1992. In the few minutes he gave to the Jewish question during his hearing before the High Court (one page out of twenty-seven in the record), he presented his actions as being a screen against the commissioner for Jewish affairs, whose influence he knowingly overestimated, and the High Court was in no position to dispute his testimony. He spoke of abolishing the police assigned to Jewish affairs, which was formerly under the Commissariat Générale aux Questions Juives, failing to make clear that he had only transferred them to his own authority in a bureaucratic reshuffling. Finally, he spoke only of German pressures, real ones, without going into either the racial ideology of Vichy, which he reminded the court had already been put into law before he accepted his position, or the question of the children under sixteen rounded up without any request from the Germans.

In his plea in 1992, Bousquet insisted at length on the fact that the investigating commission of the High Court had already gathered a certain amount of evidence relative to the negotiations with those responsible in the SS for the collaboration between the French and German police. This is an essential historical point (independent of juridical arguments to determine whether there existed "new facts" or whether the "new qualification" could be applied here). Actually, the investigation carried out against Bousquet between 1945 and 1948 was not as careless as is commonly thought. During the first phase of the investigation, in June 1945, for example, there were explicit statements on the negotiations between Karl Oberg, the SS chief in France, and Bousquet. But this element was retained largely in defense of Bousquet, who, according to the police, was supposedly safeguarding the "independence" of the French police. The question of Jewish arrests, one aspect of the police collaboration, was not mentioned.

During a second phase of the investigation in February 1948 one of the decisive reports, which came from General Information, specified without ambiguity that "Bousquet demanded from the German services that all operations relative to arrests and the handing over of foreign Jews be carried out by the French police, and it is likely that it was the various services of the French police who were charged with carrying out this task." Moreover, the file also contains the testimonies of Oberg and his associate, Helmut Knochen, which specify that the direct negotiations between Himmler (via Heidrich and Oberg) and

Laval (via Bousquet) permitted a "positive solution" to the Jewish question in France.

In other words, and this is what Bousquet points to in his defense, most of the facts were already brought out in the investigation of the High Court. These involve documents clarifying Vichy's attitude toward the deportation of Jews, even if this earlier investigation had already slanted final conclusions in a way favorable to the accused. The real question then is, why was this information ignored during the actual trial?

The 1949 indictment takes up almost sentence for sentence the arguments of Bousquet. For instance, one reads that "Laval and Bousquet could not prevent the deportation of foreign Jews from the southern zone because of the German threat to arrest all the Jews of the Paris region, but Bousquet managed to have it done by the French police." Thus, the prosecution considered excusable the facts not only that it was the French police who carried out the roundups of the summer of 1942 but also additionally that those carried out in the southern zone in August of 1942, in a region where the Germans were not allowed to interfere, happened simply by accident or by German pressure. The charge against Bousquet admitted, however, that "if, in many cases Bousquet tried to avoid the worst, he had nonetheless agreed in general to serve, by his own authority, the policy of racial persecution with which Vichy had associated itself and which the Germans would have had more difficulty carrying out alone."

At this stage two other important events come into play—the personality of Bousquet and the failure of the court to understand the extent of the genocide against the Jews. It is well known that Bousquet was deeply engaged before the war in radical groups of the southwest region. Among the jurists of the High Court was his friend Jean Baylet, a deputy of the Radical Party and publisher of the *Dépêche du Midi*. This fact is important because it was the jury who pronounced the sentence, not the judges.

During the court sessions, when Judge Noguères invited the jury members to ask questions of the accused, no one raised the question of deportations; the debate centered instead on the struggle against the Resistance, which was another important part of Bousquet's activities. Only President Noguères himself questioned Bousquet on the circulars concerning the Jews, and he was rewarded by a very long answer in which not a single statement by the accused was contradicted or even discussed. Was Baylet's influence an important element in the jury's attitude? Was it so important that it could have carried weight during the deliberations? This is possible.

However, another protagonist also played a crucial role, the public prosecutor. In his closing argument for the prosecution, he at no time mentioned the anti-Jewish policy, although it was presented clearly and succinctly as part of the indictment. This means that in his eyes the trial had allowed this part of the case to be aired and the accused had been cleared of the charge. Prosecutor Frette-Damicourt was anything but a partisan of the defunct regime. As technical councilor to the Garde des Sceaux (Attorney General or Minister of Justice) during the Popular Front, he was relieved of his functions as prosecutor of the Seine Court by Vichy in November 1940 and retired the following year.

He was therefore one of the first group of judges purged by Vichy because of his links to the Popular Front and no doubt also because he was a Freemason. If he had consciously helped Bousquet, which remains to be proved, he did it either out of a feeling of mutual solidarity with top administration officials or because Bousquet was close to him politically, not on the basis of "Pétainism," but as a fellow radical. But this is only a hypothesis. To complete the picture, it must be added that Bousquet's lawyer was Maurice Ribet, who was the lawyer of another radical, Edouard Daladier, during the aborted Riom trial that Vichy brought against the leaders of the Third Republic.

Still, it is difficult to be sure that the soft treatment accorded Bousquet was the result of not being able to conceive of the anti-Jewish policy of Vichy. The same High Court, in the trials of Pétain, Laval, and officers in the Jewish Affairs section (Vallat, Darquier), had taken into account the anti-Semitism of the accused, even though this charge was never a central one. Other trials of the time, such as those of Maurras or of the French gendarmes who oversaw the camp at Drancy, had also brought to light the ideological anti-Semitism and the murderous character of French cooperation in the persecutions. From this viewpoint, contrary to general opinion, the Bousquet trial was very atypical.

In the final analysis, it is the combination of these different factors that explains the 1949 verdict. Almost the last one to be judged, at a time when the necessity for a judicial "lapse of memory," was being debated, how could Bousquet not have slipped through the net when he also benefited from the good will of a part of the Court?

6. Did the Purge Achieve Its Goals?

Henry Rousso

At the death of René Bousquet, several newspapers ran the headline, "The Trial of Vichy Will Not Take Place." This assertion, made so often today, shows more than simple ignorance; it displays a blackout as serious as that of Vichy between 1950 and 1960, a forgetting of the extent, the dilemmas, and the dramas of the Purge that followed the war.

At the time of the Liberation, the crackdown on collaborators, leaders, and civil servants of the "French State" was in full swing. It caused disagreement within political parties as well as the resistance movements, and became the center of a debate that included the whole country. It was a lengthy process that lasted for an entire decade, from 1944 to 1953. Its gaps, its lack of unity, and its injustices should not hide its scope, which is often underestimated.

The most brutal aspect was the so-called "savage" purge, consisting of summary judgments and executions, improvised court martials, individual score settling and reprisals, and shaving of the heads of women who had had affairs with Germans. Certain estimates, usually highly fanciful or partisan in nature, claimed 100,000 dead. Actually, around 9,000 people were killed in 1944–45 without any legal procedure. More than a quarter of these took place before the Allied invasion, half between 6 June 1944 and the Liberation, and only a fourth afterward, when the jurisdiction of a legal Purge went into effect. In other words, the major part of these executions was perpetrated while the war was still on and in a climate of disorder, civil war, and insurrection.

At the time the Nazi occupiers, with the help of the French Milice, were carrying out a particularly ferocious repression of Resistance members and of the French population. Innocent people were certainly victims of this burst of violence, but the main targets of the "cleansing" were members of the Vichy forces of order and those who helped the Nazis.

The provisional government of General de Gaulle was uneasy for a long time about the grave risks of an uncontrolled Purge, and the reestablishment of legal government and national law was one of the major preoccupations of those in power among the Free French and the Resistance. From the summer of 1944 on, the judicial framework of the Purge was voted into law, and its principles were simple on the surface. Collaborators were to be judged on the basis of the penal code of 1939, but the texts should be altered to take into account special situations stemming from the Occupation.

On the criminal level, the procedures were based on the application of Articles 75 to 86, which punished "acts harmful to national defense," "secret dealings with the enemy," and "attacks against the national security." Added to these traditional crimes were those of "informing," which had caused the death of many members of the Resistance and of persecuted Jews, and "shameful acts against the nation," which aimed at those taking a favorable position toward the enemy or the Vichy government and which could not qualify as "crimes" in the legal sense. All of the ministers, secretaries of state, secretary-generals in office between 16 June 1940 (the last government of the Third Republic) and 25 August 1944 (end of the Vichy Regime) were thus automatically condemned to "National Degradation" (loss of civil rights), a sentence that could be lifted in case of "deeds of resistance."

Four kinds of courts were in charge of this Purge: the High Court of Justice for government ministers, the "courts of justice" that were to apply the penal code, the "civil chambers" for those who were accused of "national degradation," and the military courts. These jurisdictions, were composed of juries of members of the Resistance and professional magistrates, who had been severely purged between September 1944 and May 1945, during which time more than 10 percent of the 3,000 working magistrates were removed or retired from office.[1]

To the criminal Purge was added an administrative and professional one in the various ministries, in important bodies of the government, the professions, the police, the judiciary, and even in the world of film and literature (carried out by the well-known National Committee of Writers). The objective was to condemn on a professional level (by revocations, banning of the right to practice a profession, etc.), or else to clear those whose behavior in carrying out their duties had been wrongly called into question.

Altogether, according to the most recent figures, the statistical balance sheet for the Purge was anything but negligible. Out of 100 cases examined by the High Court, 45 ended up being dismissed for lack of evidence or in simple acquittals; 15 were convicted only for "dégradation nationale," of which 7 were excused (as was Bousquet); 22 were given prison sentences and hard labor, 5 of these in absentia; 18 were condemned to death, 10 of these in absentia; 5 received commuted death sentences (Pétain was one of these), and 3 were executed (Laval, Darnand, de Brinon). The score for the courts of justice and civil courts is even higher: 310,000 cases were compiled, which affected roughly 350,000 people, or almost one French person in every 100. Of these, 140,000 were dismissed before the preliminary investigation (empty files) and 43,000 afterward (insufficient charges or none at all). The 127,000 remaining files brought 58,000 judgments from the courts of justice and 69,000 from civil chambers. The courts of justice pronounced 12 percent of these acquitted, and 6 percent suffered loss of civil rights only. Seventy percent received prison and hard labor sentences (of which 4 percent were in absentia and 4 percent for life) and 12 percent got death sentences, of which more than half were in absentia and 767 ended in execution. The civil courts pronounced 67 percent as sentences of "national degradation," or loss of civil rights, 28 percent were acquitted, and 5 percent were pardoned for acts of resistance.

To this score must be added that of the military tribunals, whose activities remain obscure but who condemned to death and executed around 800 people. This means that the number of *legal* death sentences carried out was around 1,500, twice the official figure, which includes only the count from the judicial courts.[2] The total cost in lives, then, of the "savage" Purge and the legal one was over 10,000. It must be pointed out, however, that the amnesties of 1951 and 1953 brought about the liberation of a great majority of those condemned and in prison. In 1954 fewer than 1,000 were still detained.

The administrative and professional Purge was also underestimated, but it was very uneven in its different activities. Out of 1,000,000 civil servants, around 30,000 were the object of sanctions, a partial number that did not take into account all of the ministries.[3] Among these nearly half were dismissed or retired from office. For example, besides the cases of the magistrates already mentioned, the Purge Commission of the army had examined the files of more than 10,000 officers, half of all those on active duty in 1944. More than 20 percent were discharged or retired.[4] The National Commission in charge of the Purge of businesses examined more than 1,500 individual files of business owners, executives, and workers of whom fewer than 200 were condemned. In the film industry, out of 60,000 professionals, about 1,000 were sanctioned, a fourth of whom received severe punishments.[5]

Whether or not it was considered afterward to be too harsh or too lenient, the Purge was nevertheless a major social phenomenon that inevitably prolonged the tragic events of the Occupation. It left a general feeling of frustration because it raised, as today in the former countries of the Soviet bloc, difficulties that often cannot be resolved. Almost all of the accused found themselves reproached for having betrayed their country or for having attacked the nation, a view of events peculiar to the climate of a period that was unable to take into account the specific character of World War II as we see it a half-century later. The engagement on the side of the invader resulted, without doubt, less from a wish to "betray" than from a desire to see France line up beside the Nazis, for either ideological reasons (Doriot, Brasillach) or geopolitical strategy (Vichy).

However, these trials, like Bousquet's in 1949, did not give the priority we consider essential today to charges of crimes committed within the framework of the Final Solution. This was a result of the collective perception of magistrates, of juries, of resistance fighters, even of the victims themselves, who at the time, in the great majority of cases, did not demand a special punishment for crimes resulting from anti-Semitism in these trials.

Finally, and surely this is a real problem, the leaders of the Purge, like public opinion itself, traumatized by the defeat, the Occupation, and the deep divisions they had created, found themselves faced with a series of dilemmas. Should the law be respected to the letter at the risk of making the Purge process inefficacious, or should it depart from its sacred principles at the risk of placing revenge ahead of justice? For how long, and to what degree of responsibility, and on what scale in terms of sentences and condemnations should the process be conducted, knowing that a certain equilibrium was indispensable for society? No purge at all would have caused a ferment of revolt, while too much of one, especially after 1945, would have led to the same result. Was it possible to dismiss tens of thousands of civil servants, magistrates, company owners, that is, condemn the "elite," and be able to replace them at the very time when the reconstruction of a devastated country was the first priority?

The evidence shows that the choices were far from perfect. The Purge was unevenly administered in both time and place, touching certain groups (the intellectuals), and letting others slip by (company owners). Soft treatment and protection for certain ones and injustice done to others could not be prevented. Added to this was the emergence of the Cold War. In the opinion of some, communism became the principal enemy even while the enemies of yesterday were still being judged. The amnesty laws of 1951 and 1953, besides their hidden political agendas, were carried out in the context of this necessity to reestablish, even at the price of judicial amnesia, the "civilian peace" and to assure the continuity of state and nation. No one could foresee then that, in spite of its widespread impact, the oversights and the uneven treatment of the Purge, and the long silence about the role of Vichy, would once again, decades later, trouble the peace—and the conscience—of the French.

Notes

1. Alain Bancaud and Henry Rousso, "L'Epuration des magistrats à la Libération," in *L'Epuration de la magistrature de la Révolution à la Liberation: 150 ans d'histoire judiciaire,* Colloquium of the Association Française pour l'Histoire de la Justice, Paris, 4–5 December 1992 (forthcoming).

2. Henry Rousso, "L'Epuration en France. Une histoire inachevée, Vingtième siècle," *Revue d'histoire* 33 (January-March 1992), 78–105. It is a summary of this article that is presented here.

3. François Rouquet, "L'Epuration administrative en France après la Libération. Une analyse statistique et géographique, Vingtième siècle," *Revue d'histoire* 33 (January-March 1992), 106–17.

4. Jacques Vernet, *Le Réarmament et la réorganization de l'armée de terre française (1943–1946)* (Vincennes: Service Historique de L'Armeé de Terre, 1980).

5. Jean-Pierre Bertin-Maghit, *Le Cinéma sous l'Occupation* (PARIS: O. Orban, 1989).

THE TOUVIER AFFAIR

The essays and interviews included here concerning the Touvier Affair are divided into several sections. The first essays, by Jean-Denis Bredin and Tzvetan Todorov, deal with the implications of the April 1992 acquittal of Touvier by the Paris Court of Appeals, a decision that shocked the French and raised important questions concerning the nature of the Vichy regime and the viability of crimes against humanity in French law. The acquittal also raised important concerns about the French justice system itself. These and other matters are discussed by Bredin and Todorov in their essays.

The second section, dealing with the trial of Touvier in March–April 1994, is divided into three subsections. The first subsection, "Personalities," offers brief portraits of two of the more important and compelling figures in the trial, Touvier's lawyer, Jacques Trémolet de Villers, and one of the lawyers for the civil parties, Arno Klarsfeld.

It is important to realize that in the French system there can be different lawyers representing multiple plaintiffs or "civil parties" attached to the state's prosecution. In the Touvier case, there were thirty-four different lawyers for the relatives and descendants of those murdered at Rillieux-la-Pape. The prosecutor for the state was Hubert de Touzalin. The judge, Henri Boulard, had two assistants. All three judges voted with the nine jurors, and a two-thirds majority was required to convict.

In the French system, moreover, the judges, the prosecutor, and the civil party lawyers all have the right to interrogate the witnesses. This explains the unusual (for American audiences) degree of freedom of exchange in the courtroom, as evidenced in the articles dealing with the courtroom sessions, gathered here under the heading "Proceedings." The last section, "Reflections," includes a series of brief essays on important historical issues raised by the trial. They are written by Henry Rousso, who attended the trial and reported on his reactions in *Libération*, and by Tzvetan Todorov. The Rousso essays were first published in *Libération*. Todorov's essays originally appeared in his "Letter from Paris" feature in *Salmagundi*, following the April 1992 acquittal and the trial of Touvier in the spring of 1994. Todorov's essays were translated by John Anzalone.

Reflections on the April 1992 Appeals Court Decision

———

The Touvier Affair: History and Justice Abused

Of course it is not sufficient that the trial of Paul Touvier seem necessary to us—an imperative of memory, of morality—for the Law to wish it to occur. Moreover, a judicial decision is not necessarily bad just because it shocks us. A state of law can pass judgments that distress us, but the rule of law is the pillar of democracy. We must therefore try to read the decision of the Chambre d'Accusation without prejudice: 213 pages of careful work, well constructed, often well written, but 213 pages that, as one reads, seem nevertheless slanted toward an acquittal.

Eleven crimes are attributed to Touvier. The Court dismisses ten of these charges, developing in each case lengthy arguments geared to their dismissal. Occasionally, the recollection—of a victim, of a witness—seems fragile, uncertain, or lacking in credibility to the court. Occasionally, a recollection appears to be unduly slanted. When a victim says he or she "recognizes" Touvier, this recognition, "taking into account the dates and conditions under which it occurred," or given the "time elapsed or briefness" of the encounter, cannot serve as proof. It would be very difficult to enumerate all the arguments in this lengthy court decision that exclude credible testimony and benefit Touvier when there is the least doubt. Could this be a symptom of a justice

dreamed of and indeed called for by judges, lawyers, and citizens—
the opposite, in effect, of the feared advance of our inquisitory system?
The accused in this case is always presumed innocent. The Chambre
d'Accusation proceeds in order to exonerate. The judge points out and
emphasizes the smallest details that benefit the accused, while demanding irrefutable proofs of his guilt. Should we rejoice in this, taking it as a sign of desired developments in the justice system? More
reasonably, one can ask if Touvier is an ordinary man accused like
others.

The Chambre d'Accusation retained only one charge against Touvier: he ordered the massacre of seven Jews, killed by the Milice, at
Rillieux-la-Pape, in the Ain Department, as a "reprisal" on the day following the assassination of Philippe Henriot, a Vichy minister. Here
again, the court takes care to observe that "the major charge weighing
against Touvier derives from his own declarations" and that no piece
of evidence in the dossier contradicts Touvier's claim that he organized
this execution "to avoid something worse," to prevent the massacre of
100 Jews. The Chambre d'Accusation concedes that "the charges
against the accused are sufficient to make him an accomplice to several
murders, but the Court is not in a position to examine the motives of
the crimes. . . ." Does the massacre at Rillieux constitute a crime
against humanity?

In a law dated 26 December 1964, consisting of a single article, the
international norm defining crimes against humanity as imprescriptible was introduced into French law. This break with ordinary law is
subject to debate. Does the impossibility of absolving crimes against
humanity as well as our duty to memory necessitate their being imprescriptible? Or should one fear that justice, when dealing with crimes
forty to fifty years old and involving charges against very old men,
will hesitate, will stall for time, as is apparently the case here? Should
one fear something more dangerous, which is that spectacular trials
such as these would foster confusion more than they would serve to
keep memory itself alive? Everyone has the right to judge the law for
him or herself. But the judge's job is to apply the law.

This law does not define crimes against humanity. It refers instead
back to the United Nations resolution of 13 February 1946, which itself
refers back to the definition of crimes against humanity provided in
the Charter of the Nuremberg Tribunal. Eminent jurists have correctly

noted the inadequacies of the definition, Anglo-American in original, which does not possess the rigor we are accustomed to in our code and criminal statutes. According to a court decision handed down on 20 December 1985 in the context of the Barbie Affair, the Appeals Court, employing the terms of international conventions, defined crimes against humanity in the following fashion: "Inhuman acts and persecutions which, carried out on behalf of a nation practicing a policy of ideological hegemony, having been committed systematically not only against persons by reason of their appurtenance to a particular racial or religious collectivity, but also against adversaries of this policy, no matter what the form of their opposition."

No one could contest the fact that the massacres at Rillieux-la-Pape ordered by Touvier were inhuman acts committed systematically against persons "by reason of their appurtenance to a racial or religious community." It remained for the Chambre d'Accusation to verify that these acts were committed "in the name of a State practicing a policy of ideological hegemony": the Court devoted seven pages to proving that this was not the case. To arrive at this result, the Court rewrote in its own fashion the history of Vichy. The Court observed first of all that a certain "ideology" reigned at Vichy, which was nostalgic for tradition, for the rural world of yesteryear, the world of handicrafts, of an attachment to Christianity, but then observed that this "ideology" tolerated divisions and that one could therefore not speak of a "specific [monolithic] ideology." The German Reich was certainly hegemonic, but not the government of Vichy. "At no time," the Court assures us, "did the Vichy regime have either the intent or the opportunity to establish any domination or to impose a conquering ideology." The Court took care—because Touvier was an officer in the Milice— to examine the case of "the Milice in this context." "Is it possible to speak of an ideology of the Milice?" The Court conceded that this ideology held sway among certain leaders of the Milice, such as Joseph Darnand. The Court noted that Darnand, secretary general of the Milice and a member of the Waffen SS as well, swore an oath of loyalty and obedience to Hitler and adhered to the ideology of National Socialism. But for the Court, Darnand was merely an "exceptional case." According to the decision, the ideology of the Milice included diverse values: the struggle against a dissident Gaullism, a stance in favor of "French unity," against bolshevism, for nationalism, against the "Jewish leprosy," for French purity, against a pagan Freemasonry, for Christian civilization. . . . In the long run, the Court asserted, there was a "radical incompatibility" between Nazi ideology and the values of the Milice! Besides, and this is the crux of the problem, the "Milice was only one of the constituent powers of Vichy state." "If it is true the Milice as a movement had a 'hegemonic aim,' it is also true that Vichy itself was not totalitarian, and that it did not itself practice a policy of ideological hegemony." With the passing of time, could the Vichy state have become a state practicing a policy of ideological hegemony? It is futile, the Court concluded, to ask this question. It is sufficient to note that "whatever its weaknesses, acts of cowardice, and ignominious deeds," Vichy never belonged in this category.

Without much difficulty the Court's decision can make light of words: "ideological hegemony" is not a clear enough notion not to be emptied of any real content or signification if one wishes to do so. But the Court's decision obliges it to distort the history of Vichy to make it conform to its own reasoning. Darnand is made an "exceptional case" who is ultimately not representative of the Milice. The Milice itself is defined as a "constituent power," among others, of the Vichy state; and the fact that Darnand was secretary general for the Maintenance of Order in 1943 and then secretary of state for the Interior in 1944—having sworn an oath of loyalty to Hitler—is inconsequential. Because the government of Vichy hearkened to many values, among them those of "traditional France" and "Christian civilization," it did not possess an ideology properly speaking, and moreover, as the Court stated in its decision, it was founded more on "a constellation of 'good intentions' and political animosities than a system of rigorously interlinked ideas." No "ideological hegemony" in the dogmas of French fascism, taken up and adapted by the government of Vichy, or in the organization of a totalitarian state, or in the principles of the National Revolution, or in the policy of collaboration, or in the actions of a government seeking to impose on everyone, without recourse to any democratic mechanism, its values as well as its exclusions and repressions, while submitting the nation, little by little over the course of time, to Nazi domination. . . . At the end of an argument such as this, what remains of the notion of ideological hegemony?

There remained nevertheless the obstacle of anti-Semitism, difficult to ignore. The Court dismissed this obstacle, observing that, even if "the policies of the Vichy administration" were not "devoid of anti-Semitism," it was sufficient to note that none of Marshall Pétain's speeches contained anti-Semitic pronouncements and that, in Vichy France, there had never been "an official proclamation that the Jew was the enemy of the State, as was the case in Germany." Neither the Jewish Statute, promulgated in October 1940, nor the Yellow Star, nor the totality of Vichy texts excluding the Jews, nor the organized mass arrests, nor the massacres—such as the one the Court acknowledged was ordered by Touvier—were judged to be adequate to assume the status of "an official proclamation" of anti-Semitism.

No anti-Semitic ideology in Vichy France? At this point even the most impartial reader is left wondering. The tranquility of Paul Touvier is ensured, but at what price! A dangerous illustration of the supremacy of prejudice: history, the law, and justice abused.

TZVETAN TODOROV

The Touvier Affair

Just when the United States was overwhelmed by the acquittal of Rod-
ney King's attackers, a great storm shook public opinion in France in
the wake of the decision by the Paris tribunal to dismiss a different
case. The resemblance, however, would seem to stop there: not only
did ghettos in France not burn as a result of the decision, but the trial
involved acts committed nearly fifty years ago! Paul Touvier, former
milicien, was in effect unconditionally discharged in proceedings for
crimes committed against humanity in 1943–44.

To recall briefly the major events of this shady business, Touvier
enrolled as an active member of the milice in Lyons in 1943 and became
the head of the local intelligence service. In this capacity he participated in the torture, execution, or deportation of many Jews, resistance
members, or Free France sympathizers. He went underground at the
Liberation and was condemned to death in absentia. He was arrested,
but managed to escape. From then on he enjoyed the extraordinary
protection of several dignitaries of the Catholic Church, who allowed
him to live safely in monasteries. He got married and had children. By
1967 his crimes found protection in the statute of limitations, and in
1971 he was, furthermore, pardoned by the president of the republic.
But in 1973 new charges were brought against him, this time involving

crimes against humanity not subject to the prescription of limitations. After a delay successfully prolonged for years by police complicity, Touvier was arrested and charged in 1989. But in April of 1992, in a final reversal, the Court of Criminal Appeal decided that there was not cause to continue the proceedings, and rendered a lengthy public justification of its ruling. Touvier, 77 years old, was set free.

The interest of the debate aroused by this dismissal (what the French call a "non-lieu," a kind of acquittal before trial, there being "no grounds" to proceed) comes from the arguments used by the judges in reaching their decision. True, the procedure for "crimes against humanity" has only very rarely been used in France; only once, actually, in 1987 against Klaus Barbie, Gestapo chief of the same city of Lyons. And we know that the very existence of such a notion as crimes against humanity evokes a certain reticence, because it may lead to the conviction of someone who has not in fact violated the law. Now, in a country of laws, the whole law and nothing but the law must prevail: acknowledgment of the rule of law protects citizens from the arbitrary exercise of power.

The history of this singular judicial category is well-known. Informally invoked since the massacre of the Armenians in 1915, it became a reality at the Nuremberg Trials right after World War II. What motivates it is precisely the fact that crimes have obviously been committed, even if without infraction of the law, because it is the state itself, the author of the laws, or one of its constituents, that is responsible for the crimes! To deal with this novel and specifically modern situation, an appeal is made to something greatly resembling the old idea of a natural law, which logically both precedes and supersedes the positive law embodied in the statutes of individual countries. It follows, and we can so postulate, that the commission of certain acts is not excused by the fact that they conformed to the law, or that they were ordered by a superior—certain acts indeed, and specifically the act that consists in excluding from humanity some of its representatives, and then considering legitimate, as it concerns them, measures that remain illegal for other members of humanity or of the nation. It is in this sense that these crimes are rightly said to be "against humanity," against the idea of an indivisible humanity, of which each human being is wholly a representative.

In concrete terms the charges at Nuremberg retain two variables: the nature of the crime and the identity of the victim. (The final judgment actually appealed in addition to a third parameter in the form of the circumstances involved: it states that there can only be crimes against humanity in time of war, which greatly restricts the application of the notion. It must on the contrary be specified that there is no crime against humanity involving the nationals of a country with which one is at war.) The nature of the crime or the forms of exclusion of humanity include assassination (or mass murder—extermination, genocide), the reduction to slavery and torture, and finally deportation (as to a concentration camp). As for the identity of the victim, this involves any part of the civilian, noncombatant population. Such individuals—and this is essential—have been singled out because of what they are (their cultural, social, or physical characteristics), not because of what they have done. The Nuremberg court does not specify (but doubtless implies) that the authors of these crimes cannot be isolated individuals, but only agents of states, governments, or similar social authorities. A maniac who decides to exterminate all Japanese, for example, does not commit a crime against humanity, and existing laws are entirely adequate to judge him. In addition, Nuremberg establishes no restriction regarding eventual ideological justifications for these acts.

This definition of crimes against humanity is perhaps not perfect, but it has the advantage of possessing a discriminatory virtue: it includes certain acts as criminal and excludes others, instead of being satisfied with an emotional approach that can be modified according to circumstances. We know that for reasons that have more to do with politics and history than with justice, the only crimes against humanity to have reached judgment have involved the genocide of the Jews. But the efficacy of the notion can be tested by applying it to other situations: without being exactly equivalent to the slaughter of the Jews, these other crimes against humanity have indeed taken place—and deserve to be punished.

Thus for the deportation and extermination of the bourgeoisie "as a class" in the USSR during the 1930s or in Cambodia in the 1970s: those struck by this repression had done nothing; their only crime was to have been born into the wrong group. The same is true of the deportation to concentration camps, the torture, and the assassinations carried out in Bulgaria under Zhivkov until the 1960s. The victims had broken no laws; their common characteristic was only that they had not been enthusiastic supporters of the communist regime. On the other hand, in giving the order to shoot those attempting to scale the Berlin wall, Erich Honeker did not commit a crime against humanity: the victims suffered for what they did, not for what they were. The French government, or certain of its agencies, was probably guilty of crimes against humanity in persecuting segments of the Algerian population when Algeria was still a part of France. The Serbian government is doing much the same thing today by persecuting, deporting, and killing the Croats, Bosnians, and Albanians on the sole basis of their ethnic or religious identity.

In contesting the idea of crimes against humanity, it may be objected that the law has merely become the mask donned by force, for to be able to judge someone, it is first necessary to defeat him. This explains why yesterday's accomplices of Hitler or today's agents of Zhivkov are brought to judgment whereas Stalin and Pol Pot, not to mention the others, enjoy impunity. Such a statement is irrefutable, but, in my view, does not call into question the idea of crimes against humanity. To attempt to go further is not desirable: what international agency would be capable of intervening in any country in the world so as to restore justice? To count on defeat is in no way pusillanimous, for it can be also shown, thankfully for us all, that even the most heartless dictatorships eventually collapse (and the defeat of tyrants is no exception). Moreover, if a dictator knows that in the case of a change of government, or even on a simple trip abroad, he risks being judged, he might hesitate before committing crimes.

Crime against humanity is by definition independent of place: the same act is a crime wherever committed, and changing countries does not shield one from its attendant justice. The fact that, on the other hand, it should escape the constraint of time—in other words, that it is not subject to the prescription of limitations—is no doubt more problematic. To defend this requirement it is difficult to invoke the necessity of keeping alive the memory of certain crimes, first, because were this to be the case, individuals would be sacrificed in the service of the abstract idea of the good of the nation or of the State instead of being judged for themselves. And then too, because other national agencies—the schools, the media, the government and its elected officials—can take on the cause of justice and ensure the survival in the collective memory of relevant events. It can also be claimed that an individual does not remain identical to himself over time and that it is therefore unjust to condemn a man of seventy for something he did when he was twenty. And it can especially be asserted that the memory of witnesses fades and becomes confused and that it is difficult, if not impossible, to conduct an investigation fifty years after the event. Such difficulties were illustrated recently in the problems of the Demjanjuk trial in Israel. To solve them, one could propose that after a certain amount of time, crimes would be covered by the statute of limitations, but not guilty verdicts—even those brought down in absentia—pronounced immediately after the commission of crimes.

Once called on to judge its first crime against humanity in the Barbie case, French justice had to introduce the concept into its discourse. It did so in 1985, in a decree by its highest authority, the Cour de Cassation. But rather than following the definition set forth at Nuremberg, the court sought instead, either because of pressure from different groups or in anticipation of certain undesirable applications, to adapt the concept to its own needs—a dangerous practice for the logic of the law itself. On the one hand, the court expanded the definition by including among possible victims not just certain categories of the civilian population but also all enemies of the incriminated regime—in concrete terms, resistance fighters, and not just Jews—thereby erasing the distinction between war crimes and crimes against humanity. On the other hand, to offset this expansion, it restricted the category of the agents of the crimes: only those who have acted "in the name of a State practicing a policy of ideological political hegemony," that is, a totalitarian state—can be prosecuted.

The judges in the Touvier case based their verdict on two types of argument, without ever openly contesting the idea of crimes against humanity. First, ten of the eleven charges brought against Touvier were set aside because of the difficulty in establishing the truth fifty years later, but without this objection ever being cited as a principle for contesting the lack of a statute of limitations for these crimes. Sometimes, or so it seemed, witnesses contradicted themselves, sometimes their statements were too vague or implausible, and at times what they asserted was insufficient to incriminate Touvier. Then, in the eleventh case, the facts were admissible, and were, moreover, the only ones Touvier himself acknowledged. The case involved hostages shot right after an assassination carried out by the resistance. Touvier made the decision to seek reprisal and chose to have seven hostages, all Jews, killed. To hold to the Nuremberg definition, the execution of hostages would not be a crime against humanity, but "only" a war crime. However, the choice of exclusively Jewish hostages is indeed a crime against humanity. But the charge was nevertheless set aside because of still another consideration: Vichy France was not really a totalitarian state but, rather, a conservative dictatorial regime of which only certain features were the product of pure fascism.

Relying thus on the definition of the Cour de Cassation, the Paris judges contributed in demonstrating its absurdity, since the same deeds, the deportation and extermination of Jews, were crimes in Barbie's case, but stopped being crimes in Touvier's. In so doing the judges also knocked a hole in the notion of the equality of all before the law. By keeping to this interpretation they assured that, in effect, only Germans could be tried for crimes against humanity; the French were exonerated in advance, because France at the time was not a totalitarian state!

It's worth dwelling for a moment on the reasoning involved in the two arguments used to reach the "non-lieu" dismissal. The first consists in pretending to accept the law as a whole, so as to deny any application of it in specific cases: the principle of the prescription of limitations is allowed, for example, but the time elapsed is considered to be too long to permit investigation. The second, on the other hand, consists in conforming to the letter of the law by pretending to ignore its spirit (the Cour de Cassation never intended to make the prosecution of Vichy agents impossible). These two arguments are of opposite types: one favors the letter of the law, the other an interpretation that ultimately requires the assertion of the contrary of that letter. They have but one thing in common: they enable Touvier to be found innocent. But at the same time, and by this very convergence, the judges betrayed their partiality and revealed that the intention to decide a "non-lieu," not logic or reasoning, presided over their verdict.

For no one was fooled by the formal arguments. Beyond judicial considerations, and beyond the Touvier case itself, the Court sought to absolve and even to exonerate Vichy. This is why the judges took advantage of the occasion to issue with their ruling a lengthy analysis of French politics during the war, in the face of which the reader must wonder whether bad faith has triumphed over ignorance, or the reverse. What can be said of the contortions they required to establish that the Milice was not fascist, even if its commander Darnand belonged to the SS? Or that if it was fascist, that could only prove that the state as a whole was not, else why would it have needed to confide that particular (fascist) mission to this organization? Or that Pétain had never been an anti-Semitic propagandist, even though he had signed some of the harshest racial laws of his time? But what is especially worth criticizing in the judges is not that they wrote bad history, it's that they wrote history at all, instead of being content to apply the law equitably and universally.

What could have been the reason for the choices these judges made? Was it their preference for the "French state" and its ideal of "family, work, and country" instead of the republican tradition that emerges from the Revolution? One might well think so, judging by the satisfaction the verdict excited among the extreme right, and the near-unanimous reproval it aroused in the other political parties, right and left. Many other recent deeds tend to confirm this resurgence of certain values from the past: the persistent demonstrations by admirers of Pétain, the continuing rise of the extreme right, the banalization of a xenophobic, racist discourse—as if the collapse of the communist utopia had to be accompanied by the rise of a conservative dystopia. But this doesn't seem to be the whole explanation. Nothing in the previous career of these judges allows us to see in the verdict any such simplistic political choice. And we must wonder whether, beyond the particular reasons that led to it, the verdict did not reveal a more massive social phenomenon, an historical evolution of far greater amplitude in which not just the decision, but also the reactions against it as well as to some other recent events, such as the agitation provoked by the fiftieth anniversary of the rounding up of Jews at the Vel d'Hiv, were all involved.

What all these events seem in fact to demonstrate is the importance for the French today, and perhaps for other Europeans as well, of establishing their collective memory. The debate about the nature of Vichy fifty years ago is one of the liveliest on the French intellectual and political scene these days; shouldn't we find that curious? But to speak of collective memory is also to speak of collective identity, and it is as if the French, without openly admitting it, are feeling threatened in their national identity, and seek to soothe themselves by attempting to reappropriate their memory. Of course it is hardly necessary to point out any more that, contrary to what a superficial interpretation of the prevailing tenets of individualism might suggest, most individuals need, even more than personal gratification, an acknowledgment of their very existence, which they acquire by feeling they belong to a national, religious, political, or racial community.

The source of these threats is obvious. Not only individuals, but also entire populations move about with greater ease than ever before, but the bell seems to have tolled for the nation-states of Europe. Certain state functions will be transferred to the European Community, others to the regions, and the former state will be no more than one authority among others. But "Europe" cannot arouse the same kind of identification as "France," and so "France" will remain. Like the other European nations of tomorrow, it will be more a cultural and less an administrative entity. Can such a thing be possible when no religious or secular dogma has emerged to relay the political entity? No one knows. Of course, the nation-state was not designed to be eternal, and in certain cases it is in fact a quite recent development. Still, this is change of some magnitude, and we shouldn't be surprised if it provokes tense identity crises. In this part of Europe, when the rest of the continent is boiling, we will have to learn all over again how to experience our collective belonging.

The Trial of Paul Touvier

Personalities

Trémolet de Villers Prefers Forgiveness to Remembrance: An Interview with Touvier's Lawyer

Redoubtable because of his skills as a lawyer and his ability to dominate courtroom hearings at the Assizes Court at Versailles, Jacques Trémolet de Villers can be credited with several notable accomplishments since he has assumed the defense of the former *milicien* Paul Touvier. Without qualms or reservations, he is now seeking Touvier's acquittal. Is the trial a political or a judicial battle? For Trémolet, it is both. The lawyer is the representative in the 1990s of an extreme right-wing Catholic tradition that spans the history of France in this century—a rightwing tradition that prefers not to characterize itself as "extreme" but wishes to be known instead as "counterrevolutionary." And this despite the continuity of this tradition before, during, and after World War II.

The son of a powerful political figure from Lozère—Trémolet's father was counselor general for and deputy of the Center National Party of Independents and Peasants (a party on the extreme right of the political spectrum)—Jacques Trémolet began his career in the law offices of Jean-Louis Tixier de Vignancour, under whom he worked from 1967 to 1974.

When one reads the homage to Tixier written by Trémolet in 1992, one understands the degree to which Tixier is today the role model for Touvier's lawyer. In discussing Tixier's defense of the OAS, Trémolet asserts: "The Military High Tribunal had been created to condemn

Salan and justify de Gaulle. Tixier transformed it into a veritable tribunal that would eventually excuse Salan and thus condemn de
Gaulle. . . . Fortunate is the lawyer who, by the persuasive power of his
arguments alone, halts the mechanisms of domination and forces those
who control them to admit their own defeat." On a subject more
closely related to the trial of Touvier, Trémolet writes that during the
Liberation, Tixier-Vignancour "gave himself completely to the cause of
the defense. The defense of collaborators and those being purged, officers in the German army and the Gestapo of Paris and Lyon. He did
it with talent, heart, and a knowledge of military customs which created an atmosphere of sympathy, not to say complicity, between himself and the military tribunal."

"I'm not a politician," Trémolet claims today, and adds, "I've done
a great deal of work on questions of general culture and fidelity to the
Catholic Church." This "nonmilitant" participated all the same in 1960
in a very political organization, the National Front for French Algeria,
whose members included, among others, Tixier and Jean-Marie Le
Pen. In 1966 Trémolet was already lobbying for the amnesty of imprisoned OAS members.

Jacques Trémolet de Villers has presided over a number of right-
wing integrist Catholic associations, which, in concert with the Association of Jurists for the Respect for Life, have attacked the right to abor-
tion. Above all, Trémolet has linked himself to the mysterious "Catholic City" (since renamed the International Office of Works, Civic
Education and Cultural Action According to Natural and Christian
Right), where, for a certain time a number of extreme right-wing movements coexisted, in particular, the Order of Knights of Notre Dame,
which protected and hid the *milicien* Touvier during his flight from the
law. The secretary of the Order, Jean-Pierre Lefebvre, a former member
of the Waffen SS, specialized in organizing and providing support for
former SS members in France and had a mass celebrated for Joseph
Darnand, founder of the Milice.

Until Touvier's arrest, Lefebvre had 3,000 francs a month sent to him
through the Conference of French Bishops. Lefebvre died several
weeks before the beginning of Touvier's trial. One can easily imagine
that it was on the advice of Lefebvre or of the Catholic City that Touvier, arrested by gendarmes in Nice on 24 May 1989 promptly chose
Trémolet as his lawyer.

"I arrived at my office the day after Touvier's arrest, and my associates told me: 'Touvier has been arrested. . . . Who is he?—He was the chief of the Milice in Lyons. . . . So?—He has named you as his lawyer.' I went to the hospital at Fresnes prison, I met Touvier, and we got along quite well. . . . I think Touvier knew of me through my writings for *Permanence,* a review distributed in the abbeys. Besides, issues of the review were found in Touvier's suitcases. But I could have been recommended to him by the monastic authorities themselves." Since Touvier's arrest, Trémolet has found a cause reminiscent of those of his mentor, Tixier.

Trémolet claims not to be rewriting history, despite his brief before the Chambre d'Accusation of the Paris Court of Appeals, a brief that constituted a lengthy defense of Vichy, Pétain, and Laval: "I am not competent to say if Pétain was right or wrong, but the charge against Touvier made the claim that Vichy was guilty of crimes against humanity, and I showed that the opposite was in fact the case. This could appear to be a justification of Vichy, but all I did was to restate what other historians like Jean-Pierre Azéma had said: Vichy was not responsible for crimes against humanity. Besides, no Frenchman was handed over for justice at Nuremberg. Vichy, after all, was my relatives, my close friends. I am pleased, therefore, that my country is not responsible for crimes against humanity." Trémolet's defense of Vichy goes beyond mere juridical debate, however, when he affirms: "Laval was goodness itself, a man of the Left who was neither anti-Semitic nor anti-Masonic."

When one contradicts Trémolet's claims by noting that, in the postwar trials, Vichy's role in the deportation of the Jews was secondary—the accused were judged for treason or "intelligence with the enemy"—the lawyer brushes the issue aside by asserting definitively: "Vichy did not participate in the Final Solution."

And what of the fact that in his own defense plea written before his death, René Bousquet, the former head of Vichy police, acknowledged having proposed that French policemen handle the massive roundup of Jews known as the Vel d'Hiv roundups? "Was Bousquet aware of the fate awaiting the Jews? Did he participate voluntarily? I believe that neither Laval nor Bousquet did this with a light heart. It is necessary not to forget the conditions of the war itself: one was wallowing in blood."

If he had had a choice, Trémolet would have preferred to see Bousquet tried—"more interesting than Touvier's case"—but, consistent with his struggles to have convicted OAS members amnestied, he believes there should not be any trial at all: "The Touvier trial is very bad for my country and for the Church as well. . . . I've received enormous numbers of letters which prove old hatreds are stirring on both sides. I have several children, and, in high school and in the universities they hear: 'Your father is a Nazi.' I'm a partisan of amnesty, of sweeping the past aside."

Inspired by counterrevolutionary thinkers who in turn inspired Action Française and the extreme right in the twentieth century—"The Catholic City *is* Joseph de Maistre and also Barrès and also Maurras," Trémolet explains—Trémolet's theocratic conception is founded on a Catholicism that rejects any notion of evolution. A conception where one prefers forgiveness to remembrance. "The remembrance of victims? Their memory is not sustained through trials. Masses are said for them, books are written about them. I am a Catholic. I am in favor of the cult of saints. The trials that please me are the trials for canonization."

Are the victims of Vichy to be canonized? "I'm not a defender of all causes. What concerns me is that this old man [Touvier] not finish his life in prison. Let forgiveness be more powerful than remembrance. Musset said, 'Two weeks have made this death old news.' Time heals all wounds."

Curiously, for this lawyer, justice is not fundamental: forgiveness will replace remembrance and a belief in truth. Dismissing the accumulation of testimony concerning Touvier's exactions, the lawyer prefers to believe that his client is "neither a hoodlum, nor a pimp, nor an assassin." Trémolet doesn't hesitate to make a hero out of Touvier, comparing him to Oskar Schindler, the German who saved 1,300 Jews during the war. . . .

Is this a sincere belief or the tactics of a crafty lawyer? "I follow the advice of my role model, Tixier-Vignancour. He used to say: 'Never listen to your client's confessions that don't concern the case. You will never know if he is lying, and he doesn't know himself. You have the dossier of the case and as for the rest, let him speak to his confessor about it. People lie to their confessors, so why shouldn't they lie to their lawyers?'"

The Young Son Replaces His Father

Serge Klarsfeld has turned over the suit of the Sons and Daughters of Deported French Jews to his son, Arno, the youngest lawyer for the plaintiffs. The following is a portrait of an agitator.

His name is Arno, like his grandfather, who sacrificed himself to save his family by opening the door to the Gestapo on the night of 30 September 1942 in Nice after hiding his wife and his children in a closet with a false bottom that he had carefully prepared. Arno Klarsfeld is the son of Serge, the little eight-year-old boy hidden in the closet, who would later become a lawyer and a historian in order to devote his life to the memory of the deported Jews of France.

Arno is also the son of Beate, a German woman known for her struggle against the impunity offered to Nazi war criminals. At twenty-seven young Klarsfeld is a militant agitator like his mother and claims this double, triple heritage. In 1987 he went to a meeting of the Front National at Bourget wearing a T-shirt with the message "Le Pen Nazi," and got himself soundly beaten up.

The following year he went to Vienna with Beate to protest against the meeting between Pope John Paul II and the Austrian president, Kurt Waldheim, and wound up in prison.

A lawyer like his father, he became a member of the Paris bar in 1989, then passed the bar examinations for both New York and California. He became a specialist in corporate law and author's rights and represented, among others, the producers of Robert Hossein's play, "Jesus Was His Name," which was canceled in New York after it caused protests.

In spite of his long black hair, his leather jacket, his cowboy boots, his fast delivery, and his provocative self-assurance—irritating to some—Klarsfeld is already launched on a brilliant international career, always between transatlantic flights with a suitcase ready in the middle of the law office he shares with his father. But in this year of 1994 his father has passed him the torch, giving him the responsibility of pleading in his place at the Touvier trial, representing their association, Sons and Daughters of Deported Jews of France. And today we saw the youngest lawyer for those accusing Touvier come forward and declare that in the Rillieux affair there had been no German order—a legal risk that would eliminate any charge of a crime against humanity in its strictest sense and taken after sleepless nights spent poring over the 30,000 pages of the file, all meticulously separated into colored folders.

Most important of all, he has the support of his father, Serge, who wants to see the Milice judged for its crimes without the alibi of the so-called "protective shield" used by the French collaborators. Being alone and in disagreement with his associates does not bother Arno Klarsfeld. "I've faced neo-Nazis, I can certainly face my friends who are bringing these charges against Touvier." In the Klarsfeld family, turning commando actions into history is a habit.

Libération
15 April 1994

———————

Proceedings

To Defend a *Milicien*, the Lawyer Trémolet
Puts the Liberation on Trial

———————

"I have the feeling that this is the trial of the Milice, which I'm not representing," declared Trémolet de Villers. "My client's name is Paul Touvier." The day before, responding to accusations of "cruelty" aimed at the Lyons Milice, Touvier's lawyer had unveiled a dangerous part of his argument. In a stern voice, he recalled a phrase of Maurice Schumann, which had been broadcast from London. "The Milice are murderers, kill them like dogs." Then, staring at the court, he repeated the warlike motto of the Resistance fighter Henry Fresnay: "Remember that murder is easier than reform."

And finally, from Resistance writings, he took this extreme injunction: "Our duty is clear, to kill."

The plaintiffs' lawyers were well aware of where the defense lawyer was leading them. Blood against blood. Terror against terror. This was the common defense of collaborators, the traditional answer to crimes they were accused of.

In conclusion, the defense lawyer reminded the court of Voiron, a town in the Isère region. In the spring of 1944 a group of young Resistance partisans decided to execute a local Milice chief. They entered his home and murdered everyone, the man, his wife, even the baby asleep in his cradle. The lawyer showed a photograph of the child. It was a clear signal. If the Milice was spoken of in general terms, the defense would bring up particulars about the Resistance. He had already violently criticized the Resistance law courts, and now, he condemned its attitudes and excesses, but never directly attacked it. Clever in his presentation, careful, flexible, and very agressive when he thought the situation demanded it, he nevertheless tried to be balanced.

When he was told that the "Milice wasn't very popular at that time," he mentioned, without being specific, the many letters he had received since the beginning of the trial without actually stating that they proved the opposite, but letting it be understood that they did. As if to prove that French divisions remained intact.

"What was a typical day in the Milice like?," asked Judge Boulard.

"We tracked down leads on anti-nationals," answered Touvier.

"For instance, what was the most serious crime, in your opinion?"

The accused man thought for a moment, "To hand out propaganda wasn't too serious. Those who did that were taught a little lesson and then released. I liberated them," he amended.

"And what about listening to London on the radio?"

Touvier shook his head. "No, no, everybody listened to the radio from London. It was their right. They didn't go to prison because they listened to that."

"Well, who then? Who were the enemies of the New Order?"

"Those who killed members of the Milice," answered Touvier.

"And what about the Jews?" asked the presiding judge.

Touvier shook his head again. "My organization never arrested people because they were Jewish. If they were questioned, it was for other reasons."

Did Touvier remember the name of a single Jew who had been interrogated by the Lyons Milice? He gave a negative response.

From the end of the war, in the different statements he prepared to back up his request for a pardon, Touvier drew a pleasing portrait of himself as a conciliatory member of the Milice. He continued to insist that he had released the forty-two people still held by the Milice several days before the liberation of Lyon. "Little by little," he declared, "I had them leave the prison." He warmed to his story and continued,

"I did my best to liberate the largest number." As proof of his good faith, he cited the case of Jean-Pierre Rosier, the son of an important jeweler in Lyon, who was questioned by the Milice and whom Touvier had released from the Collonge château where he was being held.

"On 30 June 1944 they brought this twenty-year-old boy in to me. I asked him if he had been involved in a crime, an operation, and he told me 'no.' So, I let him go." This was an extraordinary attitude for Touvier to take. Captured in March and brutally questioned, suspected of being a member of the Resistance, all it took for this young man to be liberated was to claim he was innocent. The chief prosecuting attorney frowned.

Touvier, going still further, courteously offered to drive him back home to Chambéry in his own car. "When we arrived at the jewelry store, I told his father he must not continue his Resistance activities. If he rejoined a Maquis group, it could cost him dearly."

And today, before the court, came this statement from Touvier, ordinary words of a petty criminal. "I didn't ask for any reward. You know, I was in a jewelry store, I could have helped myself. It would have been very easy. But I didn't do it."

Later, after the war, he asked the parents to sign a deposition certifying that the liberation of their son had been unconditional. Recalling this merciful gesture at the time he was preparing his statement in 1958, he wrote, "Do this as good propaganda." Chambéry was his hometown, the Allies were advancing in western France, and it was time to think of future friendships.

"In fact," testified another Resistance fighter Touvier claimed he liberated, "He played no part in my being freed. All I can say is that he wasn't too cruel to me."

And Touvier muttered, "Well, that's something."

When it was his turn, the chief prosecuting attorney rose. "I am unable to follow what the accused claims about liberating certain prisoners during August 1944. The only certain one is Jean-Pierre Rosier. As for the others, that's something no one understands. Touvier spoke of fifty-three prisoners he had liberated, then forty-two. He contradicts himself all the time. As for me, I have only two names of people still held at that time. Two and no more."

Fatigue stifled Touvier. When words failed him, he would become angry at being old and strike his thigh with his fist, letting out long sighs. "I freed forty-two and that's all there is to it." Then he fell silent. "I can't go on, can't do any more."

Lawyer Trémolet came to his aid. "My client wanted to maintain a policy of humanity and he is accused today of crimes against humanity." There were loud reactions from the plaintiffs. "Shout your ohs and your ahs, but make it louder," retorted the defense lawyer, "because what I have to say, I'll say it louder still!"

Touvier would never say, "the Milice members," only "the French," in opposition to "the Germans." The Germans? Nothing to do with it. Confined to another place, another space, almost another time. During this period, he said, he felt isolated.

"No friends or comrades?"

Touvier responded with a scornful gesture, "I never like little gangs." He described the arrival of patriots at the time of the Liberation as "the hoodlums entering Lyon."

"Would you still call them that?" asked the judge.

"Certainly," answered Touvier. "I saw them from my window. Young men waving guns around. It didn't look very serious."

The war was over, and "Chief Paul" fled. Yesterday afternoon, at the end of the session and again this afternoon, the debacle of his flight was described, little rooms in cheap hotels, rented country parish houses. This time Touvier spoke unreservedly, withholding nothing, not forgetting or hesitating. Everything came back to him. The night spent in a cemetery, the first priest whom he woke up and who opened the sacristry door to him. Nights on the road, signal posts he climbed to feel with his fingers in order to determine the right direction to take. "I read braille, Your Honor." The friends who refused to open their doors to him, the first soup eaten in hiding, a glass of good wine, the cool apples in the straw of a friend's cellar. And these men of the church, over and over, who took him at his word and opened their hearts to him.

Paul Touvier continued without anyone dreaming of interrupting. He spoke in the tremulous voice of a long-ago storyteller. He told of his fear, his thirst, his hunger. The portrait of "Chief Paul" as a lost soldier, tracked like an animal by the new France. The lawyer, Trémolet de Villers, savored every word. This was a victim speaking.

Libération
24 March 1994

My Colleague Told Me: You Must Choose Seven Jews

For the first time during the first week of the Touvier trial the audience in the Versailles courtroom let themselves go and applauded timidly. And like the lawyers, the jury members, and the journalists, the public was also working, taking notes, underlining, crossing out things on their small pads. There were sheets of paper on every knee and a pen in every hand for, in this courtroom, the spectators were seriously applying themselves to studying the proceedings. Here the public was not just listening, it was understanding, for beyond the legal procedure history itself was having its say. Then suddenly came a little burst of applause.

Robert Paxton was speaking, the third and last historian to be called to testify. The defense lawyer, Trémolet de Villers, listened attentively. Often, with raised eyebrows, he took note of a sentence.

"The Vichy Regime," declared Paxton, "was not a passive government, waiting for orders from the Germans. It was an ambitious program in two parts, interior and exterior. Inside France, it encouraged the National Revolution, which aimed at fundamentally changing French institutions and values by setting up a dictatorial regime. It also developed a policy aimed at homogenizing the country by excluding Jews, communists, 'terrorists,' and Masons and sought in this way to be allowed into the new Europe of the Nazi Reich."

Presiding Judge Boulard was also listening attentively, noting that the Milice could have been assimilated by the German police as a "supplementary" force and that the "maintenance of order" from 1943 on was the principal concern of the Vichy regime. When one of the lawyers for the plaintiffs asked if the members of the Milice and their officers and those who inspired them had joined in a "complicity in the Final Solution," Robert Paxton answered firmly, "There's no doubt about it."

Jakubowicz, speaking for the plaintiffs, carefully enumerated the activities a Jew could not fully engage in, the relaxation he could not enjoy, the places he could not go, the things he could not own. Forbidden were the metros, the cinemas, schools, public functions, the army, sports competitions, camping, and so on. The lawyer insisted that all the heartaches and humiliations be named and that the jury members and the court learn, or remember, that Jewish children could not play freely in the public squares with other children. That they were forbidden to get dirty in the same sandpile or laugh at the same puppets.

Trémolet de Villers, Paul Touvier's lawyer, rose, and with the expression of a man who had been patient too long, he said, "A historian is not a witness. A witness is someone who has seen directly and this is why he is able to testify. A historian speaks from hearsay, and this is not testifying but giving an opinion." There were stifled movements among the opposition lawyers, and Robert Paxton listened with seeming amusement.

"In your book on Vichy France," continued the defense lawyer, "They say your version of this period is 'revolutionary,' and, before you, other historians have had different ideas. Others who come after you will certainly have different ones still. Let's say that you have been one moment in the history of Vichy."

Listening to the lawyer, Hubert de Touzalin, the prosecuting attorney, wore the same mask of skepticism he had worn since the beginning of the trial.

"Is it from a historian's opinion that a judgment can be drawn? I don't believe so," continued Trémolet. "Our legal task is the opposite of a historian's." Then, turning to the court, he said, "Your job is not to know whether Mr. Paxton is right or not, but to know as exactly as possible what happened in the time between 2:30 on the afternoon of 28 June 1944 and 7:00 on the morning of 29 June."

Turning to the jury, he continued, "You are going to judge a man. If you make a wrong decision, this is not the same as with Mr. Paxton. Someone else will write another book to say he was wrong, but you will commit a legal error." And, as he sat back down, he concluded, "That is why on the side of the defense there are witnesses, not historians."

Zaoui, one of the opposing lawyers, was pale as he retorted, "What you just said is the very foundation of those theories that deny and revise history." This accusation had already been leveled at Trémolet on the first day of the trial, and the court had remained silent, but this time it reacted spontaneously. This was the moment the applause broke out and then quickly subsided.

When Paul Touvier began to speak he surprised everyone. It was almost as if he had been forgotten. Motionless, eyes sometimes open, sometimes half-closed, sitting with his hands clasped, he had almost disappeared from the horizon. Amid the psychiatrists, his besieged family, the historians, all the repressed anger from both sides, the former Lyons Milice chief was there as an onlooker at his own trial.

But this was now over, and it was time for the facts. Yesterday, today, tomorrow, even longer, several witnesses will talk about the death of seven Jewish hostages executed at Rillieux, near Lyons, as a reprisal for the execution by the Resistance of Philippe Henriot, the Vichy Minister of Information.

"The 28th of June 1944 was a Wednesday," began the presiding judge, Boulard.

"Really, I didn't know," countered Touvier. "Anyway, if you want to talk about that, we have to begin at the beginning."

"And what was the beginning?" asked the judge.

"London."

The judge leaned over and said, "I don't see London having any part in that."

"Oh, yes," insisted Touvier. "It was London that picked out Henriot to be assassinated." A murmur was heard in the courtroom.

Touvier spoke again. "My Colleague, André Reynaud, said to me, 'We have to choose seven Jews. There's no other way.' So there was much discussion about this, but there was no way of avoiding it. It had to be done." In a quavering voice, Touvier told of how, faced with this demand, de Bourmont himself, the regional chief of the Milice, broke down.

Judge Boulard made an impatient gesture and asked, "Who took care of what?"

"Reynaud looked after everything—the details, if I can put it that way. He chose the victims, prepared the men." Touvier stopped for a moment. "The Germans were demanding thirty. I did, after all, save twenty-three lives that day."

"Why?" interrupted the judge. "Did you already have thirty in mind?"

"No."

"Well? Who were the others? Give us the names of those you saved." Then his voice hardened. "You didn't save anyone."

At that moment Judge Boulard became a different person. He

adopted the tone of a judge faced with a petty criminal who annoyed him, one who would always claim the wallet he had stolen had been found in the gutter. Without any sympathy, he questioned a small-time crook, a liar. "In permitting this to take place, you joined in the effort to eliminate the Jews."

"Oh, no," answered Touvier, making a vague gesture of denial.

"Oh, yes," insisted the judge. He fidgeted in his chair and excitedly searched for words. "You could . . . I don't know exactly . . . not carry out the order and then disappear."

"That never entered my mind," answered Touvier.

"But why not? Why not? You who loved the white knight on the poster for the Order of the Legion (S.O.L), you could have intervened and taken their part, if you had been as upset as you claim."

"I don't know why."

"You don't know why," cried the judge. "You never know why. What a strange attitude."

The judge picked up a letter of one of the witnesses. "The Milice wanted to see who was Jewish. They had the men's flies opened and they examined the men for circumcisions with the barrel of their pistols."

The awful picture broke the silence. Touvier felt the effect and shook his head.

Libération
29 March 1994

Louis Goudard, the Troublesome Survivor

If the death of seven men points the finger of guilt at Paul Touvier, the life of one man condemns him even more.

The witness who came forward said he was saved by the former chief of the Milice, and this gesture of mercy is one of the elements constituting a crime against humanity. The very existence of Louis Goudard, seventy-four, attests to the reality of a crime committed "for racial or religious motives." Thrown into the same cell with seven Jewish prisoners, all the others were executed because they were Jewish and he was not.

Louis Goudard was arrested by the Lyons Milice on 21 June 1944, a week before the Rillieux massacre. He was the regional head of information of the FTP-MOI (Independent Partisans and Immigrant Laborers Association) and was known as "little Louis." He immediately became the target of what he modestly called a "ritual beating," before being thrown into a cell for the night. It had been a broom closet and was only 50 centimeters wide and 5 meters long and had been converted into a cell. The following morning, he was no longer alone in the cell.

"The door slammed and a young man was pushed into the room. I asked him what he had done. You know in prison you didn't get to know each other, you just asked why the other person was there. He was Jewish."

He was young, tall, with brown hair, and Goudard would never know his name. "One day when I came back from the questioning," said the witness, "he helped me to get up, to lean back against the wall, and he wiped my face." Twice during his testimony, Louis Goudard had asked that he be spared a recital of the torture he had suffered. "It's too painful for me," murmured the witness, "and since I'm not one of the plaintiffs, I thought this wouldn't be necessary." But today, Judge Boulard insisted.

"The first time I was interrogated without the 'machine.' Just blows everywhere. After that, there was the tub of water, the electric prods, and then more blows, the needles under the fingernails. But these details were not the main thing. The important thing was what went on in your head between the interrogations. You know, I learned several things. First, the idea one creates of physical suffering is worse than the suffering itself. And I learned that those who crack do it when they receive the first blows." The courtroom was very quiet as he spoke. "You had to hold on till the first blow, Your Honor. If you could stand that, you knew you wouldn't talk. That was the real fear, the real anguish, the real obsession, not to talk."

Judge Boulard turned toward the accused. "Well, what do you have to say to that?"

"Electric prods?" quavered Touvier. "There was no such thing."

"But this is the fourth witness who has talked about it," cut in the judge.

"There could be ten or twenty who say that, it would be the same," replied the former head of the Milice. "Ten lies don't make a truth."

Prisoners entered the narrow cell. "They came in and left, they stayed one night or two, then disappeared the next day." The young Jew was released. Others replaced him.

Then two patriots from the Maquis of Saône-et-Loire arrived. After they had been thrown in the cell they exploded with joy. "Good news, guys. Philippe Henriot has been executed."

"But for us," continued Goudard, "This was not good news. A few hours after getting the news, the first of seven Jews rounded up was thrown into the cell. They had been arrested at work or in a café or at home or in their shops according to lists drawn up by the Milice some time before. Reserve Jews, you could say." Or "free hostages," the terrible name used by another witness.

One by one they joined Goudard, who could not remember in what order they arrived—Zeizig, Benzimra, Glaeser, Prock, Krzykowski, Schlussemann, and the young Jew who had helped him and who had been released only to be recaptured later. It was around 8:30 P.M. when the last one entered.

"We weren't allowed any soup. Night began to fall. Each one was deep in his own thoughts, certain he would be killed. It was 10:00 P.M.," continued the witness. "The young Jew I had met the first time stood up and leaned against the door of the cell. And then, very softly, he began to sing, as if for himself." On the defense side of the courtroom all eyes were on their papers as they listened. Lawyer Trémolet's assistants abandoned the sympathetic smiles they often could not suppress as they listened to the witnesses for the prosecution. "He was singing," continued Louis Goudard, "it was a passage from *Tosca*, the song of the prisoner who would be executed the next day."

There were twelve of them in the closet. In the middle of the night, the door opened. Maurice Abelard, who wasn't Jewish, was taken from the cell. An hour later, the two Resistance fighters were separated from their comrades. Seven Jews and Goudard were left. "The cell window began to lighten. It was between 3:00 and 4:00 P.M. when the door opened again. I recognized Gonnet, the Milice member, with a list in his hand. He called the roll, one by one. All the prisoners had foreign sounding names. They were lined up against the wall opposite the cell. It was then that I myself was called, the last one on the list. And I recognized Touvier, coming from the stairway just as they pushed me against the wall. We exchanged a look. Touvier had been to see Gonnet, and they talked a moment in low voices. Then Gonnet walked up to me and put his hand on my shoulder and took me back into the cell. Then day began to break and I realized I was alone." The next day, as they were distributing the soup, two detainees brushed against him and whispered, "The Jews that were with you were executed back of the cemetery in Rillieux." The witness leaned toward the court. "I realized then that I had not been one of the group because I wasn't Jewish."

After these words, the court became silent in respect for the dead. Leave quagmire and confusion to the defense. Let Touvier deny once again, with a shake of his head, hear him repeat, "There was never a hunt for Jews." But here was proof that this simply was not true, and the plaintiff's lawyers were quick to pounce on it. Once again, in a disorderly procedure, they clouded the pure crystal of the testimony with other dramas that this one had evoked, mentioning the martyred children of Izieux, deported by Barbie, or the victims of Sarajevo. They tried for too many exclamation points, tried to dramatize, wanted the affair heavily underscored, but much more serious, they drew Louis Goudard into the argument of German responsibilities. Yes? No? Who gave the order for Rillieux? The Milice? The Gestapo? Was it an inspired act? Was it collaboration or initiative? What did he think about this? In this way they transformed the implacable witness of facts into an improbable historian and thus allowed the lawyer, Trémolet, to cast doubt on everything that had been said in the courtroom. And perhaps even Goudard's resistance, his escape, his torture.

"The counsel for the defense is trying to have us believe that the witness was a traitor," cried an angry prosecution lawyer.

"Oh, you are very intelligent!" Trémolet allowed himself to retort with the satisfied smile of a man who comes out on top.

Libération
7 April 1994

"Monsieur Berthet": In Hiding among the Clergy

Paris, Brignais, Montpellier, no matter where, no matter how, Paul Touvier circled and recircled in his flight from the authorities. To escape the Resistance, many French collaborators had fled to Germany, but not Touvier. He remained in France and managed a chaotic interior exile. He assumed a secret identity as Pierre Gaillard, then Monsieur Truchet or Monsieur Paul, before adopting the name Berthet, that of his future companion. Little by little, Touvier disappeared into the unsettled conditions following the war. One day he would be a caretaker for an estate in the Somme, the next a grower of green beans for a welcoming priest. He would sometimes remain in one place three hours, and in another for two weeks. He returned to Paris around 1946, where, he explained, "Several men condemned to death would meet with each other."

A picture of the accused as an ordinary crook began to emerge.

"Once you tried to break into a bakery, didn't you?" asked Judge Boulard.

"No, not break in," answered Touvier, "just to get some bread tickets. To live on."

"And this idea that you really wanted to rob the store. . . . Was it a real holdup?"

Touvier appeared shocked. "No, of course not. A priest told me it was all right to take money from the government," he said in a soft voice.

"A priest told you that?" asked the astonished judge.

"Yes, a priest," insisted Touvier.

"But, you were stealing. You couldn't call it anything else." insisted the judge.

"They were only loans."

The presiding judge shrugged his shoulders. "What you're saying is just what I hear in common law trials."

Touvier and his counterfeit money, his special chisel for opening chests, his fake stamp from city hall, his fake papers. "But never a gun," he insisted loudly, "Not during the war or after." One day he stole a car but botched the job. A man followed him and fired, and Touvier was wounded in the arm. On 3 July 1947 someone reported him, and he was arrested and sent to the headquarters of the information bureau where an inspector threatened him.

"We're going to take you back to Lyons, and you'll be executed inside of three months." While he was waiting, someone asked him how he had managed to survive until then. Who had put him up, hidden him, helped and comforted him. Touvier gave the name of the priests who had opened their doors to him and the addresses of the secret presbyteries. He sold out those who were being tracked down all over France, as he was. He betrayed fellow members of the Milice, then a separatist from Brittainy, a woman who had engaged in the black market, several editors who continued to print the writings of collaborationists. He turned in those who had helped him to stay alive.

"The accused was an informer," shouted the attorney Nordmann angrily, "A stool pigeon." Touvier also gave the name of a Milice member who was said to have accompanied the Gestapo to Caluire to arrest Jean Moulin.

On 9 July, around noon, after another interrogation, the police left the room, and a secretary approached Touvier, who was alone.

"She said to me, 'Now's the time. I'll open the door for you.' So I escaped. I went down the stairs of those three stories like a sled, on the bannister, like you do when you're in high school." At the bottom of the stairs he stopped and caught his breath, smoothed his navy blue jacket, and walked past the control post, saluting the workers there. Then he walked past the sentry box and saluted the policeman. "After that, I started running and threw myself under a hedge like a dog who has run too long. And then I lost myself in the big city again."

The presiding judge was skeptical. "You made a deal with the police?"

"Certainly not."

"Still, it's a very unusual escape."

In a low voice Touvier responded, "That's what I've always been told. But, no. There was never a deal."

Paul "Berthet" drifted on. Monique, who had given him her name and looked after him after the failed attempt at car theft, never left him after this.

"Sometimes we walked around in Paris in the evening. And, after several outings, she became my fiancée."

Soon after his escape, Touvier contacted the priests, knocking at presbyteries and parish houses. And the doors continued to open for him.

"Did you explain the reasons for your being in hiding to these priests?" asked the Judge.

"Certainly. They welcomed me in full knowledge of the facts."

"And they shared your ideas?"

Touvier nodded his head. "More or less."

One of them actually felt so strongly about the "Touvier affair" that it became a personal battle. Monsignor Duquaire was a former private secretary to Cardinal Gerlier, the archbishop of Lyons, and would soon become secretary to Jean Villot, the number two at the Vatican.

With Duquaire's help, Touvier regained confidence and began working on his appeal for "pardon and amnesty." He met with people, officials, priests, former members of the Resistance. Responses on letterhead stationery piled up, postmarks followed each other, signatures were added to signatures. He kept and filed all the documents. He continued to plead not guilty, and to all the men and all the women he contacted, he recited his creed. He had not killed, had not plundered, hadn't denounced anyone. He was a member of the Milice because of circumstances, and he had spent more time liberating the poor prisoners than questioning them. In his own way, he was almost a resistance fighter.

With a policeman's soul, he was a fanatic about records and intelligence, about cross checking and information. In this way he became an expert in public relations. He made people feel sorry for him, and he compromised everything he came near. Even the great Jacques Brel, whom he met after a concert and whom he followed and never left. He was at every recital, every hotel on the tours. Touvier moaned to Brel, repeated his story, implored, and Brel gave in to this man so unjustly pursued. This "Berthet," this "Monsieur Paul," "so obsequious and clinging, always ready to do favors to the point of taking us over completely," Brel's wife would tell the inquirers when the truth had become known.

During a concert at Saint-Etienne, Touvier even occupied the loge of the police chief. Among the singer's entourage, he was called "The eye of Moscow."

"Oh, that's very funny," Touvier commented.

Brel paid him to search for a piece of property in the Chartreuse and then to oversee workers there. And he allowed Touvier to use the song "Voir" for a Philips record Touvier was editing explaining sex to children. Even better, according to defense lawyer Trémolet de Villers, it was for Touvier only that the singer wrote, "To see a ruffian and try to love him. . . . See the eternal enemy and try to forget."

Anne-Marie Dupuy, Pompidou's cabinet chief, begged the president to pardon the former member of the Milice. Touvier now had two children, and it was for them, she explained to today's court, that she had accepted this task. "Alas," she admitted, "I was a very good advocate for him." According to her testimony, Monsignor Duquaire, whom she said she'd only met once, subjected her to a veritable siege. She herself was the mother of three children. So, there you were. An ecclesiastic, a woman. "He played on my emotions. I spoke to President Pompidou about it, and I think that Pompidou himself decided on the basis of the children."

In November 1971 Paul Touvier was officially pardoned by the president of the French Republic. Touvier's two death sentences had already lapsed, all that was left to do was mark through the accompanying condemnations. Banishment was withdrawn as well as the confiscation of his property. He remained deprived of his civil rights for life, that was all.

Touvier emerged a free man and became "Touvier called Berthet." But not for long. The press got hold of the affair, and the scandal broke. The Milice member, Touvier, had been pardoned! He went into hiding again with his family because he feared both reprisals and the judiciary, which would soon be working on the idea of a "crime against humanity." His hideout at Chambéry was attacked, ransacked, and burned. Touvier went back to the priests, and a false notice of his death was published to put pursuers off the track. The black and brown network was reactivated.

The defense lawyer, Trémolet, rose again and shouted, "What are you doing there? Ten, fifteen, twenty trials for Touvier. A botched holdup? Car theft? Bread coupons? The execution? Go on, admit it! All you have here is an old man who isn't able to respond to your harassing, and you take advantage of him. And remember the former collaborators Touvier went around with after the war. They went to prison. That's over. Now, they're free men." He took on a look of exaggerated surprise. "Touvier met with Xavier Vallat? [Ed. note: first commissioner for Jewish affairs] Incredible! I'm going to confide in you. I saw him, too. At my home, invited there by my father. And I'm not a criminal against humanity." The lawyer bullied and threatened. "Watch out for this kind of terrorizing, saying that one doesn't have the right to meet others because fifty years ago they had a certain way of seeing things."

In his box Touvier did not react. A psychiatrist rose to confirm that his engagement in the Milice was the "ordinary rise of an unimportant man." He also said that there was a strange painting on one wall of his cell, of seven death heads.

Libération,
25 March 1994

Rillieux Was Carried Out on Orders from the Germans

The contradictory arguments are over, and Paul Touvier will speak no more. Or perhaps only at the very end, just before the court retires to deliberate. This entire week will be given over to those who have brought the civil suits, twenty-eight lawyers in five days in court sessions. Some will represent the remaining descendants of those murdered at Rillieux, Suzanne Prock, Gérard Benzimra, Georges and Henri Glaeser, René Zeizig. Others will present the case for the approximately twenty organizations and sometimes for five of them at a time.

During the Klaus Barbie trial in Lyons in 1987, the large number of witnesses for the civil suits had the effect of considerably lessening the horror of the raw accounts. The children of Izieux and the clanking of the iron train cars dissolved little by little in the fog of words. In confronting the solitary defense lawyer, Jacques Vergès, one began to wonder if it wouldn't have been better to have called only a handful of victims to contradict him, uniting in one accusation all the actors from the past. But this was not the case, and even today at the trial court at Yvelines, because of the endless hours of testimony, the danger remains of seeing the slow and painful erosion of undiluted emotion.

The lawyer Joë Nordmann came forward to the lectern that had replaced the railing in front of the witness box, and as the senior magistrate he opened the week of hearings at Versailles. An eighty-four-year-old Alsacian, he had gone underground as a Resistance fighter during the war and had been excluded from the Paris bar because he was Jewish. During the Occupation he organized the National Judicial Front, the only Resistance organization in a group generally favorable to the Vichy regime, and became editor of *le Palais libre*, a quietly circulated small newspaper. At the time of the Liberation, Joë Nordmann was named director of the Office of the Secretary General in the Justice Department and became a member of the Commission to Purge the Magistrature.

Later in Paris in 1949 he defended the communist newspaper *Les Lettres Françaises* against the Soviet dissident Kravchenko, who in 1946 had authored a book *I Chose Liberty* (*J'ai choisi la Liberté*) denouncing the prison camps in the USSR. Kravchenko was accused by the newspaper of being an agent for the West and responded by bringing libel charges against it. Kravchenko won narrowly.

Lawyer Nordmann surfaced again at the side of the North Vietnamese soldiers, and again with the Algerian patriots. He was the lawyer for Jacques Duclos, former director of the French Communist Party (PCF). He was an adviser to the Albanian government and was the lawyer who in November of 1973 filed the first complaint against Touvier, two years after he had been pardoned. Nordmann filed the charges on behalf of Georges Glaeser, son of Léo, one of the seven shot at Rillieux.

As a Jew, a communist, a Resistance fighter, an activist in carrying out the Purge, Joë Nordmann is the perfect symbol of all that the accused had fought against. Even more striking was the fact that, for the first time in this trial, a lawyer for those accusing Touvier clearly showed in his arguments that Touvier was a symbol not only of the Milice but also of the Nazis. "After fifty years in hiding, Touvier's attitude and the sealed documents both show that he continues to adhere to Nazi ideology," declared Nordmann. Surprised by the violence of the accusation, the defense lawyer, Trémolet, made a note of it. "The accused claims he never read *Mein Kampf*," continued Nordmann, "but there is little difference between it and what he has written, himself.

Hitler declared, 'The Jew is a harmful germ,' and Touvier says, 'The Jew is garbage, filth.'"

Since the beginning of the trial, the important question has been who gave the order. Who caused Rillieux to happen? Was it a German action or an initiative coming from the Milice? This is a fundamental distinction because, to be a crime against humanity, the execution must have been carried out in connection with or at the order of a European Axis country, Germany in this case. For quite some time the civil parties have maintained that the Milice acted independently, thus transforming Rillieux into a war crime. But today, although there is real division among the lawyers, a majority accept the claim of a German order. Nordmann declared, "We thought the Germans were indifferent about Philippe Henriot's death, but we were wrong. This trial has told us things we didn't know, that Hitler had personally declared that Philippe Henriot must be avenged. He himself had Georges Mandel turned over to the Milice, and the former minister was executed on orders from the Germans."

And in case the defense refuted the fact that it was a German order? Lawyer Nordmann made an orderly retreat. It didn't matter. "Touvier's boss was Darnand, and Darnand wore the uniform of the SS and had sworn loyalty to Hitler. The Milice identified themselves with the Nazis and Touvier acted on their behalf." The lawyer's arguments were like a tiny spiderweb. He admitted it was a German order, but if someone claimed the opposite, he would insist that such an order did not need to be given because, by their very essence, Touvier and the Milice were French Nazis, accomplices of the SS, already declared a criminal organization at Nuremberg. Therefore, however things appeared on the surface, Joë Nordmann was sure that "Rillieux was committed on behalf of the Germans and by their order." "Hitler," he continued, "had trained the French to be Nazis."

The argument of the old lawyer was essentially defensive, and he insisted on a lengthy preview of points which would be brought up by the defense. "So, he saved some Jews, and that makes him not guilty? He had some men killed to save others. This unworthy argument won't hold. It is a lie. If he wanted to save Jews, he would have neither arrested nor liberated them. This is a fraud, a false syllogism."

Speaking of the defense lawyer Trémolet, studiously occupied in taking notes, Nordmann continued, "Perhaps they are also going to say to you, 'Seven Jews only? And that's a crime against humanity?' " And he quoted both the Chief Prosecutor Truche and the Free French spokesman Maurice Schumann: "It isn't the number which constitutes a crime against humanity, but the complete perversion of a system whose object is to punish by death the crime of being born."

Georges Glaeser had said, "I'm not asking for revenge, I'm asking for justice," and his lawyer reminded the court of this. "Will this man be condemned in principle only? Because he is old? And leave here free once again? Freed from the court that revealed the gravity of his crimes? His age deserves indulgence and pity? What kind of pity? This man's face reflects his past. His features retrace his life, an existence of misdeeds and lies." Touvier listened with lowered eyes and clenched jaw. "Won't the old be among the damned on judgment day?" demanded Joë Nordmann, who is five years older than the accused, standing very straight, and looking at the jury. "I solemnly ask you here to return a verdict which fits this crime."

Ugo Ianucci, former president of the Lyon bar, echoed Nordmann when he said, "Just like Barbie, he is an old man being tried because he has always tried to escape justice." Ianucci is the son of Italian anti-fascists whose brother-in-law was killed at Vercors the same day as the massacre at Rillieux.

"Like Barbie," said Ianucci, "he was a member of a political police force and, as such, did not have to answer to any other organization. Like Barbie, he wanted to make us believe that he knew nothing of what went on. That it was all fiction, a joke, a fantasy. These two men denied everything and renounced nothing."

Libération
12 April 1994

It Was an Ideological, Premeditated, and Diabolical Crime

Monsieur Trémolet de Villers, Paul Touvier's lawyer, clearly showed his opinion of the arguments of the prosecution. A barometer in a black robe, he delighted in registering the importance, or lack thereof, of the claims being made by the opposition. Several times on Tuesday he made a show of yawning and finding the proceedings very tedious. Yesterday, on the other hand, he was back at his post, the alert sentinel.

Opposite him, Monsieur Philippe Bataille, lawyer for LICRA (International League Against Racism and Anti-Semitism), in carefully chosen words, painted a shockingly sad picture of the French defeat in 1940, of the exodus, of a country under the heel of the conqueror:

> Our civilization was made to seem almost pathological. Maurras welcomed the enemy as a "divine surprise," Touvier was relieved and heartened, Marianne became a trollop, a whore. The word *Republic* was repealed. Democracy disappeared and liberty along with it. Instinct and force replaced intelligence, exclusion replaced fraternity. We gave up civilization to enter a barbaric and despicable world.

While the prosecution spoke, Monsieur Trémolet took notes and remained unsmiling. "The Milice," continued the lawyer, "constitutes the embryo of a single-mindedness that is at the origin of all totalitarian states."

This was a crime against humanity and a trial of inhumanity. "The crime is an ideological one. This is its very essence. It is a diabolical crime because through one individual the criminal aims at a collective victim. There will never be just seven victims at Rillieux. These have rejoined the millions of others murdered because they were born Jewish, exterminated because they were gypsies."

The lawyer stared at the accused, but Touvier would look at no one. Since the beginning of the session, he had been turning his chair a little more toward the court so that he seemed to almost turn his back on the questioning voices.

Monsieur Bataille reminded the jurors of the victims, naming them one by one, inviting them to enter the courtroom. He spoke of the way they looked when they were still alive, then when they were dead, of their hopes just before the execution. "What were they thinking of as they faced the guns? Their wives? Their children? Their God? Their land, their country? Did they realize that, never again . . . ?" And turning to Touvier, "And you, have you come to terms with the souls of these dead people?" Touvier showed no reaction.

"I find the accused morally lacking in his calculated amnesia, his endless evasions," declare the lawyer. Turning to Trémolet he said, "But what can the defense plead in favor of Touvier? Nothing. Not the beginning of the first word of the first letter of a plea." Monsier Trémolet showed his irritation. "You are going to rehabilitate what we all hate?" cried Bataille, no longer hiding his anger. Shaking his head and tightening his lips in disgust, he pointed to the box. "The despicableness is here on this side, the civilized nation on the other, and the verdict will be the voice of this nation."

Next it was the turn of the lawyer, Zelmati, also speaking for LICRA. As he began, it was clear that there was a kind of dialogue among the lawyers. The first argued the legal background, the second would argue the case itself. Without being dramatic and in simple language and style, the lawyer managed to clarify the affair, forgetting his lawyer's robe.

In great detail he created a convincing indictment, carefully underlining all the elements of the charges against Touvier—the orders given, the orders received, the involvement of Touvier, the premeditation.

Then the lawyer Patrick Quentin rose, a last spokesman for LICRA. He spoke of the number 76303 that was inscribed into the arm of his mother-in-law, deported in March of 1944, obliged to undress the children as they departed to their deaths. "Much later, when her daughter was born and for a whole year thereafter," said the lawyer, "she could not make herself take the baby in her arms." He spoke, too, of his wife who, at their first meeting, told him she was Jewish, as though she still feared being one and admitting it. He spoke, as Monsier Bataille did, of his Jewish colleagues who are today on the bench in Versailles. Fifty years ago none of them would have been allowed to enter the door of a justice building. They would have been dead, or disappeared, beyond the reach of humanity.

"This trial is like that war, one of light against darkness," he said. And turning toward Touvier: "You have no connection with other men because you are the shame of humanity."

Then Léo Glaeser, one of the seven from Rillieux, was remembered by the lawyer Marina Cousté. When he fell before the bullets of the

Milice he had a paper folded in his wallet. This was Léo Glaeser, a brilliant lawyer who spoke six languages, an untiring champion of Jewish unity, an unarmed *résistant* fighting for the rights of all men. On this folded paper was a phrase from the German poet Heinrich Heine: "A truly brave man has no illusions about the consequences of his acts. He expects the worst."

Libération
14 April 1944

The Prosecuting Attorney Demands a Life Sentence

When he rose, Hubert de Touzalin paused and gazed at Paul Touvier. Touvier never took his eyes off the magistrate, who in four hours and fifteen minutes would demand the heaviest possible sentence for him, life imprisonment. Standing erect, the magistrate, hands clasped in front, wearing the same skeptical frown he'd worn throughout the trial, waited for the chamber to become silent.

Hubert de Touzalin is a fifty-nine-year old magistrate and a former army officer who served as a volunteer in Algeria. There, he was wounded in battle and decorated by his division. He served in the army for ten years and ended his career attached to the military courts before joining the civil judiciary. This has not prevented him from remaining a soldier at heart, and his argument was organized like a battle plan.

"I'll tell you my state of mind as I address you. I do this without personal ambition, without being overly eloquent, with no wish to compete with the historians, without wanting to preach to you. I do it with a desire to uncover the truth, deliberately, guided only by a desire for justice. Only that." Hubert de Touzalin opened his folders and the smaller ones inside, all of them on recycled paper. On one side were his notes, on the other, printed outlines the work of an economical soldier.

What was being judged here? "Paul Touvier," responded the magistrate. "The only question you will have to answer is about his guilt and if it is in the affirmative, what sentence he should receive." In a few phrases he dismissed the argument of the length of time since the crime, saying, "Time no longer stops when it is a question of uncovering acts committed against humanity." He pronounced himself "astonished" at the little time the prisoner had spent in prison. "Two years, one month, seventeen days." Later, he recalled the difficulties in putting together this case. "Ten judgments from the appellate court, seven from the criminal division of the high court, four examining magistrates."

All of this for whom? Touvier, the local man who simply carried out orders? No. "This was no ordinary subordinate who took orders directly from the military staff of the Milice in Vichy. You have been told that he had immediate and independent power and authority. That is true." Today, we would say that he was a decision maker. At twenty-nine? "Let me tell you," continued the magistrate, "that it is possible to assume this role at that age. He was judged to be good at recruiting, good at gathering information, good at commanding." When he described the organization of the Milice or that of the German police in France, Hubert de Touzalin was still a military man. As if it were a terrorist network of cells of a rebel army, he carefully took apart this "organized hell," insisting that there could be no worse danger in the army "than that of putting in Touvier's hands the secret information and the task of acting on it." He also revealed the relations between the German SS and its French regional colleagues, ranging from Paris to Lyons, and revealed that Barbie and Touvier had talked to each other. He spoke of the Milice chief's meetings with the German chiefs of police, and insisted that the Lyons Milice had certainly collaborated with the SS.

The magistrate had warned that there would be no unnecessary eloquence in his speech and the promise was kept. He became a sort of Topaze, Pagnol's grammar school teacher, going back over every important sentence, underlining each key word, even spelling it out. Hubert de Touzalin went on to speak of the reprisals demanded by the Germans after the death of Philippe Henriot. Yes, the Nazis had "considered his death unacceptable," and yes, they had felt "that it was necessary to respond with reprisals from the French themselves."

Well then, *did* Touvier and his men obey German orders? There were two answers, the first one from the magistrate. "No, there had not been a German order in a military or hierarchical sense." One after the other he carefully used the words "request," "willingness," "wish," "demand." Now, the soldier spoke: "And even if there had been an order, which I do not believe, it would not have lessened the responsibility for such an act since it would have come from an illegitimate 'authority.'"

But did Touvier know of a concerted German plan aimed at exterminating the Jews, and did he subscribe to it? The magistrate did not equivocate. Yes, and yes again. "I am convinced that Touvier knew of this anti-Jewish policy." He claimed it was very unlikely that the chief of the Milice investigations in Lyon could have been ignorant of its existence. "The crime of which Touvier is accused fits perfectly into this plan," continued the magistrate, returning once more to the grounds that constitute a crime against humanity. "The plan was a Nazi one, the active cooperation was French."

Yes, there had been premeditation. Yes, the seven Jews had been rounded up with the sole purpose of killing them. And yes, once again the German police chiefs were the "promoters, the instigators, the initial decision makers." As for the Rillieux assassinations, yes, Touvier was the immediate instigator of the killings. Yes, the members of the Milice, who acted under his orders, were the "murderers."

"The maximum punishment is called for here," murmured the magistrate. "Someone could say to me that the man is old and that to demand a long sentence for him, fifty years after the actual deed, would constitute a lack of humanity." He looked at Touvier and the defendant stared back. "The memory of the innocent victims seems to me even now to demand a very harsh verdict." The defense lawyer, Trémolet de Villers, carefully took down these last words, "This verdict must also be a verdict of principle, for justice, in order to be equitable and credible. It must be permanent and of the severity that suits it." Then, eyeing Paul Touvier, who remained as motionless as ever in his glass cage, the soldier in the red robe spoke to the aging member of the Milice. He used a simple language, reminding him of a commitment to Point 21 of the vow he took at Vichy in 1943, "Against the forgetting of crimes, and for the punishment of the guilty." Surely, he had no good reason to be protected from that vow, now. Touvier did not react but sat perfectly still. He blinked his eyes nervously, a little more rapidly than before.

Libération
19 April 1994

H E N R Y   R O U S S O

T Z V E T A N   T O D O R O V

Reflections

Klaus Barbie and Paul Touvier

Henry Rousso

"Klaus Barbie was to the SS what Paul Touvier was to Vichy and the Milice." This is a refrain heard since Monday from the lawyers bringing the charges of crimes against humanity against Paul Touvier. The comparison seems to be a good one on the surface. Klaus Barbie, chief of Section IV of the Sipo-SD in Lyon, was assigned to investigate and track down Resistance members and to organize the Final Solution against the Jews. Paul Touvier, regional chief of the second service of the Milice in Lyon, also gathered information on members of the Resistance and tracked them down. Hunting down Jews was also one of his specialities. The two men, undoubtedly in contact with each other, shared a common ideology. They had both done everything possible to escape the law, and both will remain symbolic as the only two men ever brought to trial for crimes against humanity in France. Finally, their crimes were committed in two places only a few dozen kilometers apart, located at the time in the same department of the Ain—Izieu and Rillieux.

But the similarity stops there. Barbie was at the administrative hub of a formidable service that had partly dismantled the Resistance organization by eliminating its leader, Jean Moulin. Touvier was never as effective as Barbie. And this was actually one of the surprising revelations of this trial. Looking over the mass of documents and all of the accounts of witnesses, it appears that the Milice's service of the Rhône did not have a decisive impact. Made up of marginally criminal elements more interested in pillaging the apartments of Jews than in exhaustively tracking down victims (a speciality of the Sipo-SD), Touvier's organization was like the entire Milice, a supplementary police force, a stand-in for the occupier from whom it got everything—arms, instructions, and protection. Bousquet's anti-Jewish policy and that of the regular police of Vichy, between 1942 and 1943, was even more murderous, given the number of Jews rounded up and deported.

Barbie was condemned in 1987 for having deported forty-four Jewish children hiding at Izieu. He had come looking for them in their hiding place in order to send them to camps to be executed. He rounded up *all* of the Jews he was able to capture that day, and, in doing so, he was carrying out a policy of systematic extermination, a policy created at the highest level of the Reich command.

In the Rillieux affair Touvier arrested only men, leaving out women and children. He did it as a direct punishment of the Resistance attack on Henriot. He even went so far as to tell a young Jew who was arrested soon after the departure of the seven men for the place of execution, that he "was lucky he had arrived fifteen minutes late." Touvier did not obey a government directive since it was known that Laval expressed his disapproval to Darnand regarding this kind of Milice reprisal, which always had a devastating effect on public opinion. Was he obeying a German command? Probably not.

At any rate, while the children from Izieu had been driven to Auschwitz in a secret convoy, the usual way for deportations carried out under the authority of the Final Solution, the seven victims of Rillieux were murdered and left where they fell, as an example to terrorize the population. They were chosen—Touvier spoke of a *triage*—because they were Jews and for that reason only. It was actually less risky in the last days of June 1944 to go after the innocent than the organized Resistance, which was capable of fighting back. But these executions were not exactly a part of the Final Solution. To say so would deny their singular character and would risk making them seem ordinary. And here is the underlying purpose of the new and unusual charge of "crimes against humanity." The singularity of genocide lies not only in the crime of killing humans just because they were born but also in the "industrial" methods used in their murders and in its systematic character. In principle *no* Jew was to escape the fanaticism of the Nazis. Rillieux was a crime committed in the *context* of a mass persecution. A context that gave to a Touvier, encouraged by the presence of a Barbie, the power of life and death over his fellow men.

Libération
13 April 1994

Collaborators, Those "Patriotic Traitors"

Henry Rousso

For the first time in this trial, although he said very little, Touvier revealed a great deal. He spoke in his own words, words from yesterday, eroded by time and denial and amnesia. In them one can spot the standard defense of those purged at the time of the Liberation but also reactions of the present day. The old theme was heard again, "I was a patriot."

When Pétain shook hands with Hitler at Montoire on 24 October 1940 and when Laval declared he "hoped for a German victory" on 22 June 1942, Touvier pretended he was "shocked." There can only be a feeling of total disbelief at such statements, but it does offer the occasion—one speaks of the "trial of pedagogy"—to be reminded that the most extreme of the collaborators were not simple traitors working for the enemy for mercenary reasons. One English historian has even described these men as "patriotic traitors." The phrase may be shocking, but it reveals some of the truth. World War II was not a simple war between rival nations, it was total ideological warfare. Those who were engaged on the side of the Third Reich fought because they were defending a certain idea of the world and of France. It was even one of the necessary keys to understanding how extreme nationalists could rally to the ancient enemy. It was not the Kaiser's Germany that they supported, but the Führer's, and they dreamed of a "national and socialist" regime in a France integrated into a future Nazi "Europe." They therefore dismissed the legal decisions following the war, which had condemned them for "complicity with the enemy," on the pretext that it was a "conqueror's justice."

And this was what the accused, in his inadequate words, was still trying to explain faced with generations for whom such a version was absolutely indefensible. From then on, one realized that he remained almost mute even to the point of denying his connection with the SS at a time, 1944, when the Milice was their main ally in France. And although his chief, Darnand, took full responsibility for his actions before the High Court, Touvier seemed incapable of getting free of the historical contradiction of the collaborators, which was that a handful of right-wing fanatics agreed to share, in all circumstances, the destiny of the Reich that had conquered and enslaved their country. On the other hand, Touvier must face a reality that was not so important by the end of the Occupation and must answer questions not often raised then. And here, a certain amnesia and seeming incomprehension arose at this trial. Touvier seemed not to understand why the presiding judge and the jury members returned over and over to the question of anti-Semitism. "I was not an anti-Semite," he insisted. On the subject of the anti-Jewish policy of Vichy and the fanatical anti-Semitism of his own organization, he declared, "That was not my concern," or "I didn't know about it."

Revolting? Of course. But this reaction is explained also by the fact that the collaborationists, except for a small group among the minority, who were obsessed by the "Jewish question," reasoned according to a set of representations that lumped together as the implacable enemy the Jew, the Mason, the *métèque* [the foreigner] and the communist, to which was added the entire Resistance movement. Altogether, they represented the "four confederated states" of Maurras, with the minor change that communists had replaced the Protestants in this truism of counterrevolutionary thought that had so impregnated Touvier's family culture.

Here, in Touvier, can be found that gulf that separates him from his accusers, a figure from the past, his resentment intact, and a world in which the values had been turned upside down by genocide. For the accused still belongs, and no doubt will belong forever, to another world.

"You don't understand," he said to one of the plaintiffs' lawyers, "You mix everything together." Had Touvier himself really understood?

Libération
22 March 1994

The Stakes in the Summer of 1944

Henry Rousso

In the Rillieux affair, did Touvier and the Milice act under German pressure or on orders from their own chief? Was it a crime against humanity or not? This question, which was at the heart of the trial, had only a limited importance from the historical standpoint. Rillieux, as seen through the prism of the law, was not enough to explain the relationships between the occupier, the Laval government, and the Milice in June and July of 1944. Actually, these relationships were influenced by three factors: the military situation, the routing of Vichy, and the rivalries between the leaders of the collaborationists.

The Normandy front was the chief preoccupation of the Germans. Since 6 June the fate of the Reich was being decided in France. On 25 June the Allies were in Cherbourg and had begun the encirclement that would end in a decisive breakthrough. Three days earlier, the Soviets had launched a devastating offensive in Byelorussia, and the Reich was being squeezed from both sides. In this context, the German reprisals were aimed at discouraging the population from supporting the

Maquis, and this was as much a statistical tactic as an ideological one. At the same time, the convoys continued to leave for the concentration camps.

Vichy was also in a precarious situation. On 2 June in Algiers de Gaulle formed the provisional government of the French Republic. Therefore, a clear alternative policy to the Pétain regime now existed, and it was the reason for Laval's hesitation between showing firmness toward Resistance fighters and refusing to engage in random reprisals that offended public opinion. He even tried at this time to make secret contact with the Allies. Disturbed by this, the occupiers began to make use of the declared enemies of Laval—the collaborationists Déat and Doriot—in order to maintain pressure on him. In this ridiculous game, the Milice members of the government, Henriot and Darnand, more or less supported Laval. The Milice hid behind Pétain, hoping to be an official force in "maintaining order," without being allied with the occupier as were the parties of Déat and Doriot. Even if all of this was a game, the situation nevertheless led to infighting in the Milice, evident in the carrying out of reprisals.

On 20 June Milice members assassinated Jean Zay, a former minister in the Popular Front who was of Jewish origin. The green light had come from Milice headquarters in Vichy, and the Germans had nothing to do with the affair. Laval made his disapproval known. This murder, not uncovered until later, was typical of internal political revenge, considering that Zay had been a target of French fascists for a long time.

On 28 June Resistance fighters shot down Philippe Henriot, and, in the hours that followed, the Milice went after the Gaullists, the communists, and even more, the Jews, just as they were to do at Rillieux. The murderous insanity was such that prefects alerted Laval, who warned Darnand to be on his guard. Darnand halfheartedly tried to quiet his men. At this point there seemed to be no question of a German intervention.

Several days later, on 7 July Georges Mandel, another important member of the Third Republic and a fierce opponent of Pétain, who was also a Jew, was assassinated by the Milice. In this case, the Germans were directly responsible. They organized the operation in a way that would "spatter" Vichy and the collaborators even more. Laval tried in vain to avoid the trap, and once more Darnand and his reserves were ineffectual.

These events demonstrated that, if the Milice was indeed a Nazi supplementary force, it also took care of some quarrels of its own. In any case, these actions were in accord with the policy of the occupiers. The disagreements at the summit meeting in the summer of 1944 were more over methods than objectives—and less over ideology. The reservations of a Laval had no effect, and the Milice was never *publicly* repudiated by Vichy. It is this fact that must be translated into judicial terms.

Libération
7 April 1994

Reconciliation and Rehabilitation

Henry Rousso

The Thursday court session [7 April] was the last given over to the testimony of witnesses for the defense. The lawyer, Jean-Baptiste Biaggi, seventy-six years old, is a former Resistance fighter. He was a member of the Rassemblement du Peuple Français of General de Gaulle, which was organized in 1947. After campaigning for "the return to power of the man of June 18" (de Gaulle), he broke with him during the Algerian war and rejoined the far-right leader, Tixier-Vignancour. He was part of the fringe group of Resistance fighters who worked for a "reconciliation between de Gaulle's supporters and those of Pétain," an active minority within the RPF.

Then it was the turn of a former member of the Milice: He came to speak to the court of "reconciliation." In 1944, when he was seventeen, he followed Darnand to Germany but, without becoming the least bit flustered, he explained that he had come to the court "to present the pardon of the Milice" to the Resistance fighters! And he added, "In the name of the Milice, I ask for pardon. I speak in the name of Paul Touvier." During the loud laughter that followed—and that included the judges—the chief magistrate turned toward the accused and asked him if he shared this point of view. Unruffled, Touvier replied, "I have nothing to say."

When the court had finally calmed down, a young woman historian born in 1957, whose family had often visited with the Touviers, took the stand. With all the authority of her *agrégation* in history, she calmly explained that all the horrors of the last war were equal, the Rillieux massacre, the one carried out by the Russians against Polish officers at Katyn, or even the "clouds of bombs dropped on Normandy." Unconnected to one another, these witnesses caused either laughter or indignation. But, in spite of the differences, they clarified a pivotal point in Touvier's defense—pardon and "reconciliation."

The arguments of 1994 could have been mistaken for those used by the backers of amnesty in the 1950s. The latter were recruited largely from the ranks of the RPF and the Christian Democrats of the MRP, two parties that had come out of the Resistance movement. They wanted to make up for the "injustices of the Purge" and put an end to the internal division present at the time reconciliation with Germany got under way. They cited the historical necessity of turning over a new leaf, which followed a long tradition observed since the days of the Revolution and up to the time of the Commune. This national debate, which had lasted six years, was inevitable. It should have been carried out with dignity, but instead it was marred by violent political confrontations.

Breaking with the nearly moribund solidarity of the Resistance, the amnesty supporters tried at first to counter the left and communists. In the context of the Cold War, amnesty was the necessary condition for a rebirth of the conservative right wing that had been considered to be dead at last. Discredited following Vichy, the political right had been deprived of a number of its leaders at the time of the Purge, and the debate offered a nostalgic extreme right the chance to lift its head once more and openly express a desire for revenge.

Fifty years later this same argument surfaces again and often comes from the mouths of young people born long after the war. There is the same questioning of the Purge, the same attempt to forget all the adversaries of the time, and it has brought about a return of a "Gaullist Pétainism" that is completely out of date. It is easy to see here the same request for pardon that in fact hides, as it did before, a desire for complete rehabilitation. If Touvier is today sitting in the courtroom as the accused, it is certainly because of his own endless efforts to obtain a pardon that would have afforded him not only material advantages but also a form of personal revenge. However, there are two essential differences in his case that keep the "reconciliation" theme from being effective. Amnesty was given after the war to those who were judged and condemned or who had, later, turned themselves in. A pardon, by definition, is applicable only if guilt is admitted and a pardon is asked for. At the court session on Friday Georges Glaeser, son of one of the victims, exclaimed: "I find it immoral to give a pardon to someone who doesn't ask for it."

Libération
10 April 1994

What Historians Will Retain from the Last Trial of the Purge

Henry Rousso

Did the historian learn anything from the Touvier trial? Factually, very little. However, the scholarly inquiries into the activities of the French Milice are few, and one would hope that such an assembling of witnesses and documents might add to what we now know about it.

The first surprise was the fact that very few documents were uncovered that came directly from the Milice or from the Sipo-SD that were contemporaneous with the deeds themselves. Most of the items in the case came from postwar trials, from later witnesses, or from the statements of the accused. The trial, when it wasn't confusing the issues, only confirmed what was already known.

On the other hand, less was known about the three-year investigation into the links between Touvier and the Catholic Church carried out by the Rémond Commission from June 1989 to January 1992, which furnished a description of the mental world of a collaborator. But this supplementary information told us more about the contemporary church and about certain dysfunctions of our republican government than about the Occupation itself.

The trial, however, thanks to the witnesses, provides an inexhaustible source for reflection on the respective roles of the judiciary and the historian in the establishment of truth. This is true less because of the actual material than because testimony in a courtroom differs greatly from a historical account, which must always depend on written records. In a criminal court, the spoken debate counts more than the written evidence, the jury decides after hearing oral arguments. Here in the courtroom, we are far from the discussions where "famous specialists" gather to give a sometimes laudatory discourse delivered with all the polite deference of the academic. Here the witness is most often unable to lie without being caught. This was made even more evident because most of the important witnesses had testified several times in the past, an unusual circumstance. They first testified at the time of the Purge, either at their own trial (the Milice member Edmond Fayolle or the secretary, Gilberte Duc), or in the first hearings on Touvier (the Resistance members Henri Jeanblanc, Maurice Abelard, Louis Goudard). Many were asked to appear several more times between 1950 and 1960 by Monsignor Duquaire, Touvier's protector, who needed recommendations. Later came the investigation by the commissioner Delarue in 1970. Then, in 1989–92 came the careful trial preparations of Judge Getti. The witnesses were called yet again by the Rémond Commission. Finally, the courts themselves demanded their appearance. Therefore, for a number of these witnesses, it was the occasion to deliver their final version of the facts. Added to this were countless declarations to journalists, writers, historians, and filmmakers who had been following the affair for twenty years.

The often subtle variations of these statements were not the least attraction of this trial. Sometimes they were favorable to the escaped member of the Milice, sometimes they snared him once and for all in the legal net. It was not that the witnesses lied, but certainly some "adapted" their story to the circumstances, forgetting that the Court had access to all of their previous testimony. An example of this was the testimony of Jean-Luc Feuz, Touvier's chauffeur, who tried to explain to the Court at Versailles that he had attempted a "double game" between the Milice and the Resistance. Or the testimony of Father Ducret, Touvier's director of conscience from 1953 to 1978, who had reviewed his own previous positions: "If I were asked to repeat my recommendation for a pardon, I would not do it," he said later.

The stories of victims or of their sons were less compelling than at

Barbie's trial, and the most "interesting" witness was Touvier himself. This was not the case with his counterpart, because Barbie was absent from his own trial. An entire book could not do justice to all the versions of the facts presented by Touvier. The stress of the Court sessions and no doubt his age and his fatigue had caused the mask of wax to melt. The truth came almost by accident from the old man's mouth, when he said, "It was horrible for us to think that it would be the Germans who avenged Henriot" (session of 30 March). It was therefore a question of a Franco-French revenge, after all. And later he testified, "I was not asked to choose" (April 6), which meant that Touvier himself decided to select seven Jewish victims and to exclude non-Jews such as the FTP Goudard, who was the eighth man, saved on the evening of 28 June 1944. "But he wasn't Jewish!" exclaimed Touvier. These spontaneous truths have no doubt weighed more heavily in the debates than the muddled accusations of the lawyers bringing charges.

The Court's key to Touvier's personality was the discovery of the famous "green notebook," in which Touvier between 1985 and 1988 expressed all his private hatreds. Here again, the methods were not those of the historian. No researcher worthy of the name, discovering such a document, would have used it during the lifetime of that person. Certain lawyers have exploited this miserable text in a disgusting way, and others have had the decency to abstain. To violate publicly the conscience of an individual, no matter how black it is, would not be within the scope of a crime against humanity. But such is the harsh law of the courts, as the lawyer Henri Leclerc reminded us. The telling effect was less in the display of Touvier's undying hatred (that was expected) than in the immediate and dramatic proof of the enormous lies he put forth throughout the court sessions: "I have never been an anti-Semite!" To which the presiding Judge Boulard, always the pedagogue in matters of procedure, never tired of repeating, "Only the accused has the right to lie."

The Versailles trial presented another peculiarity, the contortions of certain lawyers and witnesses due to last-minute changes in the definition of a crime against humanity. Up until the time of the ruling of 27 November 1992, which struck down the "revisionist" dismissal of the case on 13 April 1992, it was not necessary to be a direct accomplice of the Germans to have committed such a crime. Since then, it has become an indispensable condition. Jacques Delarue allowed himself to be caught in the trap, surprised by the unorthodox arguments of Arno Klarsfeld, which ran counter to those of the other lawyers for the prosecution. The commissioner-historian illustrated in spite of himself the variations of the historical interpretation. The same documents could end up with diametrically opposite conclusions. "There exists no trace of a German intervention in this affair," was a statement from his report of 1970 reiterated to Judge Getti in 1990. At the hearing of 1 April this same man "believed" now that there had been German intervention. The effect was even more appalling because two days before, in order to counteract the depositions against the accused by the historians René Rémond, Francois Bédarida, Michel Chanal, and Robert Paxton, the defense lawyer, Trémolet de Villers, proclaimed, "History is only an opinion." In his plea, he had no trouble showing that this is sometimes the case. It is a danger incurred by any scholarly assertion when it is thus used in the service of a cause, no matter how noble. In this respect, the Touvier trial should be an important historical lesson, but this sometimes gets lost in all the small details of the evidence or the legal definitions, obscuring the whole picture first presented by the academics.

Finally, two other testimonies in this case brought no reaction from the prosecution lawyers but delighted Lawyer Trémolet. In his book *Nous entrerons dans la carrière: De la Résistance à l'exercice du pouvoir* appropriately published when the trial was in full swing, Olivier Wieviorka interviewed François Mitterrand. The president informed him of his reservations about this trial, which was so late in coming, and his desire to forget the terrible internal division of the Occupation. At least the chief of state can be credited with a certain consistency in the matter. The statement brought outraged responses and a few lyrical flights of oratory from the civil complainants. However, none of these complainants had noted that two witnesses quoted by them had also been asked by Olivier Wieviorka about the opportunity for such a late judgment of former collaborators. These were the Resistance fighters Jacques Chaban-Delmas and Pierre Messmer. Chaban-Delmas was in poor health and could not make the trial, but he wrote a letter to the court, and it was read on 17 March. In it he reaffirmed his unfailing loyalty to the duty of remembering. "In the eyes of the French (. . .) events must not be forgotten with the excuse that so much time has passed." But to the historian Wieviorka he declared in 1990–91, "After decades have passed, I believe not only that men do not remain the same but I also cannot see what purpose these trials serve. I do not see what good it does. Some say, 'To recall these horrible things, well, why not?' but where does the truth lie? How can we untangle it after such a long time? I think we must let the dead bury the dead."

Chaban-Delmas, in answer to a question, admitted that he agreed with Pompidou's pardon of November 1971 when he was still the prime minister. He was later replaced by Pierre Messmer in July 1972 in the middle of the Touvier affair. Messmer, minister of the armed forces in 1963, refused to reopen the Touvier case. But he, too, at the court session of 5 April 1994 proclaimed his refusal to forget. "Men of my generation already have trouble in forgetting the crimes of the war and, therefore, crimes against humanity." Questioned by Olivier Wieviorka in 1990, he had declared, "These pursuits are without doubt legally sound since they are continuous, but they are a mistake. When one sees what is becoming of Germany, I think the moment has come to draw the curtain of forgetfulness on individual acts committed between 1940 and 1945." The same words had been used by Pompidou to justify the pardon that unleashed the whole affair.

Finally, the historian must surely remain perplexed by the waste of energy involved in trying to force open doors that were already open. Yes, the Milice was the accomplice of the Nazis. This is in all the history books. Yes, historical truth and the testimony of witnesses are fragile things, and they vary according to the times and the circumstances. This fact, too, is in all the philosophy textbooks. But the historian is not an enthusiastic public for this spectacle. Moreover, there is a certain hypocrisy in asking if this trial should or should not have taken place. Doubts and reservations could certainly be expressed, the disappointments of the trial made only a little less. But from the moment the trial began, the law had to decide, if only to avoid having the Leguay case scandal happen all over again—ten years of being indicted without a decision of dismissal or postponement—a scandal repeated in the Papon case.

In thinking about the delays one wonders whether this trial has met its "pedagogical" goal. Has it allowed the young to get to know this period a little better? It is easy to be skeptical, but only the outcome can provide an answer. In any case, there is the risk of regression. For twenty years historiography has not ceased to insist on the specificity of Vichy and particularly French anti-Semitism as compared to that of the Nazi occupier. It was even one of the major causes for the convulsive movements of the collective memory since the 1970s. A new generation was ready to break with the idea of Vichy being a small parenthesis in the history of France and the collaborators only "a handful of traitors," (de Gaulle). A desire to dissect the inner workings of Vichy and its own particular anti-Semitism was one of the real motives that had allowed, in spite of the lapse of time and numerous obstacles, the completion of a body of evidence for crimes against humanity that set in motion all that was to follow.

But because Leguay and Bousquet are dead, because Papon is still awaiting judgment, because the Supreme Court wanted to avoid asking the question of whether or not a French nation could exercise "a policy of ideological hegemony" and commit or be an accomplice to a crime against humanity, the Touvier trial was only the trial of a "collaborator." The preoccupation of the lawyers with the arguments of the existence or nonexistence of a German order in the Rillieux affair, which at times became almost ludicrous, was simply an attempt to translate into legal terms the historical fact of the partial autonomy of Vichy and the Milice and the effects of this fact.

Locked into the necessity for a direct cooperation with "a member of the European Axis," this trial, in a certain sense, found itself once more following the arguments of the Liberation and trying a crime of collaboration. But no longer was it collaboration with the *enemy*—Article 75 could no longer be applied because of prescription—but collaboration with a government that had conceived of "a concerted plan" for the extermination of Jews, an imprescriptible charge. But this proved unsatisfactory, to say the least. The lawyer Arno Klarsfeld and his dissenting defense, "Touvier acted alone," was right to plead the truth of historical fact and memory against a law whose measurements were as variable as they were skimpy.

Perhaps the real lesson of this trial lies elsewhere. The Court proceedings in Versailles were partially open. The vague concept of a crime against humanity and the difficulty of allowing into our judicial tradition the idea of imprescribtibility were frequently discussed. These discussions about a concrete case, with the fate of one man hanging in the balance, will no doubt clarify the thinking, if not the law, about these issues since the new penal code went into effect on

1 March 1994. Moreover, the Touvier defense was able to express itself a little more freely.

But the defense argued more in a legal sense than in a political one. We expected an attempt to rehabilitate Vichy, but this was only developed incidentally. We expected a trial of the Purge, which, as it turns out, was relatively understated. Rillieux? "A war crime in response to another war crime" (the death of Philippe Henriot). This was the defense strategy, but how could we believe, today, that seven Jews were dead on 28 June 1944 just because there was a war on when at the same time several million died because they were Jews? The defense lawyer, Trémolet, no doubt against his will and in spite of his talent and his undeniable conviction, drew back from a defense that was too political in a trial that was also a political trial. The possibility of a debate and the reaffirmation of our fundamental democratic values were the least one could expect from the last trial of the Purge.

Libération
20 April 1994

The Touvier Trial

Tzvetan Todorov

Certain aspects of the trial of Paul Touvier did no more than repeat the lessons one could draw from previous trials of former Nazis or from the histories devoted to those times. The sinister role played by the Milice, the French political police force created in 1943 that rapidly became the local equivalent of the SS, was confirmed and demonstrated. The overall attitude of the defendant called to mind strategies used on earlier occasions: he didn't know; he hadn't heard of the wretched racial statutes concerning the Jews established by Vichy; he was only obeying orders, and he himself hadn't killed anyone: "I wasn't the one who decided, and I didn't proceed to any execution." His regrets had pity go no further than to himself, not to his former victims.

But other aspects of the trial are more singular and deserve closer scrutiny. Touvier was prosecuted for a single crime. On 28 June 1944 Philippe Henriot, Vichy minister of Information and an active Milice member, is assassinated by the French Resistance. Reprisals are rapidly organized. In Lyons Touvier sets to work finding victims. In the Milice cell block under his orders, there are prisoners; he takes two of them, Jews, and proceeds with the arrest of other Jews of whom he finds five more. At dawn on 29 June all seven are shot in Rillieux, near Lyons.

Touvier never denied his participation in the crime; in fact, he was the first one to reveal it. But during the many years preceding his arrest, he always denied responsibility. If we are to believe him, Touvier only obeyed the orders of the local Gestapo chief, who decided on the reprisals; he himself had no choice. To look at the facts in this light, in his thinking, should exonerate him, or at least suggest extenuating circumstances for his actions. However, since the redefinition by the Cour de Cassation of crimes against humanity, his strategy had become catastrophic. Touvier admitted having obeyed the Nazis, which was precisely the condition needed to convict him. The prosecution stormed through the breach: whereas the entire investigation of the case had sought to show that Touvier had acted alone, the prosecution did a complete about-face and took Touvier at his word. Now he was accused of what he had seen as an excuse, the execution of German orders. Had he indeed acted alone, he could not have been accused of a crime against humanity! But now it was too late to turn back: Touvier could no longer deny something he had claimed so tenaciously for forty years.

Touvier's defense then focused on another argument. If we are to believe this claim, the head of the Gestapo had asked the head of the Lyons Milice for one hundred hostages. The latter had succeeded in having the number reduced and had asked Touvier for "only" thirty hostages. In his turn Touvier supposedly then proposed to turn over a first batch of "only" seven hostages; there would be no second batch. Instead of being blamed for the death of those seven, Touvier should be praised for having saved from certain death twenty-three Jews who were never executed; they should practically give him a medal for his courageous act.

It is easy to see not only that this argument is completely lacking in judicial value but that there is also something obscene about it. Those twenty-three Jews had never been in Touvier's hands for him to protect or liberate. And the seven who were murdered were real people, not virtual victims. By this measure, any assassin could claim to be a bene-factor of humanity for having spared millions, even billions of people from death!

But if we accept Touvier's argument for a moment, we discover that, far from justifying the *milicien*'s behavior, it only condemns him more overwhelmingly. His general defense, like that of many other Nazi criminals, consists of stating that he acted under the pressure of events, that he had no choice. We are usually suspicious of such claims, but we don't necessarily have the proof that these and similar affirmations are false. But in this case, Touvier himself furnished the proof: even if there were such orders from the Gestapo, it was possible to negotiate without incurring their wrath. Again, to believe him, the number of hostages dropped from one hundred to seven in a few hours. More-over, Touvier claims that "by the next day, it was no longer required." War was raging in France in the last days of June of 1944; each day brought new events. One day Henriot's death was impressive, but by the next it had slipped into the background. It would have been enough for Touvier to negotiate a bit more effectively, to delay the exe-cution for forty-eight hours, for the tortured victims of Rillieux to be kept alive. So, if what Touvier says is true, it proves his responsibility and thus his guilt.

If what Touvier says is true . . . but is it? It is in the interest of the prosecution, as we have seen, to believe him, for only in this way can the act qualify as a crime against humanity. But because it is useful to construe things in this way, does that make them true? On this point lawyers for the civil parties are divided. On one side, all but one of them maintain the convenient thesis of the prosecution. On the other, a single lawyer claims that Touvier is lying. The lone dissident is Arno Klarsfeld, son of Serge and Beate Klarsfeld, the celebrated Nazi hunt-ers. His declaration explodes like a bomb: if Arno Klarsfeld is right that Touvier made his own decision to act, Touvier is perhaps more odious, but he cannot be convicted of crimes against humanity.

The young lawyer's arguments are specific. In the first place Henri-ot's assassination offended the Milice infinitely more than the Ger-mans, who at that point had many far more urgent concerns than that of avenging a member of the French Milice, even one of the most prominent. Such a reaction, although improbable, is not impossible of course; on other occasions the Gestapo did in fact intervene in this way. But in the Henriot affair, all over France it was the Milice that took charge of the reprisals. Furthermore, a detailed report exists concerning the activities of the Lyons Gestapo chief on 28 June 1944; there is no mention in it of a demand to shoot one hundred hostages. Finally, during a trial in 1946, a Milice accomplice declared: *"we* seized the property of Jews, *we* carried out the execution"; he makes no mention of orders coming from somewhere else.

Is Touvier innocent for all that, even in view of the strange French statute? The lawyer pleads against such an interpretation, for if the Milice decided on the reprisals on its own (and Touvier was among those responsible for the Lyons branch) it was nonetheless in the service of the Gestapo. If we were to put aside the way the law is formulated (something Arno Klarsfeld couldn't permit himself to do before the court), we could say that the Milice, although French, was in effect a Nazi organization, acting in the service of an anti-Semitic ideology; in that capacity, it was guilty of crimes against humanity. The Milice didn't just serve the Nazis of Germany; it *was* Nazi.

Other aspects of the trial brought forth by witnesses or recalled by the prosecution shored up Arno Klarsfeld's hypothesis. One involves a contemporary episode. In Macon, not far from Lyons, another Milice chief named Clavier decided to take revenge for Henriot. On the afternoon of 28 June he arrested seven hostages suspected of Resistance sympathies and had them shot immediately. This gesture provoked general indignation. The prefect informed Laval, who complained to Darnand, the national chief of the Milice. He had Clavier imprisoned— by Touvier, in Lyons. Touvier thus knew that his own superiors were against reprisal, but he also knew that a "colleague" had avenged Henriot by executing seven hostages. It seems likely that this was the moment when he made his final decision: he too would have seven killed, but to "cover" himself, he would claim that the Germans gave an order about which nothing could be done. The invented "German order" was to protect him from his own superiors; only much later, after the war, was it to be used again, in order to excuse his deeds. Having repeated his alibi so often, Touvier, as happens, probably came to believe it himself.

Another indirect indication of what really occurred can be found in several things Touvier did around the same time. After the raid on Jews who would be executed had already begun, Touvier went to a Jesuit priest to ask for advice. The priest recommended that he go underground, which struck Touvier as unrealistic. But if he hadn't made the decision himself, if he were only executing a Gestapo order, would he have experienced the situation as problematic, would he have sought such counsel? At dawn on 29 June, just after the seven hostages were executed, Touvier sped to Vichy where he obtained the release from prison of a young resister whose family he knew. The next day, he went to the prison himself to get him and bring him home to his parents. Doesn't this act unmistakably resemble an attempt to redeem himself, which would once again be meaningless if Touvier had felt himself in no way responsible for what had just happened in Rillieux?

These coincidences are in no way proof, but they strengthen the hypothesis that Touvier himself was responsible for the decision. A detail must be added. If he did not spare the lives of twenty-three Jews, as he claims, he did indeed save one person from death at the moment of the execution. But far from exonerating him, this gesture, on the contrary, transforms the reprisals from a war crime subject to the statute of limitations to a crime against humanity, for which there is no such limitation: the man was not a Jew. At first, in fact, eight men were taken away, but as Touvier passed them in the staircase, he recognized one of them as an active resistor. He had him sent back to his cell. Only the Jews were subjected to reprisal. By behaving in this way, paradoxically, Touvier condemns himself.

Lessons

The Touvier trial is over, but what purpose did it serve? and what purpose is served today by trials for crimes against humanity like those of Touvier and Barbie?

Such questions have an immediate, positive answer. The trials allow for the application of the law, the dispensation of justice, and the punishment of the guilty. Barbie was found guilty of the deportation to Auschwitz of forty-four Jewish children who had been in hiding in

Izieux, Touvier of the execution of seven Jewish hostages in Rillieux. Such criminal acts are outside any statute of limitations. It is right and just that, even fifty years later, the authors of such infamous acts should be punished.

But the public attention surrounding the trials shows that, more still than the sole application of the law, what was expected of the trials was a lesson for public opinion, an example involving Law itself, or Morality, Memory, or History. And from this point of view, the results are less satisfying.

Can we say that these trials demonstrate and glorify the idea of a serene and impartial Law? Only with difficulty. First, because both depend on the strange definition of crimes against humanity fashioned by the Cour de Cassation, according to which the same acts are crimes if they are committed by Germans or anyone in their service, but cease to be so if their authors are French, acting for the sake of the French state or French institutions. And doesn't this negate one of the fundamental principles of modern jurisprudence, the equality of all before the law? Touvier's lawyer did not hesitate to remind the hearing that the massacre of fourteen thousand Polish officers at Katyn was a crime against humanity as long as it was believed to be Hitler's doing, and it ceased being one when it was learned that Stalin was responsible. Such a transformation of the verdict stains the law itself or, worse, mocks it. And, one wonders, why should we be reminded of this fact by Touvier's lawyer, who was certainly not behaving as an ardent defender of republican tradition, when what is involved is indeed one of the great republican principles, that of equality before the law?

The about-face of the prosecution in the midst of the proceedings gives the same impression that legal principles are something malleable. The entire investigation of the case tended to prove that Touvier had acted on his own. Suddenly, thanks to the judgment rendered by the Paris court, the realization occurs that formulating matters this way will not permit a guilty verdict. So, with the same conviction, the opposite claim is made: Touvier acted under orders from the Germans, and for their benefit. Some commentators criticize the notion of a crime against humanity on the grounds that it had no legal standing when the actions occurred. But they are wrong, since the great humanitarian principles underscore every code of law, and the idea of a crime against humanity only causes what was formerly implicit to appear clearly.

On the other hand, it is harder to accept that such an idea could be redefined so drastically from one year to the next, and that something that was a crime—the brutality of the Milice in its own name—ceases to be one; or that something that wasn't a crime—Gestapo persecution of the resistance—suddenly is. Are we not just adapting the law to meet the political objective of the moment, instead of allowing it to judge individual cases according to unchanging criteria?

Finally, during the trials it was often said that it wasn't just Barbie on trial, but the Gestapo; not just Touvier, but the entire Milice. And people hope for indictment of the collaborationist administration of Vichy via the trial of Maurice Papon, a former high official, who is also accused of crimes against humanity. But is it legitimate to judge and condemn an individual as an example, so as to pillory the criminal organization to which he belonged? Should we hold Barbie responsible for the existence of Auschwitz? Individuals must be judged for what they do, not for what they are or represent. This is another principle of law we have no cause to surrender.

True, moral judgment has no place in the halls of justice. Yet it can take shape on the occasion of trials such as these, in the margins of the debate. But no such things occurred during the Touvier trial. Still, a question like the following could have been asked: given that the French resistance and the London government in exile knew well the horrible practice of reprisal both the German occupiers and the Milice had put into practice, and given that the battle under way on 28 June 1944 was already essentially decided in favor of the Allies, was Philippe Henriot's assassination really necessary? To ask such a question in no way implies the lessening of Touvier's guilt, however much he might like to think so. The two acts—Henriot's assassination and the Rillieux executions—are quite distinct from one another: the latter is not the automatic consequence of the former. This should nevertheless not stop us from questioning their moral significance—fifty years later.

People also claim that such trials serve the ends of memory, that they teach the younger generations what has happened so that it will not be repeated. But some authoritative voices, like Simone Weil, who was herself at Bergen-Belsen, or Georges Kiejman, whose father was killed at Auschwitz, have been heard to wonder—rightly so to my mind—if the staging of such trials was absolutely necessary to keep memory alive. Beyond the danger, once again, of practicing justice as an example, for the teaching that might result, there are many other avenues for the preservation of memory: in official commemorations, in scholarly teaching, in the media, in written histories. The 1944 Allied landings have just been abundantly celebrated and are etched in everyone's memory. Did we need trials besides to remember better?

And furthermore, it is not at all certain that such trials really serve memory well, that they provide a precise and subtle image of the past. The floor of the court may not be the ideal space for establishing the truth of History. The results of the Barbie trial were, in this context, less than conclusive. By accepting to prosecute Barbie for his actions against the Resistance, not only was the law twisted in its ability to distinguish between war crimes and crimes against humanity, but remembrance was done a disservice as well: it's a fact that Barbie tortured Resistance fighters, but they did the same when they got their hands on a Gestapo officer. The French army, moreover, systematically resorted to torture after 1944, in Algeria for example; no one has ever been condemned for crimes against humanity as a result. Besides, by reserving the first trial for crimes against humanity to a German police official, the implication of the French in Nazi policies was rendered less rather than more visible when, as many witnesses testify, the Milice was often worse than the Germans. And finally, the historical meaning of these acts was not illuminated by the presence of witnesses like Marie-Claude Vaillant-Couturier, who had been deported to Auschwitz, but had also subsequently brought notoriety upon herself by her rejection of the revelations about the Goulag in the David Rousset trial of 1949.[1]

The Touvier trial did not lend itself to the same blurring of distinctions: Touvier was French, and he was prosecuted exclusively for something that was indeed a crime against humanity. The role of the Milice was recalled, but without any new revelations: in that context, the entire trial remained in fact at a level well beneath what can already be learned from specialist studies. And the presence of Counselor Nordmann among the lawyers in the civil case was troubling. As the pre-eminent lawyer of the French Communist Party for many years, this jurist had made himself famous for a particularly aggressive performance in the Kravchenko and Rousset trials in 1948 and 1949, when he was involved in the denial of the existence of Soviet labor camps. Can concentration camps be condemned in one case, when they have elsewhere been defended? It is true that at the Nuremberg trials Stalin's representatives participated in judging Hitler's collaborators, when in fact they were guilty of equally atrocious crimes.

Thus, if "memory" was not in fact mistreated during the trial, it was not particularly well served either. But then maybe the trial was the occasion for "satisfying the new cult of remembrance," in the words of the journalist who covered it for *Le Monde,* for proclaiming loud and clear that "memory has imprescriptible rights," that there is a "moral duty" to remember, that people should be "militants for memory." One may wonder: has it been established and accepted by one and all that memory is only and always a good thing?

Without entering deeply into so vast a question, we should remember that memory is never the integral reconstitution of the past, but always no more than a choice, a construct; and that such mental operations are not predetermined by the subject matter recurring to memory, but very much by agents who remember, with a particular goal in view. And if reconstruction of the past in itself is not a bad thing, certain uses of memory are more noble than others. Memory can serve repetition or transformation, it can have a conservative or liberating function, and these are not the same thing. Everyone has the right to remember as he or she sees fit, or course, but a community will place a high value on some uses of memory even as it condemns others; it cannot practice an undifferentiated cult of remembrance.

The same can be said for another truism often heard in the same context, that certain events, like the Nazi destruction of the Jews, are so singular that they can be compared to nothing else. It is said that they are and will remain unspeakable and unrepresentable, incomprehensible and unknowable, and therefore sacred. By saying that such an event is at once singular and incomparable one is probably suggesting something different, for taken literally it is either banal or absurd. Indeed, all events, not just traumatic ones, are absolutely singular. And it is hard to see how one can be decreed incomparable unless its sacred character is posed at the outset. To compare does not in fact mean to equate; to perceive difference, comparison is necessary. And how can those who affirm that a particular event is perfectly singular know that it is, unless they have compared it to others? So when people speak of a singular quality, what is meant is something else, namely, a superlative quality: one really affirms that a particular event is the greatest or worst crime in the history of humanity, which is, once again, of necessity a comparative judgment.

If we say, "let's remember the past so that we will behave appropriately in the present," we do not renounce the singularity of individual events, but we imply that parallels between past and present deeds are legitimate. What does justify recalling the past is its judicious use in the present, which the sole reconstruction of the past does not guarantee. Recall, once again, the David Rousset trial: those who were opposed to Rousset's attempt to combat the concentration camps at work had not forgotten their own camp experiences. Pierre Daix, Marie-Claude Vaillant-Couturier, and the other communist deportees lived through the hell of Mauthausen and Auschwitz, and the memory of the camps never left them. If they refused to combat the more recent camps, it's not because of any failing of their memory, but because their ideological principles forbade them to. As Ms. Vaillant-Couturier, a communist member of the legislature said, she refused to even consider the question, because she knew "that there were no concentration camps in the Soviet Union." In their denials, these former deportees became true negationists, far more dangerous than those today who deny the existence of the gas chambers, because at the time the Soviet camps were fully operational, and the only way to combat them was to denounce them publicly.

Even today, when the memory of World War II is alive in Europe and nourished by countless celebrations, publications and TV and radio programs, the ritual slogans about how we must not forget have no visible effect on the processes of ethnic purification, on the torture and massive executions that are taking place at the same time elsewhere in this same Europe. If trials for crimes against humanity could help deflect even slightly the policies of the states where these things are happening, they would find ample additional justification.

Note

1. See Tzvetan Todorov, "Letter from Paris: 'Old Scores,'" trans. John Auzalone, *Salmagundi* (fall 1992): 00–00.

B E R T R A M   M.   G O R D O N

Afterword:

Who Were the Guilty and Should They Be Tried?

The materials in this collection illustrate the passion with which arguments over World War II are still carried on in France. Resolution of the Bousquet and Touvier cases, by murder and conviction, respectively, leaves one still unresolved case, that of Maurice Papon, who served in the Vichy prefect corps in Bordeaux during the Occupation and had a distinguished administrative and political career in the Fourth and Fifth republics. These three cases are based on the relatively new French judicial concept of crimes against humanity, itself a concept evoked largely in reaction to the World War II Holocaust against the Jews. The issue of similarity and difference between the Holocaust and other group persecutions, prior and since, has been widely and intensely discussed since the war. From a historical perspective, however, the cases addressed in this book show a France suffering from the inevitable difficulties associated with the question of guilt encountered in countries that are defeated in war and then make a dubious peace arrangement with their conqueror, only to see their conqueror, in turn, overthrown in short order. Such was the situation for France, which was defeated in 1940, then signed an armistice with Germany, which did not remove the formal state of hostilities between the two countries. The 1940 Armistice, however, was followed in France by a publicly announced policy of collaboration with Germany, which was overturned with the Liberation of 1944. It is the issue of collaboration with an enemy, the meaning of which is continually re-written as history changes, that is at the heart of the Bousquet and Touvier affairs. Woe to the individual collaborator who, seemingly secure in his triumph of the moment, fails to pay attention when the tide turns against his cause. Joseph Darnand, the head of Vichy's Milice, who replaced Bousquet in charge of the police at the beginning of 1944 and whose *miliciens* killed Jean Zay and Georges Mandel in July of that year, was told the following month by Marshal Pétain that he would be a blot on the history of France. "You might have said so earlier," the disillusioned Milice leader replied caustically to Pétain. Darnand was executed in 1945.[1]

Collaboration and punishment in history constitute a complex and continuing issue throughout world history. In 1991 German Chancellor Helmut Kohl criticized those who wanted to purge the Stasi and other pro-Soviet collaborators in the former East Germany. Had he grown up in the Eastern zone, Kohl stated, "I myself don't know which route I would have taken."[2] In France a pattern of collaboration and retribution can be seen dating back to Caesar and Vercingétorix. Nor are women exempt from the history of collaboration and retribution. The history of the late sixth- and early seventh-century Merovingians includes episodes of betrayal by Frédégonde and Brunehaut that led to a half century of fratricidal war ending only with the violent death of the latter, who, at age seventy, was literally torn apart by being tied to wild horses running in different directions. All her descendants were strangled.

The betrayal of Charlemagne's forces by Ganelon at the 778 Ronces-vaux battle and the capture of King Jean le Bon in 1356 and his betrayal of French interests to the English are also episodes of retribution, purges, doubt, and guilt, all encompassed in the problem of collaboration.[3] During the Revolutionary wars, the Count of Artois, youngest brother of King Louis XVI, together with other antirevolutionary émigrés, fled to France's enemies, whom they tried to stir up against the revolutionary government. When the king also tried to flee, his act was also perceived as collaboration with the enemy. It contributed significantly to the overthrow of the monarchy. The subsequent defection of General Dumouriez to the Austrians further inflamed political passions, leading to the revolutionary Reign of Terror in 1792–94. Talleyrand betrayed Napoleon to the allies but escaped punishment when after Waterloo Louis XVIII returned from exile with the émigrés of 1789 "in the baggage of the foreigners" to reign over France. A feeling for expiation on the part of some in France, after the 1870 defeat at Sedan and the Paris Commune revolt of the following year, was represented by construction of the Sacré Cœur cathedral in the capital city.[4] One need only read Emile Zola's *La Débâcle* (*The Downfall*) for a literary perspective on the intensity of passions engendered by the events of 1870–71. Some twenty-five years later, during the Dreyfus Affair of the 1890s, France was again engulfed in accusations of treason and collaboration that called into question the identity and role of the army in republican France and the role of the Jewish community established there.

The *Union sacrée*, or unity of the various political factions, that was created with the outbreak of World War I in 1914 did not survive the human cost of the battles of Verdun in 1916 and the Nivelle offensive of the following year. Mutinies within the army in 1917 were followed by civilian labor strikes that required forcible suppression to keep France in the war. Political leaders such as Joseph Caillaux and Louis Malvy were prosecuted by the government of Georges Clemenceau for having had ties to the Germans. Not surprisingly, this repression raised recriminations after the war. The issues of collaboration and punishment were given new dimensions with the rise of the Russian Bolsheviks to power in 1917 and the subsequent relationship of the French Communist Party with the Soviet Union.[5]

The issues of collaboration, retribution, and reevaluation continued through the interwar and World War II years. Colonel Eugène Faucher, adamantly opposed to the Munich agreement that gave the Südetenland to Germany in 1938, resigned his commission and remained in disgrace through the Occupation for having been on the wrong side. History having turned, however, he has been more generously viewed since the war.[6] In January 1940 some seventy communists who, after the August 1939 Nazi–Soviet pact, called for opposition to the Anglo-French war against Germany, were removed from the French Parliament by the Edouard Daladier government. Reviled by Vichy after the German invasion of the Soviet Union in June 1941, they were treated as Resistance heroes for their role in fighting the Germans subsequently. Another instance of collaboration and retribution was the June 1940 case of the twenty-nine deputies and one senator, who, after the German advance into France, left on the ship *Massilia*, to continue the war against Germany from French North Africa. As Robert Paxton notes, they were detained and returned three weeks later to France as "cowardly émigrés," a term used earlier in French history.[7] The most obvious target for Vichyite accusations of dereliction of duty and treason was General Charles de Gaulle, condemned to death under Vichy for having fled France to continue the war from London.

During the Occupation, the Riom trial, which was opened in February 1942 by the Vichy government, was intended to put on trial leaders of the Third Republic, notably Léon Blum, Edouard Daladier, and Paul Reynaud, for having instigated the war by anti-German collaboration with the English. The trial was hastily suspended by German pressure when it turned to the issue of French preparedness rather than responsibility for the war. Even the Cagoulards whose name means "hooded" because they reminded an observer of the American Ku Klux Klan, and who had attempted an anticommunist provocation in 1936 as a prelude to a military countercoup, split three ways, symbolized by Vichy, Paris, and London. Some supported the Pétain government in Vichy in 1940, others agitated for a more thoroughgoing collaborationist government in occupied Paris, whereas still others joined General de Gaulle and the Free French in London.[8] In the literary world, well-known collaboration cases included Georges Simenon. A Belgian native and a widely read mystery writer, Simenon served from 1940 through 1942 as commissioner for Belgian refugees in la Rochelle. As conditions worsened with the German occupation of the southern zone in November 1942, Simenon noted that his stance was simply to take advantage of whatever opportunities the situation offered.[9]

Not surprisingly, when the tables turned again with the Liberation in 1944, more purges and chastisement were on the agenda. Much depended on when a given person was caught. For example, those caught in the immediate aftermath of the Liberation in the autumn of 1944 or exiles returned from defeated Germany in May 1945 were likely to suffer more violent and immediate retribution than those who were luckier and/or shrewder and were able to hide at least until passions cooled. Women accused as "horizontal collaborators," who were paraded in public sometimes naked and with their heads shorn, have been said to have indirectly helped those accused of more consequential acts of collaboration by deflecting and thereby diminishing initial popular anger.[10] An example of the way in which timing affected those involved in the collaboration is the case of Paul Malaguti, who was involved in a massacre of resisters by the Gestapo on 15 August 1944 in Cannes. Sentenced to death in absentia in 1945, Malaguti managed to avoid capture. In March 1992 his name headed the National Front's list of candidates for the regional elections in the Loiret.[11]

Robert Paxton has noted that retribution for collaboration differed according to groups in France, that "experts, businessmen, and bureaucrats survived almost intact; intellectuals and propagandists were more heavily purged; Third Republic deputies were rejected nearly as totally by the Liberation as they had been by Vichy."[12] To cite one example offered by Paxton of those who had worked for Vichy but did well after the war, two later prime ministers, Félix Gaillard and Jacques Chaban-Delmas, had served in Vichy's Inspectorate of Finance.[13] Paxton noted that French governments had historically changed their prefect corps upon their accession to power. The Second Republic had changed all the prefects in 1848, and those of the Second Empire had been removed wholesale in 1871. In control of the government after 1877, the Republicans had again purged the prefect corps. Paxton further points out that although the purge of prefects at the time of the Liberation was extensive, with only 20 of 87 newly named prefects drawn from the existing corps, by 1947 many of the new prefects had left the service. Half the corps after 1947 were members who had served under Vichy.[14] In his book on the purges of the French administration after the Liberation, François Rouquet emphasizes how difficult it is to estimate the severity of the retribution with any precision. Nonetheless, he shows that the purge was more severe with regard to employees of the Interior Ministry and police agents who had served Vichy, than it was, for example, against the ministries of Agriculture, Public Works and Transport, and Railway.[15] Rouquet refers to a note written by the Provisional Government to the commissioners [*commissaires*] of the Republic, who were told that to purge only the Vichy prefects while leaving in place the lower level government officials who had served the Pétain government would be condemned by the people. The commissioners were advised to maintain their intransigence in their purges, but not so far as to impede seriously the continuing functioning of the various services.[16]

In his book of documents related to the Papon case Michel Slitinsky points out that some Vichy functionaries were able to escape the postwar purges because the Provisional Government wished to avoid possible takeovers by local Resistance groups, some of which were communist dominated, at the time of the Liberation. Of the 419 officials in the Bordeaux Prefecture, according to Slitinsky, seventeen "second-level" ones were disciplined after the war. Of the 2,010 state police officials, forty-three were sanctioned. Those who were retained and promoted after the Liberation included Papon and his superior, Maurice Sabatier.[17] Whereas time worked to the advantage of some who were able to maintain their lives and careers and slip back into mainstream life in postwar France, it worked eventually against a few of the higher officials, such as Bousquet and Papon, or the most clearly compromised collaborators, such as Touvier, who, in a manner of speaking, ran out of luck in the 1980s and 1990s. Papon was one of those who made a smooth transition from Vichy to the postwar government. He served as police prefect of Paris under General de Gaulle from 1958 through 1966 and budget minister under President Valéry Giscard d'Estaing from 1978 through 1981.

First accused of crimes against humanity in 1981 and indicted two years later, Papon has yet to be tried. Delays in his trial have angered some, as seen in the assertion made in early 1995 by Sonia Combe, that the French state was still seeking to conceal its complicity in crimes committed against humanity by limiting access to the archival records of its functionaries from the Vichy years. The failure to try Papon, whose career "showed a remarkable continuity" from Vichy into the Fourth Republic, she argued, reflected the action of a state "which no longer even hides its refusal to judge a man accused of imprescriptible crimes."[18]

The "Papon Affair," as it has sometimes been called, opened on 6 May 1981 when the French weekly *Le Canard enchaîné* published an article entitled *"Papon, aide de camps"* [Papon, camp attendant], which argued with documentary support that Papon had participated in the deportation of 1,690 Jews from Bordeaux, their ultimate destination being Auschwitz. At the time the article appeared, Papon, who had had a virtually unbroken career in the French administration from 1941, was budget minister under Giscard d'Estaing, then in the final stages of a presidential election campaign that he would ultimately lose to François Mitterrand.[19] The first complaints of crimes against humanity were raised against Papon by some thirty individuals and fifteen groups on 8 December 1981, and he was initially indicted on 19 January 1983. As of this writing, Papon is the last Vichy official still awaiting trial on charges of crimes against humanity. Subprefect [*sous-préfet*] under Maurice Sabatier, who was appointed by Pierre Laval as prefect of the Aquitaine region, Papon held a lower office than that of René Bousquet, police minister. Papon was not involved in the activities of the Milice, as was Paul Touvier. Of the three, Papon saw his career least disturbed at the time of the Liberation. Unlike Bousquet and Touvier, he did not face trial, even in absentia, during the 1940s. Instead, within two months of the liberation of Bordeaux, he was named "prefect-third class," in a decree signed by General de Gaulle.[20]

Papon's career, which spanned a half century, was that of a highly successful French functionary. Born in 1910 in Gretz-Armainvilliers in the Seine-et-Marne department, he was the son of a glassworks entrepreneur who was also mayor of his hometown. As a student during the mid-1920s, Papon supported a student affiliate, then headed by Pierre Mendès-France, that backed the moderate leftist Cartel des Gauches. In general the young Papon was surrounded by a radical socialist political milieu that in the French political parlance of the day was moderate left. After service in the military Papon took an administrative position in the police services (*Direction générale de la Sûreté nationale*) in 1935. In 1936 he was transferred to another administrative post, working now under Maurice Sabatier, a civil servant who would become a patron for Papon. The electoral victory of the Popular Front in June 1936 brought Papon into the ministerial arena. He was given a post as attaché for Alsace-Lorraine in the cabinet of François de Tessan, a family relative and also a radical socialist deputy from Seine-et-Marne, who served as an undersecretary of state in the cabinet of Premier Léon Blum. From 1936 through 1938 Papon shifted among several administrative posts in the Popular Front government. When the Popular Front administration was ousted in April 1938 he returned to the civil service. With the outbreak of war in 1939 Papon was mobilized as a lieutenant and sent to the Eastern Mediterranean. Posted in Syria during the spring 1940, he was not on hand to see the defeat of France.

Demobilized in October 1940 Papon went to Vichy, where he was given a post working under Sabatier in the Interior Ministry. In a book about the "Affair," Gérard Boulanger, a lawyer for the civil complaints against Papon, notes that he received five promotions in the French civil service during the Vichy years.[21] Papon survived several ministerial crises in Vichy. Laval was dismissed in December 1940, to be followed by Pierre-Etienne Flandin, then, in February 1941, Admiral Jean-François Darlan. In April 1942 Laval, who had been pre-eminently associated with Franco-German collaboration in Hitler's New Order, was recalled to power. Shortly thereafter, on 1 May 1942, Laval named Sabatier as prefect for the Aquitaine region. Continuing to promote Papon, Sabatier named him secretary-general of the Gironde Prefecture. As all the prefects under Vichy, on 5 June 1942 Papon took an oath of fidelity to Marshal Pétain. According to Maurice-David Matisson and Jean-Paul Abribat, who wrote a book about French collaboration with the Germans in occupied Bordeaux, Papon signed somewhere over eight hundred deportation orders, including many concerning children.[22] It is, of course, the signing of such deportation orders, with most, if not all, of those concerned ending in Auschwitz, that is the basis for charges of crimes against humanity. In his book Boulanger cites a memo over Papon's seal to the German security police that tells them that he has ordered the French police to intern Jews caught while trying to flee from the Occupied Zone, where Bordeaux was located, to the then-safer Unoccupied Zone. The note states that this action was taken "according to your wishes."[23]

Papon appears to have escaped possible reprisals at the time of the Liberation because of Resistance connections. He claimed to have initiated Resistance "behavior" as early as the beginning of 1941.[24] Roger Samuel Bloch, of the Marco-Kléber, an offshoot of the Kléber intelligence network, which funneled information about German troop positions and movements to the Free French, stated that Papon had been an "occasional agent" at the end of 1943.[25] The dating and significance of Papon's Resistance activities have been much contested and, from a legal standpoint in France, awaits determination in the course of a trial. What is clear is that Papon was able to continue his career, virtually unimpeded, after the Liberation. The Provisional Government's desire to preserve the continuity of orderly rule in France and preclude the possibility of communist uprising appears to have worked in his favor. Boulanger notes that by the end of the Occupation, Papon had removed himself from deportation activities.[26] According to Slitinsky, during the period from the Allied landings in Normandy to the liberation of Bordeaux on 28 August 1944 Papon used his prewar personal ties to establish a relationship with Gaston Cusin, named commissioner of the republic for Bordeaux by General de Gaulle. Eager to maintain administrative order and ignorant of Papon's involvement in the deportations, Cusin, according to Slitinsky, reappointed Papon. On 22 August 1944, the very day on which the local Bordeaux Resistance Committee relieved Papon and the other Vichy functionaries of their duties, Cusin named him prefect of the Landes.[27]

Papon's status was confirmed in late October 1944 by de Gaulle, who named him "prefect-third class." He was also mentioned as having been an "agent" for the Jade–Amicol Resistance network. The Provisional Government determined that purges of the prefect corps would be carried out by the Interior Ministry on the advice of local committees of Liberation. In February 1945 the Purge Committee of the Bordeaux Committee of Liberation recommended that Papon be replaced and that his rank and salary be lowered. Additional complaints were brought by the Committee of Liberation against Papon during the year 1945, but his career continued its ascent.[28] He was appointed subdirector [*sous-directeur*] of Algerian affairs in the Ministry for Algeria in 1945, and the next year he was made *chef de cabinet* in the office of the Secretary of State for the Interior. In 1947 Papon was prefect for Corsica. On 19 November 1948, he was named Knight of the Legion of Honor for "eighteen years of public service and wartime military service." The next year he was prefect in Constantine (Algeria).[29]

Papon continued his ascent in the French civil service through the Fourth Republic years, and in March 1958 was named police prefect of Paris under radical socialist Premier Félix Gaillard, mentioned earlier by Robert Paxton as a veteran of Vichy. Papon, who held this post until December 1966, was in charge of the Paris police at a turbulent time when France was deeply involved in the war against Algerian independence and during the transition from the Fourth to the Fifth Republic. He presided over the repression of a demonstration by Algerians in October 1961 in which some two hundred people were killed. Among the dead, Bertrand Le Gendre notes, were some who had been drowned in the Seine.[30] In the 1968 National Assembly elections Papon was elected as Gaullist Union pour la Défense de la République [UDR] deputy from the Cher. He was reelected under the banner of the Gaullist party in 1973 and again with the party, renamed the Rassemblement pour la République [RPR], in 1978. In 1973 his book, *Le Gaullisme, ou la loi de l'effort,* was published. A defender of Gaullism shortly after the death of the General, Papon commented little on the war years in his book. He wrote, however, that de Gaulle "had been first of all the man of refusal, of resistance—even to facts, always to power and to 'fatality.'"[31] In a section entitled "The refusal of the easy [way] [*Le refus de la facilité*]," Papon wrote that history had taught that the choice of the apparent easy path had never resolved difficulties. "As, moreover," he wrote, "the choice of the easy [way] is accompanied generally on the political sphere by a comforting demagogy, the effects of this choice are poorly perceived by the citizens. True security, in effect, depends on the ability of a people to take in hand its own destiny and accept the challenges. Such is the teaching of Gaullism, which has given numerous proofs of it, notably by the decolonization."[32] From 1973 until 1978 when he became budget minister, Papon served as the reporter for the Assembly's Finance Committee. Engaged in his own defense following the opening of the "Affair" in May 1981, he decided not to run for reelection. Two years later he opted not to stand for reelection as mayor of Saint-Amand-Montrond (Cher), a position he had held since 1971.[33]

Papon defended himself by claiming that he had used his position under Vichy to save people who might otherwise have suffered at the hands of the Germans and that he had also served as an undercover Resistance agent. He added that the accusations against him were being made for unspecified political reasons.[34] To authenticate his status as a resister and thereby clear his name, Papon asked in 1981 for the convening of a special Honor Jury of Resistance notables. Meeting in Lille, the Honor Jury validated Papon's affiliation with the Resistance networks Jade–Amicol, as of 1 January 1943 and Kléber as of 1 December 1943. It also indicated that he should have resigned his Vichy post in July 1942.[35] Daniel Mayer, however, who presided over the jury's deliberations, argued that Papon had acted correctly in staying at his post because had all the prefects resigned, it would have been harder for the Resistance to have become organized.[36] In the proceedings of the Honor Jury was a statement by Sabatier claiming total responsibility for the actions of the Gironde Prefecture during the Occupation. Judicial investigations of Papon continued after 1983, but in 1987 they were annulled by the Criminal Appeals Court on the grounds that Sabatier had expressly assumed responsibility for Papon's actions under Vichy. Jurisdiction was given to the Arraignment Court of the Bordeaux Court of Appeal.[37] In 1988 Papon published *Les Chevaux du pouvoir*, a book in which he defended his activities as prefect of police for Paris. Discussing the transition from the Fourth to the Fifth Republic, Papon described a de Gaulle who in 1940 had "condemned an archaic doctrine, even [if] clothed in the authority of Marshal Pétain, a military capitulation disguised as political capitulation by the makeshift 'governors.'"[38]

With the reassignment of Papon's case in 1987, a new investigation was launched, followed by a yet another, headed by Annie Léotin, councilor of the Bordeaux Arraignment Court, in 1990. In October 1992 her investigation produced a new indictment of Papon for crimes committed against humanity.[39] This is where matters stood until Touvier's conviction in April 1994 of crimes against humanity, the first such conviction of a French citizen. Not surprisingly, attention turned again to Papon, who in the meantime, had filed civil complaints against the *Nouvel Observateur* and lawyer and author Gérard Boulanger for defamation of character in their accounts of his wartime activities. In June 1994 a Bordeaux court ruled that Papon's suit against Boulanger be delayed until the crimes against humanity changes had been adjudicated. Both sides claimed to want a quick trial on the crimes against humanity charges. On one side stood those who wished to punish Papon and make his case instructive for those too young to have experienced the war. On the other side was Papon with his supporters, who wished to clear his name.[40] Commemorating the anniversary of the July 1942 Vel d'Hiv roundup of Jews, the Union of Jewish Students of France in July 1994 charged that political as well as judicial authorities in France did not wish to see Papon judged. Banners reading "After the SS Barbie, the *milicien* Touvier, the high functionary Papon?" were unfurled in demonstrations.[41] In *Le Monde*, Bertrand Le Gendre wrote that the more dramatic case of Touvier had marginalized Papon's in public attention. Whereas Touvier had been prosecuted by the official organs of the republic, Le Gendre noted, in the case of Papon it had been civil claimants who had bought the charges.[42] In September 1994 Justice Minister Pierre Méhaignerie stated that the magistrate in charge of preparing the Papon dossier had been relieved of all other responsibilities, presumably to focus on preparing a trial. Méhaignerie indicated that he expected that a trial "could take place during the course of the next year [1995]."[43] By March 1995 with the case still untried, one of the lawyers for the plaintiffs in the case against Papon threatened to use a provision of a new penal code, drawn up in March 1994, to bring charges against officials who interfered with the judicial process, an oblique threat against anyone delaying the trial. Boulanger publicly considered asking the European Court of the Rights of Man in Strasbourg to condemn France for failure to ensure a speedy trial, a violation of the human rights of the plaintiffs. Serge Klarsfeld, on the other hand, expressed confidence, at least in public, that the case would be resolved soon.[44]

The tangled story of Papon's involvement in the deportations and in the Resistance, the latter of which may have preserved his career, is for those in possession of the documents to sort out and, ideally, for French justice to resolve. Central to any trial of Papon, as well as Touvier and, had he lived, Bousquet, is the relatively recent legal notion of crimes against humanity and their definition in France. Although the idea of crimes against humanity was evoked in a 1915 declaration by France, Britain, and Russia denouncing Turkish massacres of the Armenians, the concept did not enter international law until the post–World War II trials of German and Japanese leaders. Pierre Truche, *procureur général* [prosecutor general] at the Paris Court of Appeals on duty during the trial of Klaus Barbie in Lyons, noted that in the Tokyo trials of World War II Japanese leaders and the Nuremberg war crimes trials, the idea of crimes against humanity was inextricably linked with war crimes, the former subsumed in the latter. The same was true of the trials of collaborators in France in the years immediately after the Liberation. This changed in 1964 when the French Parliament wrote crimes against humanity into law, specifying that such crimes were legally imprescriptible, meaning that there is no statute of limitations for these crimes. Those accused of committing them might be tried at any time during their lifetime. Such a legal concept is used in neither

Anglo-American nor international law. As statutes of limitations came into effect regarding war crimes, to punish someone for having worked for Vichy and the Germans in France, it became necessary after 1964 to prove that crimes had been committed against humanity.[45] Truche noted the unique quality of the law regarding the imprescriptibility of crimes against humanity in that its application was after the fact of the crimes with which it deals.[46]

The 1964 law did not define crimes against humanity, referring instead to a United Nations resolution of 13 February 1946 that was based on the charter of the Nuremberg Tribunal and that cited racial and religious persecution. Although the 1964 French law made no mention of specific groups, it has been invoked only in cases relating to the Holocaust. It was used as the basis for charges brought by civil parties against Touvier in 1973, who was indicted eight yeas later, and the indictments of Jean Leguay, Papon, and Bousquet, drawn up in 1979, 1983, and 1991, respectively.[47] In a decision of 1985 involving the trial of Klaus Barbie, the French Supreme Court of Appeal [Cour de Cassation] defined crimes against humanity as "Inhuman acts and persecutions which, carried out on behalf of a nation practicing a policy of ideological hegemony, having been committed systematically not only against persons by reason of their appurtenance to a particular racial or religious collectivity, but also against adversaries of this policy, no matter what the form of their opposition."[48] The effect of the 1985 ruling was to include acts against the Resistance in the category of crimes against humanity, blurring the distinction between such acts and crimes of war. By specifying that crimes against humanity could have been committed only on behalf of a "nation practicing a policy of ideological hegemony" the 1985 ruling in effect limited the concept to crimes committed during World War II. At a time when the Barbie trial raised the possibility that French actions during the Indochina and Algeria wars might also be categorized as crimes against humanity, the Court of Appeals narrowed the concept, applying it virtually exclusively to World War II and the Holocaust, which by implication was seen to differ qualitatively from other persecutions, past and present. Furthermore, as Tzvetan Todorov has shown in his first essay in the present collection, the verdict of Touvier's innocence in 1992 on the basis that the Vichy government did not fit the criteria of a nation practicing ideological hegemony systematically against members of racial or religious groups, effectively cleared Vichy of such crimes. Because the appeal of the 1992 verdict used to retry Touvier was based on legal technicalities, the court's definition of Vichy as nonhegemonical and nonracist still stands. Henceforth to prove that a crime against humanity has been committed, a person must be shown to have served not Vichy France but Nazi Germany directly.[49] In March 1994 the new penal code in France differentiated genocide from other crimes against humanity:

> Genocide is constituted [by] the fact in execution of a concerted plan tending toward the total or partial destruction of a national, ethnic, racial, or religious group, or of a group determined by any other arbitrary criterion, to commit or to cause to be committed against members of this group one of the following acts: willful attack against the life, serious attack against the physical or psychological integrity, submission to conditions of existence of a nature to produce the total or partial destruction of the group, measures seeking to impede births, forced transfer of children.[50]

Other crimes against humanity defined in the new code are "Deportation, reduction to slavery, or the massive and systematic practice of summary executions, of removal of persons followed by their disappearance, of torture or inhuman acts inspired by political, philosophical, racial, or religious motives, and organized in execution of a concerted plan against a group of civil population."[51]

The new definitions, however, did not alter the 1992 court finding that effectively cleared the Vichy government of having committed crimes against humanity. Eric Conan and Henry Rousso have pointed out in their book *Vichy, un passé qui ne passe pas* that many of those who hoped that Touvier's trial would highlight the autonomy of Vichy's role in the Holocaust and the fact that there were French citizens who participated in it independently of the actions of the German occupation authorities, found that Vichy was now exonerated and that Touvier had to be shown to have been obeying German directives to have committed crimes against humanity. *"Militants de la mémoire"* [militants of memory], however, had wanted to establish Touvier's connection to a Vichy government, willfully autonomous in its contribution to the Holocaust. Touvier was condemned, but Vichy was exonerated.

The *"militants de la mémoire"* had won their battle but lost the war.[52] If, Conan and Rousso reasoned, the purpose of trying Papon was to show the complicity of Vichy, through the agency of its bureaucracy, with those perpetrating the Holocaust, the whole issue had become moot. Whatever Papon might or might not have done, at most he could be shown to have been, like Touvier, a minor factotum in the Nazi enterprise of genocide. Implied was the suggestion that it no longer made any sense to try Papon.[53] Obviously cognizant of the fact that to prove crimes against humanity in the French post-1992 legal climate, Papon would need to have been shown to have directly served the Germans, his attorney, Jean-Marc Varaut, has argued that his client had no ties to the German authorities during the Occupation years. Bertrand Le Gendre, however, writing in *Le Monde*, cited documents signed by Papon that indicated the contrary. One, dated 1 February 1943, authorized the police "to escort a convoy of Jews," and a second, dated 24 August 1942, stated that the instructions of the SS are to be followed [*il y a lieu d'exécuter les instructions des SS*]."[54] At this point a trial to highlight the role of Papon as a Vichy functionary, abetting the Holocaust at French as opposed to German instigation, now seems out of the question.

Historically, the Papon Affair is part of the larger story of collaboration and resistance and their shifting meanings as a shifting present continually rewrites the past. Criminal procedure in France has extended the complexity of the Vichy problem beyond 1944. Limited amnesties in 1946 and 1947 and broader ones in 1951 and 1953 left only the most serious offenders in prison.[55] In reality, however, the Vichy period did not end in 1953 or even in 1983, when, by one account, the last imprisoned collaborators had been released.[56] The imprescriptibility of crimes against humanity, written into French law in 1964, has carried the Vichy era, so to speak, down to the present.[57] In *Vichy, un passé qui ne passe pas*, Eric Conan and Henry Rousso suggest that the Touvier trial will turn out to be the last of the post–World War II trials and that, as such, it will mark the turning of a page in French history.[58] It appears, however, that the Vichy episode still has some time to run before it is consigned to the history books. Statements made in 1994 about his Vichy past by President François Mitterrand to both author Pierre Péan and journalist Jean-Pierre Elkabbach, the latter in a one-and-a-half-hour-long television interview, generated a reaction showing that Vichy's history was still not complete.[59] With reference to a reception hosted in March 1995 by Mitterrand for Fidel Castro, an American columnist used the French President's Vichy confessions to portray him as an inveterate collaborator with dictatorial governments that trample human rights.[60] Thus, the history of Vichy is not quite finished and will remain so at least until the Papon case is resolved in France, either by trial or by the death of Papon. This history will be complete only after the passing of the last surviving participants, within the next ten to fifteen years.

The Bousquet and Touvier affairs, together with the unfinished business of Papon, have focused much of the attention of the press and the scholarly community on the three individuals in a quest for traumatic resolution as in a Greek drama. Taken together, the affairs have deflected much of the attention away from questions of the larger historical structure of France's continuing struggle with military failure, occupation, collaboration, retribution, and reevaluation. The details may differ, involving the occupation by an outside power, as in the case of Jean le Bon, or internal processes such as the civil wars of the Reformation, or by some combination of both, seen during the French Revolution, the 1871 Commune, and Vichy. Most of those involved in the various episodes of collaboration in French history undoubtedly found ways to escape the momentary vengeance that followed when events turned against them. The formalization of guilt on the persons of the relatively few who had the lack of foresight or bad luck to be caught is what historically allows France to bring closure to a process that will inevitably reappear in European history, given the large number of conflicting ethnic or regional boundaries that are still in doubt. Northern Ireland, Azerbaijan, Bosnia, Serbia, the Basques, and for that matter, the continuing tension between Flemish and Walloons with Brussels caught in the center, all provide potential loci for the kinds of conflict epitomized by the Bousquet, Touvier, and Papon affairs in France.[61] The future is likely to offer a virtually endless sequence of collaboration occasions, followed by accusation and counteraccusation both in France and around the world as there is no shortage of opportunities. In 1990, for example, Jean-Louis Bourlanges, a member of the Simone Weil group in the European Parliament, denounced the "eternal party of the collaboration" that he saw extending from Ganelon through Laval and Marcel Déat, a prominent World War II collaborator with the Germans, to Jean-Marie Le Pen, who Bourlanges criticized for collaborating with Saddam Hussein in the Gulf crisis of 1990.[62] Wherever the French language is in some kind of conflict, there is a collaboration problem, extending from the Québecois struggle to retain their language against a surrounding sea of Anglophones to the defense of the French language and the Berbers against Arabization tendencies in North Africa. From Vercingétorix to the Québecois and the North Africans the struggle over collaboration of and with French identity continues.

Notes

1. Bertram M. Gordon, *Collaborationism in France during the Second World War* (Ithaca: Cornell University Press, 1980), pp. 175, 279.

2. Cited in Bertram M. Gordon, "The Morphology of the Collaborator: The French Case," parts 1 and 2, *Journal of European Studies* 23/89–90 (March–June 1993), 3–4.

3. See Gordon, "Morphology," p. 6, and Pascal Balmand, *Histoire de la France* (Paris: Haiter, 1992), pp. 98–99.

4. See René Rémond, "Introduction," in *Le Gouvernement de Vichy, 1940–1942* (Paris: Armand Colin, 1972), p. 7. For discussion of the "Franco-French war" on a long-term basis, see also Rémy Handourtzel and Cyril Buffet, *La Collaboration . . . à gauche aussi* (Paris: Perrin, 1989), p. 25.

5. See, for example, the open letter in 1925 of Charles Maurras to Abraham Schrameck, who was Jewish and served as Interior Minister with the moderate leftist *Cartel des Gauches* cabinet, in Jean-Luc Pinol, "1919–1958, Le Temps des droites," in *Histoire des Droites en France*, vol. 1, ed. Jean-François Sirinelli (Paris: Gallimard, 1992), pp. 304–305. See also Yves-Marie Hilaire, "1900–1945 L'Ancrage des idéologies," in ibid., p. 535.

6. Renewed attention to the career of Faucher was expressed in a paper presented at the 1993 meeting of the Western Society for French History. See Richard F. Crane, "*Un Résistant avant la Résistance:* General Louis Eugène Faucher and the Crisis of Appeasement—Abstract," in *Proceedings of the Western Society for French History*, 21 (1994), p. 323.

7. Robert O. Paxton, *Vichy France, Old Guard and New Order, 1940–1944* (New York: Norton, 1975), p. 29.

8. Gordon, *Collaborationism*, p. 60.

9. Patricia Highsmith, "Desperate connections," *Times Literary Supplement*, 17 April 1992, p. 4.

10. François Rouquet, *L'Epuration dans l'administration française, agents de l'état et collaboration ordinaire* (Paris: CNRS, 1993), p. 130.

11. Alain Choufflan, "Du PPF de Doriot au FN de Le Pen, Malaguti, l'homme qui nie son passé," *Le Nouvel Observateur*, 5–11 March 1992, p. 30.

12. Paxton, *Vichy France*, p. 333.

13. Ibid., p. 337.

14. Ibid., pp. 341–42.

15. Rouquet, *L'Epuration*, p. 115.

16. Ibid., p. 117.

17. Michel Slitinsky, *L'Affaire Papon* (Paris: Alain Moreau, 1983), p. 156. Slitinsky, a member of an association of relatives of deportees, himself had been targeted for deportation but had managed to escape and survive the Occupation (see pp. 99–102). He was one of the complainants against Papon, who sued against the publication of the book as defamatory. The book was allowed to be published, but its preface, by Gilles Perrault, was suppressed.

18. Sonia Combe, "Vichy, les archives et les historiens 'raisonnables,'" *Le Monde*, 31 January 1995, p. 18. See also Laurent Greilsamer, "L'Ensevelissement judiciare du régime de Vichy," *Le Monde*, 10 June 1993, p. 15. Writing just after the murder of Bousquet, Greilsamer lamented the delays in trying Bousquet, Touvier, and Papon.

19. Maurice-David Matisson and Jean-Paul Abribat, *Psychanalyse de la collaboration: Le Syndrome de Bordeaux 1940–1945* (Marseilles: Editions Hommes et perspectives, 1991), p. 89.

20. Ibid., p. 38.

21. Gérard Boulanger, *Maurice Papon, un technocrate français dans la collaboration* (Paris: Seuil, 1994), p. 33.

22. Matisson and Abribat, *Psychanalyse de la Collaboration*, p. 29. Boulanger calculates the figures of those deported from Bordeaux to Drancy, from where most were sent to Auschwitz, as approximately 2,000 between 1942 and 1944, pp. 179–180.

23. Boulanger, *Maurice Papon*, p. 181.

24. Papon, Letter to Marie-Madeleine Fourcade, 21 May 1981, cited in Matisson and Abribat, *Psychanalyse de la Collaboration*, p. 33.

25. Boulanger, *Maurice Papon*, p. 218.

26. Ibid., p. 244.

27. Slitinsky, *L'Affaire Papon*, pp. 20, 141–42.

28. For a fuller account, see ibid., pp. 142–43.

29. Matisson and Abribat, *Psychanalyse de la Collaboration*, pp. 40–43.

30. Bertrand Le Gendre, "De Vichy à la V{e} République: Maurice Papon, le caméléon," *Le Monde*, 23 April 1994, p. 15.

31. Maurice Papon, *Le Gaullisme, ou la loi de l'effort* (Paris: Flammarion, 1973), p. 16.

32. Ibid., pp. 60–61. Papon's text in French reads: "Comme au surplus le choix de la facilité s'accompagne généralement sur le plan politique d'une démagogie sécurisante, les effets de ce choix sont mal perçus par les citoyens. La véritable sécurité en effet dépend de l'aptitude d'un peuple à prendre en mains son propre destin et à assumer les épreuves; tel est l'enseignement du

gaullisme qui en a donné de nombreuses preuves, notamment par la décolonisation."

33. Slitinsky, *L'Affaire Papon*, pp. 8 and 23.

34. Ibid., p. 159.

35. Matisson and Abribat, *Psychanalyse de la Collaboration*, p. 47. The complete text of the Honor Jury's recommendations is published as Annex III in Slitinsky, *l'Affaire Papon*.

36. Cited in François Caviglioli, "'Objet: Arrestation des juifs,'" *Le Nouvel Observateur*, 13–19 December 1990, p. 44.

37. Matisson and Abribat, *Psychanalyse de la Collaboration*, pp. 48–50.

38. Maurice Papon, *Les Chevaux du pouvoir. Le préfet de police du général de Gaulle ouvre ses dossiers, 1958–1967* (Paris: Plon, 1988), p. 34.

39. Ginette de Matha, "L'Audition des parties civiles dans l'affaire Papon a commencé," *Le Monde*, 2 October 1992, p. 10.

40. Maurice Peyrot, "La Justice repousse une plainte de Maurice Papon," *Le Monde*, 15 June 1994, p. 15. Papon appealed the decision to suspend his suit against Boulanger. See "Procès Papon," *Le Monde*, 26–27, June 1994, p. 9.

41. J. K., "Manifestation de l'Union des étudiants juifs de France," *Le Monde*, 17–18 July 1994, p. 7.

42. Le Gendre, "De Vichy à la Ve République," p. 15.

43. Anne Chemin and Edwy Plenel, "Un Entretien avec le ministre de la justice," *Le Monde*, 24 September 1994, p. 9.

44. Laurent Greilsamer, "L'instruction du dossier Papon devrait être terminée avant l'été," *Le Monde*, 15 March 1995, p. 12. See also "Affaire Papon," *Le Monde*, 10 March 1995, p. 12.

45. Pierre Truche, "La Notion de crime contre l'humanité: Bilan et propositions," *Esprit* 181 (May 1992), p. 83. See also Michel Kajman, "L'Eternelle actualité de la répétition du pire," *Le Monde*, 21–22 October 1990, p. 8.

46. Truche, "La Notion de crime contre l'humanité," p. 79.

47. See Henry Rousso, "L'Epuration en France, une histoire inachevée," *Vingtième Siècle* 33 (January–March 1993), pp. 101–102.

48. Quoted in Jean-Denis Bredin, "The Touvier Affair: History and Justice Abused," this volume, p. 111.

49. Tzvetan Todorov, "The Touvier Affair," this volume, p. 119.

50. "Le Crime contre l'humanité et ses définitions," *Le Monde*, 20–21 March 1994, p. 10.

51. Ibid.

52. The term *militants de la mémoire* was written on the badges of members of the Sons and Daughters of the Deported Jews of France who had come to attend the Touvier trial in March 1994. See Dominique Le Guilledoux, "Les Militants de la mémoire," *Le Monde*, 19 March 1994, p. 11.

53. Eric Conan and Henry Rousso, *Vichy, un passé qui ne passe pas* (Paris: Fayard, 1994), p. 158.

54. Cited in Le Gendre, "De Vichy à la Ve République," p. 15.

55. Rousso ends the post-Liberation purge with the amnesty in 1953. See

Henry Rousso, *The Vichy Syndrome: History and Memory in France since 1944*, trans. Arthur Goldhammer (Cambridge: Harvard University Press, 1991), p. 53.

56. Herbert R. Lottman, *The Purge: The Purification of French Collaborators after World War II* (New York: Morrow, 1986), p. 269.

57. Discussing the postwar purge in Belgium, two historians have argued that a half-century *"malaise"* has followed the war. See Luc Huyse and Steven Dhondt, *La Répression des collaborations, 1942–1952: Un passé toujours présent* (Brussels: CRISP, 1993), p. 10.

58. Conan and Rousso, *Vichy, un passé qui ne passe pas*, p. 139.

59. See Pierre Péan, *Une jeunesse française, François Mitterrand, 1934–1947* (Paris: Fayard, 1994), p. 7, and Emmanuel Faux, Thomas Legrand, and Gilles Perez, *La Main droite de Dieu, Enquête sur François Mitterrand et l'extrême droite* (Paris: Seuil, 1994), p. 103. Regarding Mitterrand's television interview, see Sylvie Pierre-Brossolette "Mitterrand rattrapé par l'histoire," *L'Express*, 22 September 1994, 8–9.

60. A. M. Rosenthal, "Kisses for Castro," *New York Times*, 17 March 1995, p. A15.

61. See, for example, Roger Cohen, "Tribunal Brings First War Crimes Charges since World War II against Serbs," *New York Times*. 8 November 1994, p. A6.

62. Valérie Dousset, "'Le Pen, c'est Ganelon!'" *Le Figaro*, 24 August 1990, p. 5.

BIBLIOGRAPHY

Algazy, Joseph. *La Tentation néo-fasciste en France de 1944 à 1965.* Paris: Fayard, 1984.

Andrieu, Claire. "Réponse d'une historienne." *Esprit* (December 1994), 205–08.

Arendt, Hannah. *Eichmann in Jerusalem: A Report on the Banality of Evil.* Harmondsworth: Penguin Books, 1963, 1964.

Assouline, Pierre. *L'Epuration des intellectuels, 1944–1945.* Brussells: Editions Complexe, n.d.

Azéma, Jean-Pierre, and François Bédarida, eds. *La Régime de Vichy et les Français.* Paris: Fayard, 1992.

Bauman, Zygmunt. *Modernity and the Holocaust.* Ithaca: Cornell University Press, 1989.

Belot, Robert, *Lucien Rebatet: Un Itinéraire fasciste.* Paris: Seuil, 1994.

Bernstein, Richard. "French Collaborators: The New Debate." *The New York Review* (25 June 1992): 37–42.

Best, Geoffrey. *War and Law since 1945.* New York: Clarendon, 1994.

Billig, Joseph. *Le Commissariat général aux Questions juives (1941–1944).* 3 vols. Paris: Editions du Centre, 1955.

Birnbaum, Pierre. *La France aux Français: Histoire des haines nationalistes.* Paris: Seuil, 1993.

Boulanger, Gérard. *Maurice Papon: Un Technocrate Français dans la collaboration.* Paris: Seuil, 1994.

Bouthors, Jean-François. "Le Président, la France et la mort." *Esprit* (November 1994), 99–103.

Burrin, Philippe. *La France à l'heure allemande.* Paris: Seuil, 1995.

Burrin, Philippe, Jean-Marie Domenach, Stanley Hoffman, Dominique Moisi, Robert O. Paxton, and Ronald Tiersky. "Symposium on Mitterrand's Past." In *French Politics and Society* 13 (Winter 1995): 4–35 (Stanley Hoffmann, Goerge Ross, Laura Levine Frader, Arthur Goldhammer, and Gretchen R. Bouliane, eds.).

Carpi, Daniel. *Between Mussolini and Hitler: The Jews and the Italian Authorities in France and Tunisia.* Hanover, N.H.: University Press of New England, 1994.

Carrier, Peter. "Rewriting Vichy after Fifty Years." *Contemporary Review* 261 (November 1992): 232–35.

Chebel d'Appollonia, Ariane. *L'Extrême-droite en France de Maurras à Le Pen.* Brussells: Editions Complexe, 1988.

Cismaru, Alfred. "Antisemitism in France." *The Midwest Quarterly* 34 (Spring 1993): 283–93.

Cobb, Richard. *French and Germans, Germans and French: A Personal Interpretation of France under Two Occupations, 1914–1918 / 1940–1944.* Hanover, N.H.: University Press of New England, 1983.

Conan, Eric, and Henry Rousso. *Vichy, un passé qui ne passe pas.* Paris: Fayard, 1994.

Delperrié de Bayac, Jacques. *Histoire de la milice, 1918–1945.* Paris: Fayard, 1969.

Dreyfus, François-Georges. *Histoire de Vichy.* Collection Vérités et Légendes. Paris: Perrin, 1990.

Farmer, Sarah. *Oradour: Arrêt sur mémoire.* Paris: Calmann-Lévy, 1994.

Faux, Emmanuel, Thomas Legrand, and Gilles Perez. *La Main droite de Dieu: Enquête sur François Mitterrand et l'extrême droite.* Paris: Seuil, 1994.

Finkielkraut, Alain. *Remembering in Vain: The Klaus Barbie Trial and Crimes against Humanity.* Trans. Roxanne Lapidus with Sima Godfrey. New York: Columbia University Press, 1989.

"France: Judging History." *The Economist* 323 (25 April 1992): 56–57.

Froment, Pascale. *René Bousquet.* Paris: Stock, 1994.

Frossard, André. *Le Crime contre l'humanité.* Paris: Laffont, 1987.

Gordon, Bertram M. *Collaborationism in France during the Second World War.* Ithaca: Cornell University Press, 1980.

Greilsamer, Laurent, and Daniel Schneidermann. *Un Certain Monsieur Paul: L'Affaire Touvier.* Paris: Fayard, 1989.

Grenier, Richard. "Laying the Nazi Ghost." *National Review* 46 (16 May 1994): 26–.

Guéhenno, Jean. *Journal des années noires (1940–1944).* Paris: Gallimard, 1947.

Gumbel, Andrew. "Vichy Slaughter." *New Statesman & Society* 7 (25 March 1994): 20–21.

Hilberg, Raul. *Perpetrators, Victims, Bystanders: The Jewish Catastrophe, 1933–1945.* New York: Harper Perennial, 1992.

"I Was Good and He Was Evil." *Newsweek* 121 (21 June 1993): 44.

Jankélévitch, Vladimir. *L'Imprescriptible: Pardonner? Dans l'honneur et la dignité.* Paris: Seuil, 1986.

Jaspers, Karl. *The Question of German Guilt.* Trans. E. B. Ashton. New York: Capricorn, 1947.

Judt, Tony. "Truth and Consequences." *The New York Review,* 3 November 1994, 8–12.

Klarsfeld, Arno. *Paul Touvier, un crime français.* Paris: Fayard, 1994.

Klarsfeld, Serge. *Vichy–Auschwitz: Le rôle de Vichy dans la solution finale de la question juive en France—1942*. Paris: Fayard, 1983.

———. *Vichy–Auschwitz: Le rôle de Vichy dans la solution finale de la question juive en France—1943–1944*. Paris: Fayard, 1985.

Kupferman, Fred. *Le Procès de Vichy: Pucheu, Pétain, Laval*. Brussells: Editions Complexe, 1980.

Lambert, Bernard. *Dossiers d'accusation: Bousquet, Papon, Touvier*. Paris: Fédération Nationale des Déportés et Internes Résistants et Patriotes, n.d.

Lambert, Pierre Philippe, and Gérard Le Marec. *Partis et mouvements de la collaboration: Paris, 1940–1944*. Paris: Jacques Grancher, 1993.

Laughland, John. *The Death of Politics: France Under Mitterrand*. London: Michael Joseph, 1994.

Legatte, Paul. *"Une Jeunesse française."* *Le Monde*, 12 September 1994, 2.

Lévy, Bernard-Henri, ed. *Archives d'un procès: Klaus Barbie*. Paris: Globe, 1986.

Lindenberg, Daniel. *Les Années souterraines (1937–1947)*. Paris: La Découverte, 1990.

———. *"L'Histoire de Vichy: Avancées et reculs."* *Esprit* (November 1994), 72–76.

Lipstadt, Deborah E. *Denying the Holocaust: The Growing Assault on Truth and Memory*. New York: The Free Press, 1993.

Lottman, Herbert R. *The Purge: The Purification of French Collaborators after World War II*. New York: Morrow, 1986.

Maier, Charles S. *The Unmasterable Past: History, Holocaust, and German National Identity*. Cambridge: Harvard University Press, 1988.

Markham, James M. *"Fugitive Nazi Collaborator Seized from a Catholic Priory in France."* *The New York Times*, 25 May 1989.

Matisson, Maurice-David, and Jean-Paul Abribat. *Psychanalyse de la collaboration: Le Syndrome de Bordeaux: 1940–1945*. Marseille: Editions Hommes et Perspectives, 1991.

Marrus, Michael R., and Robert O. Paxton. *Vichy France and the Jews*. New York: Schocken, 1981.

Mayer, Arno J. *Why Did the Heavens Not Darken? The "Final Solution" in History*. New York: Pantheon, 1990.

Michel, Henri. *Le Procès de Riom*. Paris: Albin Michel, 1979.

Moati, Serge, and Jean-Claude Raspiengeas. *La Haine antisémite*. Paris: Flammarion, 1991.

Mongin, Olivier, ed. *"Que faire de Vichy?"* Special edition of *Esprit* (May 1992).

———. *"Que reste-t-il de la Résistance?"* Special edition of *Esprit* (January 1994).

Mongin, Olivier. *"La France de Mitterrand ou le royaume de l'anachronisme."* *Esprit*, November 1994, 83–98.

Monzat, René. *Enquêtes sur la droite extrême*. Paris: Le Monde-Editions, 1992.

Morgan, Ted. *"L'affaire Touvier: Opening Old Wounds."* *New York Times Magazine*, 1 October 1989, 32–.

————. *An Uncertain Hour: The French, the Germans, the Jews, the Barbie Trial, and the City of Lyon, 1940–1945*. New York: Morrow, 1990.

Novick, Peter. *The Resistance versus Vichy: The Purge of Collaborators in Liberated France*. New York: Columbia University Press, 1968.

Ophuls, Marcel. "Le Prince et le professeur." *Le Monde*, 22 September 1994, 2.

Ory, Pascal. *Les Collaborateurs, 1940–1945*. Paris: Seuil, 1976.

Paris, Erna. *Unhealed Wounds: France and the Klaus Barbie Affair*. New York: Grove, 1985.

Péan, Pierre. *Une Jeunesse française: François Mitterrand, 1934–1947*. Paris: Fayard, 1994.

Rassat, Michèle-Laure. *La Justice en France*. Paris: Presses Universitaires de France, 1985.

Reisman, W. Michael, and Chris T. Antoniou, eds. *The Laws of War: A Comprehensive Collection of Primary Documents on International Laws Governing Armed Conflict*. New York: Vintage, 1994.

Rémond, René. "La Complexité de Vichy." *Le Monde*, 5 October 1994, 1–2.

————. *The Right Wing in France from 1815 to de Gaulle*. 2nd ed. Trans. James M. Laux. Philadelphia: University of Pennsylvania Press, 1966, 1969.

Rémond, René, Jean-Pierre Azéma, François Bédarida, Gérard Cholvy, Bernard Comte, Jean Dujardin, Jean-Dominique Durand, and Yves-Marie Hilaire. *Touvier et L'église: Rapport de la Commission historique instituée par le Cardinal Decourtray*. Paris: Fayard, 1992.

Riding, Alan. "French Angered at Ruling on Nazi Collaborator." *The New York Times*, 15 April 1992.

————. "Rulings Jar France into Reliving its Anti-Jewish Role in Nazi Era." *The New York Times*, 10 May 1992.

————. "Vichy Aide Accused of War Crimes Is Slain in France." *The New York Times*, 9 June 1993.

————. "France Confronts Vichy Past in War Crimes Trial." *The New York Times*, 16 March 1994.

————. "War Crimes Trial Opens in France." *The New York Times*, 18 March 1994.

————. "At His Trial, Frenchman's Memory of Nazis Is Dim." *The New York Times*, 27 March 1994.

————. "Frenchman on Trial: Testing the Role of the Nazis." *The New York Times*, 3 April 1994.

————. "French Lawyers Assert Man Tied to Jews' Death Was Nazi." *The New York Times*, 14 April 1994.

————. "Frenchman Convicted of Crimes against the Jews in '44." *The New York Times*, 20 April 1994.

————. "Mitterrand's 'Mistakes': Vichy Past Is Unveiled." *The New York Times*, 9 September 1994.

Roman, Joël. "Lucidités rétrospectives: Quand des historiens font la leçon." *Esprit* (November 1994), 77–82.

Rousso, Henry. *The Vichy Syndrome: History and Memory in France since 1944*. (Cambridge: Harvard University Press, 1991).

"Scandalous Sanctuary: France Arrests a Fugitive." *Newsweek* 113 (5 June 1989): 44.

Singer, Daniel. "Mitterrand Le Petit." *The Nation,* 10 October 1994, 380–82.

Sirinelli, Jean-François, ed. *Histoire des droites en France. Vol 1: Politique.* Paris: Gallimard, 1992.

———. *Histoire des droites en France. Vol. 2: Cultures.* Paris: Gallimard, 1992.

———. *Histoire des droites en France. Vol. 3: Sensibilités.* Paris: Gallimard, 1992.

Slitinsky, Michel. *L'Affaire Papon.* Paris: Alain Moreau, 1983.

Soucy, Robert. *Le Fascisme français 1924–1933.* Paris: Presses Universitaires de France, 1989.

Steinberg, Jonathan. *All or Nothing: The Axis and the Holocaust, 1941–1943.* London: Routledge, 1991.

Sternhell, Zeev. *Neither Right nor Left: Fascist Ideology in France.* Trans. David Maisel. Berkeley: University of California Press, 1986.

Taylor, Telford. *The Anatomy of the Nuremberg Trials: A Personal Memoir.* New York: Knopf, 1992.

Thalmann, Rita. *La Mise au pas: Idéologie et stratégie sécuritaire dans la France occupée.* Paris: Fayard, 1991.

Todorov, Tzvetan. "Letter from Paris." Trans. John Anzalone. *Salamagundi* 97 (Winter 1993): 21–28.

"Touvier's Troubling Trial." *The Economist* 311 (3 June 1989): 49–50.

"The Touvier Trial: Old Wounds." *The Economist* 331 (23 April 1994): 53.

Trémolet de Villers, Jacques. *Paul Touvier est innocent.* Paris: Editions Dominique Martin Morin, 1990.

———. *L'Affaire Touvier: Chronique d'un procès en idéologie.* Paris: Editions Dominique Martin Morin, 1994.

Valensi, Lucette. "Présence du passé, lenteur de l'histoire, Vichy, l'occupation, les juifs." Special issue of *Annales Economies Sociétés Civilisations* 48 (May–June 1993).

Valls-Russell, Janice. "From Dreyfus to Touvier: Remembering Anti-Semitism in France." *The New Leader* 77 (9–23 May 1994): 8–9.

———. "The Touvier Controversy: Confronting Collaboration in France." *The New Leader* 75 (29 June 1992): 9–11.

Vergès, Jacques, and Etienne Bloch. *La Face cachée du procès Barbie.* Paris: Samuel Tastet, 1983.

"La vérité sur la Milice." *Le Choc du Mois* 53 (June 1992): 25–44.

Vidal-Naquet, Pierre. *Assassins of Memory: Essays on the Denial of the Holocaust.* Trans. Jeffrey Mehlman. New York: Columbia University Press, 1992.

———. *Le Trait empoisonné: Réflexions sur l'affaire Jean Moulin.* Paris: La Découverte, 1993.

Wadham, Lucy. "Vive l'histoire: Is France Finally Accepting Its Part in the Holocaust?" *New Statesman & Society* 5 (1 May 1992): 18.

Wallace, Bruce. "Crimes against Humanity: A Trial Focuses on French Collaboration with Nazi Germany." *Maclean's* 107 (4 April 1994): 28–29.

Weisberg, Richard. *Poethics and Other Strategies of Law and Literature.* New York: Columbia University Press, 1992.

Weston, Martin. *An English Reader's Guide to the French Legal System.* Providence, R. I.: Berg, 1991.

Wieviorka, Olivier. *Nous entrerons dans la carrière: De la résistance à l'exercice du pouvoir.* Paris: Seuil, 1994.

Zuccotti, Susan. *The Holocaust, the French, and the Jews.* New York: Basic Books, 1993.

CONTRIBUTORS

Sorj Chalandon is a reporter for *Libération* who covered the Touvier trial for the newspaper.

Lucy Golsan has taught French at George State University and Wesleyan College and has served in the Peace Corps as Professor of English at the University of Budapest. She has lived and worked in Paris, where she completed a DEA degree in art history at the University of Paris III. She has recently completed a translation of Gustave Geoffroy's biography of Claude Monet and is currently translating Elisabeth Badinter's *Emilie, Emilie, L'ambition féminine au XVIII siècle*.

Richard J. Golsan is Professor of French at Texas A & M University and Editor of the *South Central Review*. He has published extensively on the Occupation and its aftermath in the *French Review*, the *Journal of European Studies, l'Esprit Créateur, SubStance*, and elsewhere. He also edited *Fascism, Aesthetics, and Culture* (UPNE, 1993).

Bertram Gordon is Professor of European History at Mills College. He is the author of *Collaborationism in France during the Second World War* (Cornell, 1980) and the editor of the *Historical Dictionary of World War II France: The Occupation, Vichy and the Resistance 1938–1946*, to be published by Greenwood Press in 1997. His recent articles include "The Morphology of the Collaborator: The French Case," *Journal of European Studies;* "The Formation of de Gaulle's Political Philosophy: Legacies of the Belle Epoque," *Historical Reflections\Réflexions Historiques;* and "The Problem of the Vichy Syndrome," forthcoming in *French Historical Studies.*

Pierre Laborie is Professor of History at the University of Toulouse-Le Mirail and author of *L'Opinion Française sous Vichy* (Seuil, 1990).

Annette Lévy-Willard is a senior political writer for the Parisian daily *Libération*. She specializes in the extreme right and cases involving crimes against humanity. She has done exposés on French television on Jean-Marie Le Pen, and with her husband, Ludi Boeken, she has made documentaries on the extreme right in Europe and the United States for the BBC. Lévy-Willard is also the author of the best-selling autobiographical novel *Moi Jane, cherche Tarzan,* to which she is now writing the sequel.

Robert Paxton is Mellon Professor of the Social Sciences and the Director of the Institute on Western Europe at Columbia University. He is the author of several books on Vichy France, including *Parades and Politics at Vichy* (Princeton, 1966), *Vichy France: Old Guard and New Order* (Knopf, 1972, now in paperback with Columbia), and, with Michael Marrus, *Vichy France and the Jews* (Schocken, 1983). He is also the author of *Europe in the Twentieth Century* (Harcourt Brace, 1991) and Co-Editor of *De Gaulle and the United States* (Berg, 1994). Paxton testified at the trial of Paul Touvier in 1994.

Denis Peschanski is a Researcher at the Centre National de Recherche Scientifique and is the author of *Vichy 1940–1944* (A. Tasca, 1986).

Henry Rousso is Director of Research at the Centre National de Recherche Scientifique (*Institut d'histoire du temps présent*). He is the author of *Un Château en Allemagne* (Ramsay, 1980); *The Vichy Syndrome: History and Memory in France since 1991* (Harvard, 1991), and, with Eric Conan, *Vichy, un passé qui ne passe pas* (Fayard, 1994). Rousso covered the Touvier trial for *Libération*.

Tzvetan Todorov is a researcher at the Centre National de Recherche Scienti-fique and is the author of many books including, most recently, *On Human Diversity: Nationalism, Racism, and Exoticism in French Thought* (Harvard, 1993); *Une Tragédie française* (Seuil, 1994); and *The Morals of History* (Minnesota, 1995).

INDEX

We index only substantive treatments of names and terms that appear on nearly every page, such as Bousquet, Touvier, and Jews, providing major subtopics. Other proper names may be indexed exhaustively, but we do not index names given only passing mention in the text.

University Press of New England publishes books under its own imprint and is the publisher for Brandeis University Press, Dartmouth College, Middlebury College Press, University of New Hampshire, University of Rhode Island, Tufts University, University of Vermont, Wesleyan University Press, and Salzburg Seminar.

Library of Congress Cataloging-in-Publication Data

Memory, the Holocaust, and French justice : the Bousquet and Touvier affairs / edited by Richard J. Golsan ; translations by Lucy Golsan and Richard J. Golsan.
    p. cm.—(Contemporary French culture and society)
  Includes bibliographical references and index.
  ISBN 0–87451–733–8 (cloth : alk. paper).—ISBN 0–87451–741–9 (pbk. : alk. paper)
  1. Jews—France—Persecutions.   2. Holocaust, Jewish (1939–1945)—France.   3. War crime trials—France.   4. Bousquet, René, 1909– .
5. Touvier, Paul, 1915– . 6. World War, 1939–1945—Collaborationists—France—Biography.   7. France—Politics and government—20th century.   I. Golsan, Richard Joseph, 1952– . II. Series.
DS135.F83M46   1996
944′.004924—dc20   95–35728
∞